LITTLE
VICTIM

Other Books by Harry Keeble with Kris Hollington

Crack House

'A true-life account of an honest cop's successful
effort to stamp out crack houses on his turf, this is a fact-filled,
very readable and at times disturbing book. Raid it and
weep . . . truly shocking. Much like its subject
matter, this is gripping stuff'

5 stars, *Maxim*

'In his blistering book, *Crack House*, hard-nosed cop
Harry Keeble tells how, for nine bone-crunching months, he and
his men rampaged through London's seething drugs underworld'

5 stars, *News of the World*

Baby X

'Powerful and moving. I didn't think I could be
shocked any more until I read *Baby X*'

Cathy Glass

'The subject matter is obviously heavy . . . But the pace
crackles from case to case – with Harry's fight to save neglected
and abused kids taking him around the world'

5 stars, *News of the World*

Terror Cops

'This is the first time a counter-terrorism officer
involved has written the inside story of Operation Overt.
And it's a truly fascinating insight into the lives of terror cops,
and the painstaking evidence-gathering that went into
this large-scale operation. A terror-ific read'

5 stars, *News of the World*

LITTLE VICTIM

THE REAL STORY OF BRITAIN'S VULNERABLE CHILDREN AND THE PEOPLE WHO RESCUE THEM

HARRY KEEBLE *with*
KRIS HOLLINGTON

SIMON &
SCHUSTER

London · New York · Sydney · Toronto

A CBS COMPANY

First published in Great Britain by Simon & Schuster UK Ltd, 2011
A CBS COMPANY

1 3 5 7 9 10 8 6 4 2

Simon & Schuster UK Ltd
1st Floor
222 Gray's Inn Road
London WC1X 8HB

www.simonandschuster.co.uk

Simon & Schuster Australia
Sydney

A CIP catalogue record for this book is available
from the British Library.

ISBN: 978-1-47112-704-5

Typeset by M Rules
Printed and bound by CPI Group (UK) Ltd, Croydon, CR0 4YY

For Keith

CONTENTS

AUTHOR'S NOTE

It is important to ensure that the details of some of the individuals encountered through my work (witnesses, police officers, social workers, teachers, etc.) are not described in a way that would enable people to recognise them. And of course it is also necessary to protect the identities of children and parents whose stories are detailed in this book. I have, with the exception of names that are in the public domain, protected the identities of some people by changing names and altering some background details. Those cases that are a matter of public record are reported in their original detail.

FOREWORD

When *Baby X* was published in January 2009, the reaction took me completely by surprise. Within a couple of weeks it was in the bestseller lists and to my continued amazement it remained there for some months.

The reaction was also evident in my inbox. Emails started arriving from all over the UK, some from people working in child protection (especially social workers) and many more from adults who had been abused when they were children.

Many of the social workers who got in touch said that they felt – quite rightly – that their profession has been given a raw deal in the media in recent years. A series of high-profile cases has seen the blame quickly thrown at those on the front line, who were often suspended before being sacked. It was only some years later, upon the completion of serious case reviews (most of which are never made public), that they were exonerated. All too often, blame for the failures we see in child protection reaches much further than one individual.

I hope this book goes some way towards showing what it's really like for front-line social workers in child protection, the good and the bad, and helps to explain why we, as a first-world, twenty-first-century society, are still letting down some of the most vulnerable members of our community.

To all those who wrote to me with their own personal stories of being abused, I was deeply moved by every single message I received. Your stories revealed much bravery and courage.

Others made me smile as you described how you had gone on to find happiness and satisfaction in life, despite suffering horrendously as children. It was also eye-opening for me, for although I have dealt with many historical cases of child abuse, many stories revealed deep thoughts and feelings I had not heard before.

The young children I dealt with rarely understood what had happened to them. They had no knowledge of sexual abuse and so found it very difficult to put their experiences into words. It was heartbreaking to hear them try. They were so innocent, so honest, as they struggled to express themselves – after all, they can't make up stories about something they know nothing about.

Very often, until someone notices something is wrong, children suffer in silence. They experience very strong feelings: fear, depression, guilt, shame, confusion, helplessness and despair. As those who wrote to me have made abundantly clear, adult survivors of childhood abuse are able to describe these thoughts and feelings, as well as fully understand the actions of adults who abused them.

Reading your innermost thoughts has been an honour and privilege and has widened my understanding tremendously. Where I have tried to help, I hope my assistance has proved useful and I hope this book, which many of you asked for, encourages more people to come forward to talk about their experiences.

Do keep writing to me. You are not alone; child abuse is a huge problem, much bigger than most people realise. It is possible to survive and find meaning and happiness in your life and there are many people who are ready and willing to help you.

This book, which describes a truly incredible year in the life of Hackney Child Protection, is dedicated to all the little victims – young and old – and to all those social workers, past and present, who have done an extraordinary job protecting the most vulnerable people in our society.

Harry Keeble
harrykeeble@btinternet.com

CHAPTER ONE

A YEAR IN THE LIFE

'Hi, John, I'm Harry.'

'Fuck off! Just fuck off!'

Easier said than done when you're stood on the roof of a building six floors up – actually make that a crumbling Victorian building with nothing but a suspiciously crooked chimney pot for company – oh and I was perched on a tiny handkerchief-sized piece of flat roof, a drop in front of me, a long sheer drop to the left, right and behind.

A stiff breeze whistled at my back. I held on to the pot a little more tightly. Ten yards away, John, fifteen years old, six feet tall and very angry, was crouched behind a raised part of the roof.

A voice shouted behind me from an open window. It was the care home manager. 'Harry, the negotiator's arrived!'

Thank God for that.

First thing that January morning, John had gone AWOL from the children's home – for the third time in seven days. He was what we call a 'regular misper' (as in missing person) and even though these things are usually a waste of police time, of course we have to go through the routine of responding to the form faxed to us from the children's home.

John, whose face was a familiar sight to many of Hackney's finest, had been quickly spotted in the high street by two constables. Instead of surrendering, he took off and they gave, well, I wouldn't exactly call it a 'chase', more like a 'follow'. It's not the same athletic pursuit you would associate with chasing a burglar over back-garden fences or someone running from a stolen car.

John jogged along, the two police officers not too far behind, grateful that they weren't being forced into a frantic chase – besides, running with all the gear they carry these days is a lot trickier than it looks.

To their relief, John headed back towards the children's home and straight to his room. 'Good lad,' they thought as they climbed the stairs, huffing and puffing from the mild exertion.

Even better, John didn't lock his door or barricade himself in. 'Crikey, what a good boy,' the officers thought, 'he really has "read the script". Just a few words and then we can write off his umpteenth missing person report, be on our way and solve some proper crimes.'

One of the cops gently pushed the door ajar.

'Oh bugger,' he said.

No John.

The window was open. He peered out of the window to see John hopping across the roof, climbing over chimney pots, surrounded by six storeys of air. He reached for his radio.

Standard police tactics came into force. A cordon was quickly put in place around the building, closing streets, attracting a lot of attention and sucking up Hackney's precious police resources.

Once all the necessary officers and cars were deployed around the block, any member of the public calling the police station about burglary or shoplifting would be told: 'We're very sorry, we're dealing with a serious incident, we'll get to you as soon as we can, please be patient.'

One car would be left to deal with emergencies while the rest of Hackney's uniformed police officers spent the rest of the day getting stiff necks, reporting any rooftop activity to those in charge.

Lucky me, I was the one who picked up the Child Protection bat-phone. I was on the scene in a few minutes. I found Adam, the manager, a tired, unhealthy-looking man with pale skin. He had all the physical signs I associate with stressful jobs that don't allow for a private life or exercise.

Adam's job certainly involved a great deal of time at his desk. On a shelf in his office were two ring folders bulging with statutory regulations and policies. One contained forty-seven separate procedures, ranging from how to deal with bullying, discrimination and substance abuse, to what to do if a child tries to make contact with a member of staff once they have left (although this advice runs to several pages it can be summarised as 'Don't').

Staff are expected to keep three simultaneous daily logs. The first is a handwritten diary noting the movement of staff and children in and out of the home; no Tipp-Ex corrections are allowed and all unused parts of pages must be crossed through and initialled. The second is a 24/7 record of the children's activities, registering, for instance, if a child gets up for a glass of water in the night. The third is an individual log compiled each day for each child, noting their movements and behaviour. All these logs and diaries must be stored for a minimum of seventy-five years – partly in case a child makes an allegation of abuse against a care worker. There are so many files like these that they're kept in a special storage unit in a disused salt mine in Kent.

It's very easy to end up puzzling over why people like Adam are drawn into this line of work. It's certainly not for the pay. There's no one to register their successes and pat them on the back, no commendations hanging on the wall: 'For rescuing Annette, aged fourteen, from prostitution' or 'For freeing Dominic, aged sixteen, from the horrors of crack cocaine'.

The only reward for people like Adam is the belief that they've made a difference. For some this fades over the years, as does the effort they put in and the distance between them and the children only increases and with it the sense of failure.

As Adam and I climbed the stairs, I told him that he did an amazing job. I was aware of the fact that the cops all too often blame places like care homes for failing to control these troublesome teenagers. I was also aware that if Adam lost hope, then the kids would lose a vital safety barrier between them and a life of misery and despair.

'Has John been suicidal before?'

'No, not at all.'

'Depressed?'

'No. He's extremely boisterous; he just wants attention. I've had a few wrestling matches with him before when he's tried to get the entire home up in arms.'

'Has he been in care long?'

'Since he was ten.'

'Parents?'

'His father's halfway through a long prison sentence for GBH. His mother last visited him three years ago. She's more concerned where the next can of strong cider's coming from.'

'Right.' Here was a fifteen-year-old boy, starved of his parents' love, desperate for the gap to be filled. The various carers did their best, and they helped him survive but there was no way they were ever going to fill that hole.

It's hard for the police to stay objective with kids like John. John's first introduction to the law was when he had been caught shoplifting. All the officers saw was an aggressive and rude acne-ridden teenager in a cheap tracksuit calling them 'wankers' and telling them to 'fuck off' – not the best of starts to any relationship. But of course, in John's case, his behaviour was the symptom of many tragedies. He didn't choose this life, he didn't want to become a pain in the arse, but shoplifting, running away and staying out all night was all he had.

It seemed as though everyone but the care home manager had had enough of John. 'John's been diagnosed with everything,' Adam told me, 'given every possible excuse; things like "school refusal disorder" and "oppositional defiant syndrome".' (To you and me that's rebellious behaviour to cops, teachers and social workers.)

'I'm starting to think he's got "corporal punishment seeking disorder",' Adam continued, 'he just wants someone to take control and push him in the right direction, although God knows which way that would be. He'd probably make a good cop,' he said with a smile. 'Seriously,' he continued. 'He looks and sounds like a monster but if you spend enough time with him, you get to see a chink of light now and then, a real interest in what's going on around him and a natural savvy you can't teach. And his vocabulary's much better than anyone else's in here. He's just had the worst possible start in life. How does the poem go?'

I knew it well. '"They fuck you up, your mum and dad . . ."'

'That's the one. Larkin, isn't it?'

It was very hard for most people to see John as emotionally vulnerable. It didn't help that he was six feet tall and looked like he could quite easily box middleweight at Olympic level.

Beat cops don't have time to get behind the facade, they have to deal with what they see going on in front of them to stop crimes being committed and that often means arresting, handcuffing and imprisoning the offender. This wasn't exactly the best therapy for someone like John, who had the loneliness of an orphan and the anger of a young man betrayed and unloved by those who should have cared more than anybody else. Now all he had was constant reminders – thanks to TV programmes and adverts – of what he didn't have, what everyone else takes for granted: a family.

Those programmes and ads twisted like a knife in John's heart; loving mums and doting dads were a cruel fiction to him. He never got to see a version of his father on TV, the father who came home drunk and high, who slapped his own flesh and blood around for half an hour or so, and who called him a 'useless little cunt who will amount to a pile of fuck all'.

As the first hour came and went, John steadily became – to the police, care home workers and the people who were stuck in traffic jams thanks to the roadblocks – a selfish nuisance. Everyone, including me, just wanted him off the roof and back at the home, and then we could all get on with the rest of our days and leave the staff to it – until the next time of course.

Mainstream cops have no time for attention-seekers. They spend their days charging around Hackney giving emergency first aid to young people with gunshot and stab wounds, tending to victims of muggings, robberies, arson, rape and murder. People like John 'waste police time'. The problem is that it's people like John who need more time than anyone else. If we spend the time on him now then there's less chance we'll have to rush to a future crime scene of John's making. After all, it's young lads like John whose short intense lives full of rage and frustration end in a hail of bullets or in a cold flash of steel.

Armed with an emotional snapshot of his life and hence totally out of my depth, I foolishly decided to engage. I clambered out of the window and onto the roof and, walking on all fours with all the speed and grace of a tortoise, I managed to get up to the apex. Gingerly resting my hands on a beautiful but wonky Victorian chimney pot, I manoeuvred myself onto a small section of flat roof about ten square feet, probably someone's en suite below.

I've got a bad feeling about this, I thought, as I tried not to think about crashing through the old roof into someone's bathroom.

Trying not to shake, I looked over the roof to see John poke his head over a parapet about ten yards away. He spotted me.

'Fuck off!' He disappeared again.

A lot of people are going to have stiff necks by the end of today, I thought, as I looked down and saw dozens of locals looking up and shielding their eyes from the sun. The eyes of Hackney were upon me.

'Great,' I muttered, 'just great.'

My mouth was dry. I should have had something hot to drink before coming up here. Although the sun was out, the January wind was freezing. What a start to the year, to the first day back after the holidays, Christmas pudding barely digested and here I was playing silly buggers on an icy roof.

The roof was constructed of flat dormers and steep tiled sections and John was quite happily jumping from one to the other like a mountain goat. I eased myself down onto another tiny flat square and stood up.

'John?' I called out hopefully.

'Fuck off, copper.'

'Why don't you come inside? It's dangerous out here.'

'No way.'

'Look, you're not in trouble with the cops, OK? Just come inside.'

'I'm not coming back in. I hate it in there. It's full of idiots telling me what to do. I just want to do my own thing, so fuck off.'

I turned around at the sound of a soft 'Hey!' It was the hostage negotiator who was now clinging to another chimney pot just a few yards from a window that opened onto the roof.

'He doesn't want to engage, so good luck,' I said quietly. 'I'll keep you company just in case.'

The negotiator nodded and tried to get John's attention. John ignored him and continued to amuse himself by hopping from one part of the roof to another.

I missed my crack dealers. You knew exactly where you were with a crack dealer. They dealt drugs, I arrested them; occasionally we had a good old punch-up but that was pretty much it.

I never knew what was coming next in Hackney's Child Protection Team. I had to admit that this was part of the attraction and part of what made me want to sign up but it was at times like these that I looked back on my crack-house raiding days with rose-tinted spectacles.

Working in child protection is one of the most challenging fields there is. The team investigates all forms of abuse (whether physical, mental, sexual, as well as kidnappings) carried out against a child by family members, extended family members, main carers, babysitters, youth workers and school workers – because in most cases of child abuse, that is exactly who's responsible.

In Hackney, cases arrive by the truckload each week, covering everything from rape to ritual abuse, from allegations of assault and/or inappropriate sexual behaviour made against teachers (about 900 in the UK last year, 79 of which led to criminal investigations)[1] to unacceptable behaviour from doctors, from paedophiles stalking schools to runaway kids on rooftops.

'I'm having no joy here,' the negotiator said twenty minutes later. 'I think we'd better let boredom and hunger do its work.'

After a long and tedious hour, I started to get the feeling that John was looking for a way to get past us. I stood up and looked behind me. The neighbouring building was but a short hop away – albeit over a sheer drop. If John made it, it was part of a large square of buildings and he would probably be able to lose us by escaping inside, or start a brand-new rooftop situation. I had visions of helicopters, fire engines, giant trampolines and enormous cordons spreading through the borough. As far as attention-seeking went, this was right at the top of the chart and would be more than enough to keep him on the roof for the rest of the day and into the night without any dinner. It didn't bear thinking about. Besides that, I had plenty of urgent referrals sitting on my desk. I wanted this over and done with.

I got myself into a position where I could spring forward and tackle John before he could dodge past me. This was not something I wanted to do at all but I hoped that seeing I was ready for him would be enough to put him off. I'm six feet five and thirteen stone. With my arms wide open on this tiny square of roof it would take someone with the devilish skills of Maradona to get past me.

However, this new activity did not go unnoticed by those below and I thought I could hear some yells of encouragement, whether for me, John or for us both I had no idea. I glanced down. This was a part of the world where kids saw crime scene cordons on a daily basis and thought they were entertainment. I could see kids John's age with phones pointing up at us. I was today's live show.

I soon realised that they were encouraging John to jump. Great, I thought, that's all we need. I really hoped John wasn't able to hear. If he did jump, and they were confronted with the horrific physical and emotional consequences of their actions (if a jumper lands feet first then the thighbone tends to travel through the body and out of the shoulder), then I bet they would soon be screaming and crying. Cowards. I watched with relief as the cops below removed them. Off they went. Good riddance.

I turned back to face John and started to wonder if I had been a bit premature, getting myself into a position where I could capture him. John wasn't suicidal; he wasn't literally on the edge and about to jump, so why take the risk?

Just then John jumped and landed on the flat piece of roof right in front of me with a thud.

Oh Christ.

If we fell over the ledge where he'd just come from then the four-foot drop would leave us bruised, but fine. Anywhere else and we were dead.

My body tensed as John edged towards me, looking for a way past. I took a breath, tensed and prepared to give him the biggest, most desperate bear hug of his life.

Suddenly a voice behind me yelled: 'Don't do it, Sarge!'

It was the negotiator. What the hell? That wasn't part of the plan! John saw my hesitation, seized the moment, leapt and elbowed past me and onto the other part of the roof. I felt myself teeter back and as my heart leapt I waved my arms in rapid circles, clawing through the air for what felt like an eternity to bring myself gradually back upright. It was probably just a second or two but it was enough time for my life to flash before my eyes. I sat down, swore, got my breath back and looked up.

John was ten feet away and smiling at me. He'd got past me. He'd beaten the cops, outplayed us all day long; this was a great victory for him. Now all he had to do was leap a five-feet gap and it would be helicopters and trampolines all night long.

Instead of making a run for the other building, however, John walked confidently back to the window where the negotiator was sitting, and climbed inside – of his own free will. This victory had been enough. I looked at the negotiator. He raised his arms in a shrug as if to say 'Whaddya know?' and disappeared inside after him.

I was simply relieved to be alive. And at least we'd got John down before the fire engines and helicopters drew the TV cameras. I climbed in and started to head downstairs. My phone rang. It was Rob, my avuncular boss.

'Harry, what's the point of you having a job phone if you don't answer it? Where on earth have you got to?'

Damn. I'd left my phone in my jacket pocket, inside the building. 'Well, I—'

'Never mind, get yourself down to the Hackney Downs estate. Craig will meet you.'

Rob gave me the address as I jogged downstairs and into the street.

'And a Happy New Year to you to,' I muttered to myself.

Yes, another day in the life of Hackney Child Protection was well and truly under way.

CHAPTER TWO

HACKNEY'S ROSE

Hackney is one of the most demanding areas to police in the UK. About 225,000 people (according to a 2007 study) are packed into this small borough. Forty-seven per cent of kids live on or below the poverty line. Burglary figures are almost three times the national average, while robbery levels are an astonishing eight times higher.[1]

Personally, I loved the area and the people in it. Although I now lived with my family in a leafy part of Hertfordshire, I had cut my police teeth in Hackney, working as a beat officer in the early nineties. This was where the action was, where impossible challenges awaited us every day. Here, there was no regeneration, thank goodness – it was a happy mess. Old was swallowed by new all right, but with a bargain basement entrepreneurial air.

I passed by officers who were rolling up crime scene tape and opening the cordon and jogged past tagged steel shutters, teenagers in the purple school uniform of Bridge Academy queuing outside a corner shop – 'Ownly 1 Shcoolchild at Time' read the memorable warning. I passed a bus shelter full of kids. Someone had scrawled 'Hackney Girl run tings' in thick black marker over the timetable. Some of them had faces and expressions older than their years. God knows there were enough risks for kids in Hackney without the dangers that came from those closest to them.

It's an intense place to live; never silent, the cries of a thousand languages echo through the borough and every kind of road vehicle roars, coughs and splutters over speed humps and dodges the traffic-calming twists and turns near the high street before becoming mired in East London's larger arteries. Pedestrians ignore every single piece of road safety advice; no one waits for the green man here. Like me they're all in a hurry to get somewhere that's important to them, whether they're criminals, local town hall officials or the underground artists overflowing out of fashionable Shoreditch and into the cheaper Hackney side of Bethnal Green Road.

A man in trendy black skin-tight jeans was passing a man coming out of a mosque dressed head to toe in white. Next to the mosque was a Baptist church. Turkish Cypriot cafes line the high street and I passed a procession of Kurds protesting about the treatment of their people in Kurdistan. At any moment I could be called to deal with someone from any one of those groups.

As a cop, I also knew Hackney's dark side, its shadowlands; I knew which gangs dealt which drugs on which streets, where the Turkish Cypriots drew their territorial lines to the north, where the Somalis bought their khat, which schools had the worst gang problems.

Hackney is packed full of contradictions; the crime-free Jewish area of Stamford Hill sits right next to Clapton's infamous Murder Mile. The rich live beside the poor; million-pound houses, way above the average price for London, sit squarely just a couple of streets away from some of London's most deprived council estates, infamous warrens of deprivation.

The borough is only a few minutes' commute from the City and for many the risks and inconveniences are outweighed by the potential return on a property development. Rich people abuse children too and we were often called to the posh homes as well as the council flats.

As I walked along Downs Park Road I passed massive ancient trees shading a burned-out Fiat, the black of the fire long faded to brown. The road was badly potholed. For some reason, some of Hackney's streets were as smooth as glass while on others you could kiss your car's suspension goodbye.

These contradictions are largely thanks to its people. About a third of the population of Hackney were born outside the UK. It meant we saw every kind of possible abuse that's ever been recorded and some which hasn't. For example, we were the first to come across ritual abuse of children who had been declared witches by their community.

It's not easy being a criminal in Hackney. There's a lot of competition here, whichever field you enter. Hackney also has the unfortunate distinction of being the place where you are more likely to hear the sound of gunshots than anywhere else in Britain. But it's not the 'general public' that are being shot. It's the teenage underclass. Gang members open fire on one another, not over money or drugs, but mainly over 'respect'. Kids join gangs for security and for prestige. That surge of well-being they get from believing that they are part of something and are valued is a false one. All too often they don't realise it until they are staring up at a paramedic's face.

These were the kids we often tried to rescue. Damaged children often turn to gangs because they don't get affection at home. They've often suffered abuse from their parents. Many criminals, whether hit men, robbers or crack prostitutes, had families: girlfriends, wives and kids – kids that needed to be saved from violence if they were to have a shot at a decent life.

The kids most at risk lived in rough estates with aggressive, sometimes drug-addicted parents, some of whom were armed. Occasionally, we'd find ourselves trying to gain access to the homes of some of London's toughest gangsters so we could take their kids away.

I jogged into the Downs Park estate and found Craig waiting for me by the lift. It looked like a bomb had gone off inside. And it stank like a week-old corpse.

'Stairs it is then,' I said.

Young Craig and I began our five-floor ascent and were soon breathing heavily, sucking in the smells of breakfasts from every continent on the globe, tinged with the unpleasant tang of ammonia. Gang graffiti covered every other wall. Criminals had set up shop in estate stairwells to evade the CCTV cameras recently installed on the estates. Nobody had thought to put cameras in the stairwells. Instead of driving crime out, the cameras had pushed it closer to people's front doors.

As we climbed, Craig told me that the fax had rolled in from social services earlier that morning. A neighbour had reported the sounds of several screaming children coming from the flat throughout the week.

'Great way to start the New Year, eh, Harry?' Craig huffed, his breath steaming in the cold air, as we arrived at the door. I smiled grimly and didn't mention my early morning rooftop adventure.

I'd known Craig for a couple of years. He'd arrived at Hackney's Child Protection Team some time before me, when it was a poorly funded department in desperate need of more officers to cope with the never-ending demand. He was in his late twenties and had one of those youthful faces that often led people to make comments about policemen getting younger and led criminals into a false sense of security, thinking that they could pull the wool over his young eyes. Despite his baby face,

Craig was a seven-year veteran of child protection and took his work very seriously. He was a tenacious and dedicated investigator.

The need for detectives was so great that Craig had gone from walking his Hackney beat on a Friday afternoon in uniform to investigating child rape in a suit on Monday. It was a daunting prospect (it usually took about four to seven years to become a detective) but fortunately Craig had the courage and determination to see it through.

I'd found my rapid transformation from uniformed sergeant to besuited detective equally unsettling but at the same time I'd been excited by the prospect. I'd come to Hackney from the neighbouring borough of Haringey, where I'd led a five-man drugs squad on a non-stop war on crack. We'd had a lot of success, closing a hundred crack houses of all shapes and sizes in just twelve months. At the end of the year I was asked if I wanted to join a glamorous new anti-drugs task force.

I turned it down in favour of Child Protection. Why? Because of the children and crack babies I'd seen in the crack houses. And because eight-year-old Victoria Climbié had been tortured to death a few streets away from where I'd been raiding drug dens. I hated the fact that it was the children who suffered most from the drugs trade; I felt the police were letting them down – these kids were the most vulnerable members of our society, after all.

To make certain, I was given the opportunity to spend some time at a North London Child Protection office, in a sort of 'suck it and see' experiment. It was known amongst the more macho police circles as the 'Cardigan Squad' and had a low status; its officers were seen as the 'poor cousins' or 'Cinderellas' of the Met. They had hardly any trained officers and no budget to speak of. Our little drugs squad didn't have any computer technology but Child Protection was supposed to be a serious department with countless cases requiring major resources. Yet the software was slow and unwieldy; it could take all day just to research four or five cases when they should have been able to do that many an hour.

I was amazed to discover that officers investigating serious offences against children weren't actually trained detectives. They were simply regular police officers with a job title. As I studied the files, I realised I was staring at the faces of kids we'd 'rescued' from the horrors of crack cocaine. What was the point of handing them over to Child Protection Teams only for them to disappear, eventually showing up years later as crack addicts and prostitutes?

I'd come to Hackney Child Protection thinking that the department needed a good boot up the backside. This illusion was soon dispelled by the dedicated team who worked on some of the most complex cases I'd ever seen. I was out of my depth quite soon.

That I'd stuck with it was thanks to my colleagues, but none more so than our boss, Rob, who took the time to steer me through some really tough investigations. Not many people have the stomach, heart and mind for what we do – the demands of interviewing paedophiles and their victims as well as studying thousands of photos and hours of films of child porn, searching for clues that could rescue the children trapped in the nightmare world of those videos, is not something that most people can do without suffering psychologically.

There was no response to my loud policeman's 'I mean business' knock on the door, so I repeated it, this time with considerably more force.

Silence. Except, listening carefully with my ear to the door, I could make out the sounds of thumping and children shrieking from somewhere in the flat.

God, what the hell's going on here? I thought. I was about to upgrade my knock to my size-ten boot when the door cracked open and an African woman peered out at us.

I flashed my warrant card. 'Hi there, police, may we come in please?' It wasn't really a question, we were going in no matter what, but I always liked to keep things as friendly and polite as possible.

The woman, who was wearing a large bright orange and red dress and hat to match, frowned and said nothing. Slowly, reluctantly, she swung the door open.

It was a three-bedroom council flat with good-sized rooms and in a few seconds Craig and I were surrounded by children who poured into the hallway. They quickly filled every available space, yelling at the top of their voices.

'What the . . .?' Craig said as we stared at one another open-mouthed at the sheer volume of children.

The kids, who were still coming into the hall from all directions, all seemed to be laughing. It was a very surreal moment. The woman, who was still frowning, said nothing and led us down the hall into the lounge.

I couldn't see any signs of abuse. The flat was clean, so were the kids, several of whom were in nappies – which I noted were all unsoiled. Often I would come across kids in yellowing nappies so full the elastic had been stretched. They'd look at me, crying their eyes out, while their mum clung on to her can of strong cider. Although they'll never remember it in later years, this pain blights their early life. Toddlers in this state don't scream after a while because they become so used to the pain; they're just miserable (although in some extreme cases babies have died from nappy rash, due to blood poisoning). Some suffer in this way as their carers are downright lazy, others because they cannot cope.

But that was clearly not the case here. The kids quickly grew boisterous with our presence. Even though they ranged in age from eighteen months to seven, there was a healthy pack mentality: we were on their turf; we had upset their routine and they wanted to know why.

I counted seven in the lounge as we sat down, and could hear others playing elsewhere in the flat. Some were drawing, others were playing with a variety of brightly coloured toys in the simply but cleanly furnished room. They were totally unafraid and seemed to me to be completely contented.

'Who are you?' one boy asked confidentially. I took him to be about seven and quite probably the pack leader.

'Harry,' I answered, 'and what's your name?'

'Hayden. What football team do you support?'

'Arsenal. Where's your mum?'

'She's at work. Who's your favourite player?'

I'd seen this before – but in an entirely different location. This was a crèche – except this one was illegal and the woman running it, sat opposite us, was very frightened, although she proved herself a natural by quickly silencing the children.

'Play quietly now,' she said firmly in a strong Nigerian accent, 'and let me talk to these men in peace.'

Sure enough, the kids quickly settled down. I made the proper introductions, which only served to increase her anxiety.

'My name's Omorose, but everyone calls me Rose.'

'Auntie Rose!' Hayden corrected.

She smiled, albeit with anxiety. She knew troubled times were ahead.

'We're going to have to report this,' I said. 'It's clearly not legal. You do realise that, don't you?'

She said nothing for a moment; no doubt there would be tax issues and probable financial penalties for an illegal crèche. Plenty for her to worry about.

'What about the children?' she asked.

Ouch. That question filled me with guilt. The kids were her first concern, not the Inland Revenue or Ofsted. It would have been a lot easier had she simply been a money-grabbing businesswoman who didn't care about the kids. Then we would have simply removed the kids and prosecuted, nice and easy. I could already tell this was going to turn out differently.

'We're not going to take the kids away, I can see that they're not in danger.' I did wonder how she might react if the kids ever got out of hand, as I'm sure they would and, of course, why some who were old enough weren't in school.

'But what about tomorrow?' Rose demanded. 'These children's mothers depend on me, how else can they go to work? Without me, they cannot work, they will be unemployed and have to rely on handouts.'

While this wasn't our problem, Craig and I were sympathetic. We knew only too well, having worked the night shifts, that there's a whole other world out there, a world that most Londoners never get to see.

As a beat officer working the early shift, I'd once caught the night bus into town from home. When it arrived, even though it was 4.30 a.m. and the streets were deserted, inside there was standing room only. This is the 'other' rush hour; the one that transports the people that keep the cogs of the City of London turning; the men and women who prepare the way for and look after the city – the security guards, caretakers, street-sweepers, sandwich fillers, newspaper sellers and coffee-makers. A hundred and fifteen buses ferry 104,000 passengers every night, half of whom (according to Transport for London) are people travelling to or from work, mostly on minimum wage jobs. In the last decade the use of night buses has gone up from 14 million to 38 million passenger journeys per year, a reflection of the rapid expansion of minimum wage jobs in London.

As the bus stopped at the massive estates between Stamford Hill and Stoke Newington, I marvelled at the large crowds that surrounded each bus stop. People either desperate to get to work

on time or desperate to get home to bed after a long night's club-
bing battled to get on the already overloaded bus.

I decided to make room and walked the last ten minutes
through the deserted streets, past a homeless man asleep in the
door of a KFC, grateful for my life, grateful that my job paid me
enough so that I could save up for a car.

Of course, many of these poorly paid workers were parents. As
is so often the way with London's poor, these parents had found
in Rose a solution to the problem of childcare, just one part of
the massive illegal – but often extremely practical – underground
economy.

'Hayden's mother is single,' Rose told us in her rich Nigerian
accent. 'She's over forty and works from 6 a.m. in the City as a
cleaner. She makes £600 a month. She has to drop Hayden off
and then I take him to school for 9 a.m. She's back home by
three, so picks him up. Without me she has no job. There aren't
enough places. Even if she could find somewhere to leave her
son, she can't afford childcare. We are just trying to help free
ourselves from the poverty trap.'

'Rose, if you're going to do this, you need to do it legally,' I
said.

I felt awful. This was a community trying to solve its own problems in its own way; there was no obvious need to take these kids
into care. Craig and I left Rose in the lounge for a quick conflab.

'I think she deserves a medal,' Craig said quietly, 'not to be
shut down and prosecuted.'

'Maybe, but we both know there's plenty that could go wrong
here for these kids – no matter how noble the intentions – that
could land Rose in serious trouble. We'd better call social services and wait for the parents to arrive. Perhaps between us we
can figure out some solutions for the mums.'

I called Hackney Social Services, one of the most overworked
departments in the UK. Dev answered the phone. He was one of

the friendliest people I'd ever met; most people mistakenly saw him as incredibly naive – he was anything but. Dev had an almost magical Derren Brown-like ability to see through lies, combined with incredibly sharp observational skills that would have turned Sherlock Holmes green with envy. He also had an incredibly thick Indian accent and a curious way of phrasing sentences. It had taken me a few weeks to be able to understand him.

'Ah, Harry, I must say as much as I like to hear your voice, the sound of it has made my heart sink somewhat. I'd set aside today to write a report and two core assessments. And now there's no one else here. Let me have a fast word with my manager and expect I'll be there in twenty minutes.'

Sure enough, Dev was with us in good time to greet the dozen or so mothers who gradually started to roll up to collect their kids. As I expected, all of them were single and had been working in the City in low-paid jobs. They were nearly all Nigerian or West African. Most of them had been at work since 5 a.m., which of course meant that they had had to get their kids up at that time, hardly ideal.

All of them, without a shadow of a doubt, were totally committed to their kids and would not be able to afford childcare – let alone find someone prepared to take their kids from before 5 a.m. Only one of them had ever cropped up on the child protection radar (and that was for something entirely innocent); they were good mothers determined to work, determined to do the best for their kids, to build a future for them. For many, breaking out of poverty requires an iron will, sacrifice and a hundred per cent dedication – and it's twice as hard if you're a single mum with a child.

As a father of three kids myself, one newly born, I knew all too well the problems of finding good and affordable childcare. Across the UK, the cost of a nursery place ranges between £125 and £375 per week. Inner London is the most expensive with an average cost about 25 per cent higher than the rest of the UK. If the baby is under two years old, prices go up even higher as babies require more hands-on care.[2]

Many nurseries also charge penalties if children are collected late (although wealthier parents are sometimes happy to pay the fine for the extended babysitting service). State-funded nurseries have a huge waiting list and the system to claim money for help with nursery care is so complicated that many people don't even realise that they're entitled.

Rose had no overheads and insisted that she ran it on her own. There were pictures in her flat of her with a man I took to be her husband, but nothing recent, so I wondered if perhaps he had passed away. Even so, I guessed that someone would have joined her for the school run and beyond – after all, she couldn't leave all the youngest kids behind while she dropped the others off at school.

I took no pleasure from dismantling this nursery, although I marvelled at the fact that Dev, whose family had moved to the UK from Mumbai when he was a child, was working with Rose and the ladies from Lagos on how to work within the British child care system.

'Even if they qualify for tax care credit, they have to pay £4,000 a year,' Rose said. 'On a pre-tax salary of £15,000 how are they going to manage? They pay me less than a quarter of that.'

'Rose, you must register as a child carer,' Dev said. 'I'm afraid it's the only way this will work.'

'Impossible!' she huffed.

'It might not be as difficult as you think,' Dev said. 'You might be able to backdate registration and possibly the, er, "tax issues". If the taxman sees you are trying to make amends then he might be a bit sympathetic. Let me help you.'

None of us got the impression that Rose was particularly money-motivated. I think she liked kids and loved doing something that was so obviously useful. Like many people living in the poorer part of Hackney, she was distrustful of the 'system', and thought she would never be able to work within it.

By the time Craig and I waved off the last child and we began heading back to the station to try to write it all up, I was feeling pretty sad.

'Those ladies will get little sympathy from their employers,' Dev said. 'It is a great pity.'

'You're not wrong there, Dev,' Craig said with a sigh.

They'd soon find themselves out of work and on benefits. Back to square one. We had just dismantled a perfectly formed (albeit illegal) Hackney ecosystem. As usual, there are no winners in child protection.

Thirty minutes later Craig and I arrived back at Stoke Newington police station and slipped through the sliding glass doors into the busy and modern front reception. It was full of police officers going about their business in a professional and confident manner. Every time I saw scenes like these I couldn't help but think how far we'd come since the dark days of the 1980s when Stoke Newington was at the centre of one of the largest corruption scandals the Metropolitan Police had ever seen, with many officers accused of beating up locals and dealing in drugs. Living in Hackney then had been like living in a police state in a Third World country. In those days the crack dealers were untouchable, at night we had twenty-eight cops on the street, they had more street dealers than that outside the Shell petrol station in Stoke Newington Road. If you came across a stabbing victim and they told you to 'Fuck off', you called them an ambulance and did as they asked. Hackney was by no means perfect but thank God those dark days were long gone.

I zipped up to the canteen, picked up a machine-made macchiato and stepped into our simply furnished but spacious and modern offices. These days – ever since the inquiry into the death of Victoria Climbié – we had a sensible budget in that we were given all the money we needed to do our job. Lord knows we needed it – but we were still desperately short of officers. Even today, many cops still need to get the message that child protection is a great job for detectives and doesn't deserve its low status. Oddly enough, social services see it the other way around, with child protection regarded as the high-status job.

Clara, the office manager, greeted us. 'Hello, Harry, where've you been this morning, then?'

I'd known Clara ever since I started work as a young PC in the early nineties. She was more like my favourite aunt than a colleague. A local girl who took no nonsense, Clara was respected by all. Somehow she kept us all in order and made sure the office ran like clockwork. In this line of work we couldn't afford to screw up, and making sure our interview suites weren't double-booked and that there were always enough people on hand to make arrests, protect children, attend court hearings and meetings with social services was a full-time job that Clara handled brilliantly.

'Oh you know, chasing troubled teens over the rooftops of Hackney. Is Rob in?'

'In the interview suite with Lucy and a five-year-old girl.'

'How long have they been in there?'

'About an hour.'

Our 'suite' was actually a specially built flat attached to the police station with its very own secluded entrance, so the little victims wouldn't be confronted by the frightening chaos of the entrance to our modern grand police station.

I sat down in front of my computer and looked through the dozen or so child-related reports that had come in from various other police departments overnight. Many of them had been written in the small hours and I soon found myself trying to get my head around some of the syntax. Tired cops trying to write dry reports after having been awake all night can be forgiven for writing sentences that are, how shall I put it, rather 'challenging'. I've certainly been guilty of that myself.

'Harry?'

I looked up. Rob had just walked into the office and was waving me over.

'A word in your ear please.'

Lucy was with him. Tall, thin, dark-haired and green-eyed, 28-year-old Lucy had started in Child Protection shortly after me. She was as tough as any male cop, had faced many horrors without flinching and was a skilled evidence-gatherer as well being a natural with kids – a skill that's truly priceless in Child Protection.

Robert aka 'Rob' or the 'Fat Controller', as in *Thomas the Tank Engine*, led our squad of fifteen. A detective inspector, Rob had quickly become my mentor and friend; he was the unit's rock, always completely behind us no matter what crap we ended up dumping on his desk. Always remaining calm, he knew exactly what to do even when we encountered some new, unbelievable horror or awkward situation – which was all the time. He wasn't afraid to let us make decisions without him, refreshing in these days of blame culture. 'The worst decision,' he said, 'is to make no decision at all.'

Rob refused to stay in a separate office and worked instead amongst us, right in the thick of things – this also meant it was impossible for us to keep anything hidden from him. Child Protection was Rob's life calling, he was always at the office before anyone else and never failed to put in a twelve-hour day – even though he was near retirement and on some days looked closer to seventy than fifty-five. He enjoyed informality and never wore a suit. His wife Mona was lovely and we'd often walk into the office to find our desks covered in freshly baked goodies, courtesy of her. Pictures of his grown-up kids and grandchildren covered his desk.

A modest man, his desk drawers were full of awards and commendations buried under case reports and he never complained, no matter how short-staffed we were or how hard he had to work. He could have taken it a lot easier but he simply wouldn't hear of it. Honestly, the man deserved a medal.

Rob pushed his glasses back on his balding head as I quickly told him about this morning's unusual discovery.

'Yes, dealing with childcare issues isn't easy,' he said.

As police officers, we all knew that managing work and family life was a tricky balancing act. Working in Child Protection is never a nine-to-five job and every day we faced sudden developments that threw our personal lives into chaos. Thanks to the long and unpredictable hours, police officers invariably have to find flexible ways to deal with childcare. For example, two detective constables who both gave birth to baby daughters within a few months of each other thought they'd come up with the perfect solution. They were the same rank, worked in the same station and were close friends. Their daughters were about the same age, so it made sense to share both job and childcare. They split the forty-hour week, both working two ten-hour days. One looked after both of the girls while the other worked their shift. They also covered for one another when a case demanded overtime, which was often – it's pretty hard to find a child-minder with that kind of flexibility. It was great for the kids, who became like sisters.

Unfortunately, a few weeks after starting this arrangement, the two detectives found an Ofsted inspector on their doorstep, accusing them of running an 'illegal child-minding business'. They thought the inspector was mistaken and invited him into their homes to explain the situation – that they were police officers and friends. But they were technically breaking the law, so that was that. The kids' dads were also police officers who worked long and irregular full-time shifts so both children had to go into a nursery at a cost of £260 each. The mums were told that they would be subjected to random surveillance to make sure they didn't try it again.

If this had happened in our department, then they would have been turned into useless detectives. We simply couldn't down tools at the end of the day – possibly leaving a kid in danger – to pick up our children from nursery. I could only imagine that the colleagues of those women would end up resenting the fact that they would have no choice but to flee the office.

There must have been thousands of parents doing this who had no idea that they were breaking the law. Thankfully, in 2009, the Children's Secretary, Ed Balls, saw sense. Now if you want to share childcare with your best friend then you no longer have to undergo criminal record checks and take childcare courses to make your arrangements legal.[3]

Most police officers weren't lucky enough to share childcare with friends and colleagues, so many of us spent a fortune on child-minders and, despite my best efforts, I missed school plays, sports days and parents' evenings.

Lucy showed us how it was done. She managed to balance home life and work – even though her son had several medical problems that required a great deal of attention.

'There's no easy solution,' she said when I asked her how she did it. 'I'm lucky, I suppose, in that there's flexibility here. I can write up reports from my local station near home if I need to. I try to come to Rob with the problem already sorted if possible.'

'Take note, Harry,' Rob said with a chuckle.

Clara interrupted us. 'Just had a call from the Homerton,' she said seriously. 'It looks like we might have a baby shaker.'

She handed Rob her notes of the call. Rob's smile vanished as he looked up at Lucy and me. 'I want you two on it. Better start by calling the husband.'

CHAPTER THREE

BABY SHAKER

The phone rang and went to voicemail. 'Hi, Will, my name is Detective Sergeant Harry Keeble, please can you call me back straightaway. It's urgent.'

Urgent was an understatement. I was about to deliver the news that would see Will's life crumble around him, that would see him go through shock, rage and grief, before he accepted the fact that nothing in his life would ever be the same, that what he experienced today would shape every day that followed.

He called a minute later. I could hear tannoy announcements in the background; he must have just come out of the Tube. 'Will, I need you to come to the Starlight Ward of Homerton Hospital.'

'What the fuck is going on?' I realised that his anger wasn't directed at me but because he had just turned the corner and seen the uniformed officer standing on guard outside his front door, helping preserve the scene of the crime.

'Will, go to your front door and ask for Lucy, she'll bring you here. I can't talk to you about this over the phone.'

'Right.'

I rang off and quickly called Lucy, who had gone with the

uniforms to secure the scene for forensics, hoping to God she answered. She picked up on the third ring.

'Lucy, it's Harry. The husband's outside and doesn't know.'

'Leave it to me.'

There's only one way to break news like this: concisely and clearly, so there can be no misunderstanding.

Twenty minutes later I was standing in front of Will in the quiet parents' room, part of the small paediatric inpatient section of Homerton Hospital, the fifteen-bed Starlight Ward.

Will was in his late twenties, good-looking, wearing expensive clothes with a haircut to match; in happier times Will easily could have been the poster boy representing the success of life in the City. Now, however, he looked utterly crushed and confused. He brushed his dark hair back with shaking hands. He was still in shock; the tears were yet to come. Will was as yet unable to deal with the incomprehensible: that his baby daughter Emma lay in a coma and on a life-support machine and that his wife, Anne Marie, was under suspicion of being responsible. Emma's twin sister, Jo, had been taken into our care when we'd arrested Anne Marie – for how long would be determined by the events to come.

Lucy had packed a bag of a few essentials: changes of clothes and toiletries for the mum and dad. They wouldn't be going home anytime soon. Forensic teams in white jumpsuits had started going through their house; the middle-class neighbours watched with horrified curiosity, wanting to know what tragedy had befallen their outwardly perfect neighbours.

The paediatrician, shining his penlight into Emma's sightless eyes, had seen lots of tiny specks – burst blood vessels, possibly caused by violent shaking.

A baby's head is large and heavy. It makes up about 25 per cent of the infant's total body weight. Its neck muscles are too weak to support such a disproportionately large head. If someone grabs the baby's shoulders and shakes it, the brain bounces within the skull cavity, bruising the brain tissue. The brain swells, creating pressure and leading to bleeding at the back of the eye, which can cause blindness. Sometimes, blood vessels that feed the brain are torn. Blood can collect inside the skull, creating more pressure leading to seizures, lethargy, vomiting, and irritability, or in extreme cases coma or even death.

Around two hundred cases of shaken baby syndrome (SBS) are diagnosed each year – but not all of them correctly. At the time of this case, in 2005, the Court of Appeal had heard four appeals of SBS in just one month; two convictions were upheld, one conviction was dismissed and one conviction was reduced from murder to manslaughter.[1] There remains a great deal of debate as to what symptoms and physical signs prove that a baby has been deliberately shaken.

These remained debates for the courtroom, however. At that moment, I was wrestling with a tough decision, a decision that was entirely mine. In any other case the suspect would have been told to strip on a large white piece of paper before changing into a white suit. Their clothes and anything that had fallen from them while they changed would be bagged, tagged and studied.

Anne Marie, my only suspect, was currently in the bed beside her daughter, however, and so potential evidence was being contaminated. We had already passed the 'golden hour' of the police operation, the most valuable time to collect physical evidence. I also didn't want her to see Will, not yet anyway, as this would mean more contamination and if I let them talk together there was the danger they would create a 'story', making our job that much more difficult.

But that's their ten-month-old baby in there, I thought. Should we arrest them and further tear their lives apart at a time like this? What if we've got it wrong?

Just as I was getting Will to sit down with a cup of weak and sweet machine tea so I could start briefing him on what I planned to do, the paediatrician came in.

'May I have a word, Detective Sergeant Keeble? In private.'

I nodded and we stepped outside into the corridor; I could see the bright walls of the Starlight Ward just down the hallway.

The doctor was about my age, in his mid-thirties; he looked fresh and alert and clean-shaven. This was how his day had started, with a baby in a coma.

'I have the best job in the world,' he said, 'but sometimes it's the worst. Emma's not going to make it. I'm about to tell the mother that we're going to turn the life support off.'

Oh God. This made my rooftop brush with infinity and the closing of the crèche look like a jolly day at the fair. I wondered how the doctor would deal with this at the end of his day. Could he brush it aside or did he have someone to talk it over with at home?

I thanked him for letting me know.

'What do you want to do?' he asked.

I sided with humanity and let the mother stay with her daughter. Once she'd said her last goodbyes, then she'd have to come with us. I decided I had to give the father the option of being there too. I couldn't know how he would react – perhaps the anger would suddenly pour out. I doubted it, but you never knew, so I would have to be there too. The doctors broke the news in private. They were then taken into a special quiet room while Emma was taken off the machine, brought in and gently handed over.

Anne Marie, who was a few years younger than Will, cuddled her daughter, telling her how much she loved her. For a little while, they were a family together again. Emma looked so alive, so healthy, but her last little bit of life quickly ebbed away.

Leaving her at that point, saying goodbye was the hardest

thing Will and Anne Marie would ever have to do. There's nothing in life that can prepare you for facing something like that, nothing.

The following day, Lucy and I were in our interview suite with Anne Marie, who had spent the night in a cell. She was now wearing a fresh change of clothes and staring at a steaming mug of tea. Video cameras and tapes recorded everything. Rob was watching on a TV screen in an adjoining room, from where the recording devices could be controlled.

We started gently, but we didn't have to talk for very long before it came pouring out.

'Yes, I lost control,' Anne Marie said. 'I found it hard bringing up twins. Everyone seemed to think motherhood was hard work but that everyone just coped. I couldn't cope. I didn't know what to do; I didn't know why I didn't feel like all the other mums seem to feel.

'While Will was at work, I spent my days in despair. He was on his way up. The idea was that we would put everything into his career so that we'd be able to afford the life we wanted. Me a full-time mum, looking after the kids and our beautiful home, making sure they went to the best schools and had the best holidays and so on. Will was home late and left at the crack of dawn. When the door slammed behind him I felt like I was locked in, a prisoner in an inescapable trap of our own making.'

'Did you talk to Will?' Lucy asked.

'No. I went to see my GP. He said I was depressed and that he could prescribe medication but I didn't believe for one moment that I needed tablets. Only crazy people, weak people take tablets, right?'

She stopped talking for a few moments. We didn't need to answer that question and I watched the untouched tea steam for a few seconds, waiting for her to continue.

'I was too proud. I thought I was a strong woman and refused help but it was a mistake. I should have used my strength to accept help, to tell Will what was going on.'

'It doesn't sound as if Will could be there for you,' I said.

'What could I do? He was working every hour God sends, first in the office, last out, as well as studying for exams and working shifts covering the foreign markets … I don't know what did it in the end. I – I – can't … Oh God, how can we be talking about this?'

I glanced at Lucy. A slight, almost imperceptible nod told me that she thought Anne Marie was able to continue, at least for now. We had reached the critical moment very quickly. The plan had been to guide her slowly but Anne Marie's thoughts had raced ahead; thoughts of where her baby was now, thoughts of the mortuary and the post-mortem, the realisation that she was never going to see Emma again, the shock repeated in wave after wave until exhaustion set in and unadulterated grief took over.

'The last thing I remember … sitting in the lounge. I felt like I could never go outside again. Emma and Jo weren't crying, I was. I was sobbing as I looked at them. I wanted a rest; I wanted something to change so that these feelings would go away. At that moment … At that moment I … There was something building inside me; tension, pressure and that was it, that's all I remember.'

Anne Marie's pent-up frustration and despair had erupted into an uncontrollable rage. There was no single trigger event. Her depression, unnoticed by her husband, had pushed her beyond her limit. That was it. That was all that it took. The torrent of emotions that came with postnatal depression out of control had led to the death of her daughter. It was now up to a court to decide her future. In this case, it's not actually murder, it's infanticide, when the mother kills her newborn child (under twelve months) while the balance of her mind is disturbed as a result of giving birth.

In the months after the birth, Anne Marie had been repressing her depression, her irrational – as she saw it – desire for help, thinking she shouldn't need it. Pride in the superficial success of her family made it impossible for her to admit her deeper feelings to anyone. She might have confided in Will if he hadn't needed her to be strong for the sake of his job, a job that would provide the family with a lifetime of security. This created a huge, overarching sense of despair, despair Anne Marie managed to resist for a long time before her sudden and fatal emotional crash.

The sentencing guidelines for infanticide are the same as those for manslaughter, that where the defence of 'abnormality of mind' is used (this is defined as a state of mind so different from that of ordinary human beings that the reasonable man would term it abnormal). Although custodial sentences are sometimes given, it's become increasingly rare for a mother who kills her baby when it's less than twelve months old to go to prison, unless very exceptional circumstances are involved.

We interviewed a shell-shocked Will next; he had clearly realised that their fast-track plan to a secure future had backfired in the worst possible way.

'I should have realised but we were caught on the rollercoaster and couldn't get off. When I think about it now, it seems so crazy, so . . . so inhuman what I was doing. Some days there was nothing to do but we all stayed late anyway, nobody on my floor wanted to be the first to leave. The one who stayed latest was the one who got noticed and had a better shot of promotion. Then you had to be one of the boys, so we'd work late and then party late. I didn't tell Anne Marie about that bit. I thought she wouldn't understand, that going to these bars and strip clubs were just as much a part of the job as being on the trading floor. All the project managers did coke and they loved getting us newbies to try it for the first time, getting us hooked with them. They shagged the dancers, paying them £200 a time, and threw cash at them; they were all from Eastern Europe and worshipped us. Then I was somehow supposed to find time to study for my exams. Emma ... Oh God ...'

Lucy leaned across the table. 'Will, you don't have to go on if you don't want to,' she said softly.

'It's OK,' Will said, 'I want to get this done now.'

I could see he was physically holding himself together by keeping his muscles taut. As soon as the first sob came, spasms of grief would follow and he would be lost to fatigue and grief. With an effort, he continued.

'Emma and Jo kept me going. I thought if I could just pull myself together and get through this then it would all be OK.'

Will and Anne Marie were already exhausted when parenthood began. The coke wouldn't have helped, of course. The line between high jinks and addict is hard to see; few realise they've crossed it until it's too late and I suspected that this had further blinded Will to his wife's mental illness.

'The only one doing well out of our life plan was the company. I worked like a slave, made them a fucking fortune and look where it's got us. I was working too hard to notice, until it was too late. Now I've got to pay for it.'

In Will's eyes, his job, the very thing that was supposed to provide for his family, had destroyed that family. He had lost Emma; his wife, already depressed and going through bereavement, would soon be on trial. I couldn't see Will returning to work. Then there was Jo, their other daughter. Eventually social services would decide what to do about Jo.

Will's whole world may have caved in, but it was now that he needed to fight. He had to fight for his surviving daughter and see his wife through a trial, if he could.

CHAPTER FOUR

NEVER TO RETURN

The monster looked at me coldly.

'No comment,' he said, sneering.

David was in his early thirties, handsome, self-assured, smug and smart. I hated the clever ones. They were the worst kind, the most dangerous kind. Evil shone clear and bright in David's eyes. He was a predator of the highest order and delighted in the game he was now a part of. The only reason we were here at all was thanks to a neighbour whose suspicions, I believed (although motivated by jealousy), were bang on.

His victim, I was a hundred per cent certain, was Anna, a beautiful fourteen-year-old girl, the younger daughter of David's girlfriend, an attractive thirty-something called Karen who lived on one of the borough's estates. These zigzagging H-blocks were known by criminals as 'The Snake', thanks to the twisting corridors that connected them (lots of places to lie in wait for the unwary).

Anna had agreed to an interview and did everything she could to defend David. All it had done for me, however, was confirm my worst fears. It wasn't surprising to learn that boys pursued Anna at school. She was beautiful but innocent and romantically minded. She adored teen girls' magazines, rom-coms and liked the social aspect of school, although she found the lessons difficult. Anna revealed that she felt as though her mother had not paid her or Sue, her sixteen-year-old sister, much attention in recent years.

Karen had once had hopes of becoming a professional singer before Sue and then Anna had come along courtesy of a session drummer, ending Karen's dreams. Their father had left when Sue was three and the girls had no memory of him, although they hated not having a dad. And then David had come along. The perfect boyfriend. The perfect father.

'It was brilliant when Dave moved in,' Anna told me. 'Before, Sue, my older sister, and me could never persuade Mum to let us go to a party on the estate. One day we were driving her mad, telling her we was bored and that we never got to have any fun, when David came home. He'd been seeing Mum for just a few weeks and had already moved in. He was working on a building site.

'Just as Mum was telling us we weren't going to no house party, David came in. He asked us "what party?" Mum said we wanted to go to some party with a boy from our school. It was in the same building as us and his parents had said it would be OK and his older brother was gonna be there to make sure it didn't get out of hand.

'David gave us permission. He said Sue being sixteen was old enough to look after me. He said to give him the address and he'd pick us up at midnight. He had a bottle of wine with him and said him and Mum would welcome the privacy for a few hours. We were amazed when Mum agreed. He's brilliant, a real miracle worker. He's made all of our lives so much better.

'He's good-looking, he's a builder and always loaded with cash and he loves spending time with Sue and me. He knows about our music and movies we're into and always listens to what we have to say. Mum never seems to be that interested, to be honest. I think he likes Sue more than me. She's older, sixteen, so closer to his age, I suppose. I'm still too young really, you know, being fourteen.

'He takes us on days out, he buys us takeaways, make-up and other treats. Even better than that, he gives Sue the occasional fiver and the odd packet of fags. She loves that; she's made all her friends jealous.'

Although it seemed from these comments as though David was after Sue, he wasn't.

He wanted Anna.

David wasn't a paedophile, not in the 'normal' sense. The law says that anyone under eighteen is a child. A paedophile is someone who has a sexual interest in a child. So does that mean that a nineteen-year-old who sleeps with his seventeen-year-old girlfriend is a paedophile? No, of course not. The term 'child' is a legal one. A paedophile would not find a mature-looking fourteen-year-old girl attractive. They much prefer pre-pubescent kids. There is a difference between under-age sexual activity and paedophilia. This is why the law has specific offences regarding under-thirteens.

David had chosen carefully. Anna was fourteen.

'Was there ever a moment you felt uncomfortable around David?' I asked Anna.

Her response sent a chill down my spine.

'Well, there was one time. But it was nothing, really. Mum and Sue had gone out together for the evening. Some party at a neighbour's. David said he didn't fancy it and he was going to have an early night as he had work in the morning. Once they'd gone he got a DVD and some crisps – it was *Love Actually*.'

'Did you sit together to watch it?'

'Yes, and David gave me some wine. I knew I shouldn't have but I felt grown up, that at last I was having some special time with David. He'd always been doing stuff with Sue and Mum, going out and so on, so when he put his arm round me it felt really cosy, like ... like he was my dad, like I was getting some special time with him at last. We were laughing at the film, the wine made me feel giggly.

'Then he put his hand on my leg.'

As Anna told this story, I noticed that her skin had flushed and then paled and that she started to breathe more quickly.

'What happened next?'

Anna's hands jerked nervously as she spoke. She said it was nothing but it was clear to me this was anything but the case. She was back there now, reliving the first burst of anxiety she had felt in David's presence; reliving the instinct to fight or run. Unable to do either, she had fallen into a kind of paralysis, something that many young victims experience.

'He didn't do anything else,' Anna said. 'Nothing happened. Look, he's done nothing wrong, all right? Can I go home now?'

David had carried out what paedophiles call a 'taster'. This, to any child protection officer, is a veritable fifty-foot-tall neon warning sign that screamed extreme danger. A 'taster' is an act that crosses the line of decency but is something that can still be explained away if the victim reacts badly – and without fear of arrest. It was clear to me that David was an intelligent predator who would prove extremely difficult to catch.

Sadly, Anna had passed the taster test. There'd been no shouting and no reaction and she'd shown David that she would be willing to put her family's happiness before her own welfare. She wasn't going to ruin the best thing that had ever happened to them by accusing David of anything inappropriate. If she did, it was very likely that she'd simply end up alienating herself.

Thanks to the complaint, we'd been able to arrest and interview David in the hope he would break down and confess under questioning.

He poured scorn on my efforts to be friendly, to build a rapport. I made sure he had coffee, I let him smoke, I smiled and looked him in the eye as we talked and my tone implied that this was all a bit of a fuss about nothing and no one was really going to care if he'd got a bit 'over friendly' with Anna. The idea was to put him at ease to try to get him to admit to the kind of abuse that would earn him a long prison sentence.

I thought I'd mastered this technique; after all, I'd been taught by the master – Rob – but it was soon clear I still had some way to go. David was a non-com ('no comment') through and through, no matter how long I kept going, until I'd ran out of questions and started repeating myself. David was certain we had no evidence and believed Anna wouldn't talk, so he was quite happy to sit there and wait the process out.

Karen, Anna and Sue's mum, had been at a party the previous night and, although she was sober, she was still the worse for wear when I spoke to her. She was aggressive and rude before I'd even put the allegations to her. When I did, she really flipped, telling me it was neighbours who were jealous of her good fortune in finding someone like David.

She was in her mid-thirties and although she was attractive and dressed to kill in tight jeans and a Libertines T-shirt that emphasised her ample bosom, her rock-and-roll lifestyle was clearly starting to show in the deepening lines that surrounded her features. She scowled with barely concealed anger as she answered my questions.

'When did David move in?'

'A few months ago.'

'When did you start going out with him?'

'A couple of months before he moved in.'

'That was pretty quick, wasn't it?'

'Not really. We had room and, besides, he could pay his way. He chipped in a hundred pounds towards the rent and bills.'

I bet that saved him a fortune in rent – and I bet the council never knew. And then there was the prospect of regular sex.

'What's he like with the kids?'

'He treats them like his own. Not like that monster who calls himself their dad. He cleared off long ago, the useless bastard!'

Again, there was no way Karen was going to say anything that implicated David in any crime, let alone abusing her kids. She was either in denial or David was careful. I suspected it was the latter.

'And?' Rob said, peering over the top of his glasses when I came into the office afterwards.

'Non-com,' I replied, 'and the girlfriend and daughters are defending him to the hilt.'

'Turn him loose then.'

Seeing my expression, Rob continued. 'I'm sorry, Harry, I know what you think but it's the worst-case scenario for us at the moment. David's a "never to return". We haven't got the evidence; there's no DNA, no willingness from the family. All we've got is an anonymous tip-off.'

We called cases like this one 'never to return' because the suspect is arrested, brought in and interrogated before being bailed 'never to return' for lack of evidence and a lack of desire to prosecute from the family.

I hated myself for agreeing but Rob was right. Our chances of getting this guy locked up were zero. I'd hoped that someone would let slip a vital piece of information but we had nothing.

David had painstakingly planned and covered every single detail – he was a sociopath of the most dangerous order.

What made it worse was that I could see he knew that I knew. He also knew that I was helpless to stop him. This victorious encounter with the Child Protection Team only made the game more exciting for David while simultaneously reinforcing Sue and Karen's belief that he was a good man wronged by a jealous neighbour, whom they already suspected of reporting the abuse.

As I re-entered the interview room, David couldn't help but gloat. 'Face the facts, mate,' he sneered. 'You're barking up the wrong tree. Now why don't you let me go before I sue for harassment?'

Bastard. I turned him loose, with much politeness. I did my utmost to try to make sure that he didn't think that he'd got to me but it didn't work. I was deeply upset and this was impossible to hide. I escorted him out of the station where he turned and looked at me. His handsome face cracked into a sneer as he reached around Karen's shoulders, Anna and Sue in tow.

Each week, we talked about the cases as 'a family'. Clara would appear with a tray fully laden with pots of strong tea and coffee, the smells of which relaxed us all and put us in the mood for a chat – even if the topics were hard to listen to.

It was vital. All we had was each other. We couldn't talk about these cases to anyone else. None of us really wanted to burden our families with the traumas we witnessed, so talking about it with each other was essential, otherwise the pressures could build, causing psychological damage, jeopardising the cases we worked on. Rob chaired the meetings. He was our friend, counsellor and confessor, and we could say anything we liked and keep it between us.

All police officers have cases that get away from them; this is an inevitable part of policing. We're there to see justice is done and sometimes the system – which does a fine job of protecting the innocent – can't help but sometimes favour the guilty. Although we understand this, it doesn't make it any easier to bear when someone like David walks back to the family home with a sneer on his face, knowing that you're helpless to save a young girl from abuse.

I said as much to the room.

'Look, Harry,' Rob said, 'you've not been in this job all that long. It's easy to get caught up in cases like this, to let them eat you alive. You must never forget you are an officer of the law. All you can do is follow each and every case to the very end in an effort to protect the children and present the best possible evidence in court, should it be needed.

'Obviously, there are limits to what we can achieve but the system runs the way it does for a reason. We are on a quest for justice. Not everybody gets what they deserve and the courts aren't always able to put the bad guys away for long enough. But that isn't going to put you off, is it? No matter how difficult or delicate the case might be. Besides, Anna's case isn't over yet and when it does appear on our radar again – and believe me it will – then we will answer the call and make that family safe.'

'Harry,' Clara said, 'it's a terrible case, I know, but don't dwell on it too much.' She tapped her watch.

Clara was reminding me I was due to sit in on an interview.

'I know, thanks, Clara. Rob, you're right as always. Can't say that makes me feel any better though.'

Rob nodded. 'And neither should it,' he said.

I knew how the job worked and that it worked that way for a reason. I needed to get a grip. I was here to do my utmost to protect children and that was exactly what I was going to do.

I walked to the interview suite, took a seat in the camera room and watched as little Jack, six years old, blond-haired, blue-eyed, entered the interview suite, followed by Helen, the newest member of our team, and sat down.

CHAPTER FIVE

THE SELFISH GIANT

Helen and Jack had spent the last twenty minutes getting to know each other in the 'lounge', which was furnished just like an ordinary family home. The decor was ten years out of date but tasteful. Landscape prints on magnolia walls; comfy, functional furniture. There were several toys for children of various ages, along with a TV, DVD player and a selection of films. Everything was done to try to make those brave children who stepped through our door as comfortable as possible.

The suite where we held the interviews was just across the hall. It was slightly smaller and similarly furnished. The one crucial difference was the tiny cameras and microphones, one hidden in each corner, which fed images to the control room, where I was getting settled. This was easier said than done. It was a tiny space and every time I moved I banged my head, elbows or knees on the desk, wall or ceiling. It was also extremely stuffy; there were no windows and the heat from electronic equipment soon turned the little room into an ozone sauna.

As I panned the cameras to the correct setting and checked everything was on and recording, I saw Mike, a young, keen and idealistic social worker, enter the interview room. My heart went out to him. Mike had missed this one.

I hadn't worked with Helen before and didn't know too much about her except that she was in her mid-twenties and had joined the team just a few weeks earlier. She was strong-willed, decisive and was quick to bond with children of all ages. Interviewing children is one of the most difficult things a police officer can do and took anything from a few minutes to several hours. These sorts of interviews, although traumatic for all concerned, are fascinating to observe – none more so than in this case as it was Helen's first time leading the interview, so her inexperience couldn't help but add a certain sense of tension.

I'd sat in as Rob, who was the undisputed master of interviewing both children and abusers, went through some of our interview techniques with Helen one more time.

'It helps to remember that the child often wants to help us but doesn't always know what we need. Of course, we want to help the child and build a safe future for them – but we all have to help each other in just the right way. If we ask the wrong question or phrase a question incorrectly, or make a misleading prompt we could end up with inadmissible evidence and the child could end up being unnecessarily traumatised.

'Don't forget that kids get post-traumatic stress disorder as well as adults. Kids with PTSD do everything they can to avoid the subject of abuse in interviews, so we need to make sure they enter the room as relaxed as possible, otherwise they will stay silent or change the subject.'

That's why the lounge is there, to help the child relax, get used to us and gives us a chance to show that we're warm, caring and friendly (not like the gun-toting cops they might have seen on the TV) before we get to the formalities. The interviews have to be as short as possible so the child doesn't become tired, bored or confused and it's generally best to ask questions that end in short definitive yes or no answers.

'Younger children who are Jack's age and below are especially difficult,' Rob continued. 'There often comes a time when leading questions become necessary. The most important thing to remember is that the child's safety comes above everything else. If they are the only piece of evidence we have and it is likely they will be returned to a dangerous environment, then it's up to you to use your questions to get the child to safety. The solicitors can argue about that in court months later. Of course, you should avoid loaded questions like: "He touched your penis, isn't that right?"

'Remember also that children should be treated like children. It's OK to praise kids for trying hard and doing their best. This is completely normal in all other adult–child situations and is expected. But be careful; don't undermine the integrity of the interview by only praising the child when they give answers that you want to hear. Similarly, you should in no way criticise a child's answers or interrupt a child unnecessarily. Suggesting that a child should know the answer to a question, when they may in fact not know the answer, is also inappropriate.

'Needless to say, some kids are harder to handle than others, some will be downright rude. But we need to treat them the same. Condescending attitudes or game-playing, e.g. 'I bet you don't remember the colour of his hair', undermines children's confidence and will render them silent. Similarly, children should not be frightened into answering questions, e.g. 'We need you to answer the question otherwise we can't help you.' Even telling a child that they can have a break after they've finished answering the next question can be construed as coercive.

'Of course, interviewers can't be completely objective but competent interviewers do not approach cases with their minds made up. The purpose of an interview is to determine whether abuse took place, not to confirm it.'

This was easier said than done in this case. I'd met Jack's eighteen-stone thug of a dad and there was no question in my mind that he was a real prize monster.

'Although it's impossible for us to work this way,' Rob said, 'researchers have found that interviewers who don't know the facts of a case get more disclosures from children than those interviewers who do. This says something about how you should approach these interviews. Be as brief as possible, but at the same time leave no possibility unexplored.'

For both adults and children the interview is sometimes like a form of hypnosis; the isolation of the subject in a neutral room, followed by a period of acclimatisation and relaxation, gradually leading to the reliving and exploration of past events before the subject's carefully orchestrated return to the present.

After putting Jack at ease, spending a couple of minutes talking about school, about his favourite subjects, friends and games as he took in the new surroundings of the interview room, Helen gradually got to the nub of the interview.

'You live in a house in Hackney with your mum and dad, don't you, Jack?'

'Yes.'

'Any brothers or sisters?'

'No.'

'What does your dad do?'

'Nothing.'

'He doesn't have a job?'

'No, he can't work 'cos he's sick.'

'Does your dad sometimes shout while he's at home?'

'Yes.'

'How does that make you feel, when he shouts?'

'Scared.'

'What do you do when he shouts?'

Jack put his hands over his ears and shut his eyes.

'Does your dad shout at your mummy sometimes?'

'All the time. She screams sometimes.'

'Does he shout at you?'

'Yes. Especially at the weekends, when he drinks a lot.'

'Does he frighten you when he's drinking?'

'Yes. He's different, not like normal. He falls over a lot and I try to hide.'

'Does he frighten you when he's sober?'

'Not as much.'

'Do you go out together as a family?'

'No.'

'Do you play together?'

'No.'

'Does anyone ever hit you?'

Jack paused. The crunch question. You can never quite tell how a child will react when you get to this part of the interview. A child may test the water and reveal a small part of the abuse to see how we react to the disclosure of 'the secret', so it's vital to be accepting at this point, so that the child feels safe and will reveal more about the abuse. Helen had got the tone just right; these were straightforward questions, spoken softly, clearly and in a friendly voice.

'My dad.'

Helen nodded and waited for a moment.

'A lot,' Jack said. 'He hits me a lot.' Then he looked at Mike. 'He told me not to tell you. I wanted to come with you when you came round.'

Mike looked down at the table, clearly heartbroken.

'Can you remember what he said?' Helen asked.

'Yeah. I was at the top of the stairs, Dad was at the bottom. He swore a lot.'

In his quiet voice, Jack repeated his dad's words of hatred. 'He said the social are at the door. He said I should say nothing, or I would be really for it.'

'And what did you tell Mike when you spoke to him during that visit?'

'I said I loved my dad and was happy. I said he never hit me.' Jack stopped and looked down.

'It's OK, Jack. You're doing great,' Mike said. 'I don't mind that you didn't tell me. I understand. You had a good reason.'

Jack nodded.

'Did your mum ever try to stop your dad from hitting you?' Helen asked.

'She can't. She wants to but he's too strong and she gets very tired.'

'Why is she so tired?'

'She can't sleep at night 'cos she's frightened too. She sleeps in the morning. Falls asleep watching TV.'

'And what happened at the weekend?'

Jack stayed quiet.

'Jack? Can you tell me what happened?'

Silence.

'It's OK, you don't have to but it would be helpful if you could tell us a little bit about what happened.'

This was a great piece of open-ended questioning. Judging by how smoothly the first part of the interview had gone, I thought Jack might be able to answer.

Jack nodded. 'OK. Dad chased me down the hall. It really hurt. He hit Mum too. She was going to wash the sheets after, 'cos of the blood and that's when he hit her again and she didn't get up . . .'

He stopped. Helen waited a moment before starting to wind up the interview.

'That's fine, Jack, you've done really well. Would you like a rest now? We can go back into the other room.'

'Yes please.'

I watched as Helen and Jack left the interview suite together.

Once they'd gone, Mike placed his elbows on the table and held his head in his hands. I heard him say: 'How the hell did I miss that? How?' before I switched off the equipment.

A few weeks earlier, Jack's teacher, Mrs Williams, noticed that Jack, who was a quiet lad at the best of times, was even more withdrawn that day. She asked him if he was OK.

We totally rely on the vigilance of teachers, very often the people who are second only to the parents in terms of closeness to the children. These moments are so precious, so crucial to the child's welfare, for if the teacher is able to combine their observation with tact, skill and a basic knowledge of child protection, then a disclosure that might save a child's life may well follow.

Each school has a designated representative who is responsible for referring potential cases to the police and social services. The effectiveness of this role varies from school to school. I've been in some schools in Hackney where a teacher has simply been given a folder and the title. As is the case with many aspects of child protection, its importance is only realised when it's too late.

Fortunately in this school, they were on the ball and Jack trusted his teacher enough to tell the truth. 'No, Mrs Williams.'

'What is it, Jack?'

She could see the tears welling up in his eyes as he fought to stay composed. 'Don't worry, Jack, come with me.'

She took his hand and they walked to the deputy head's office. 'Now, Jack, just tell me, what is it?'

'It's my dad. He got drunk and hit me. He did it Saturday night.'

'Where did he hit you?'

'Around the face, he slapped me.' Mrs Williams studied Jack's face but could see no injury.

'Are you hurt anywhere else?'

'No, Miss.'

'OK, Jack, I'd like you to go back to class now. If you want to talk again at any time, just ask for me, OK? You have been very brave, I'm very proud of you.'

As Jack made his way back down the corridor, Mrs Williams picked up the phone and dialled Hackney Social Services.

Mike took the call. Like many social workers, little had changed for him since the report into the death of Victoria Climbié. His caseload was off the chart (not that anyone kept a record of the number of cases). Haringey's guidance stated that the recommended maximum number of cases was twelve. Victoria Climbié's social worker Lisa Arthurworrey had nineteen cases, many of which involved child protection. Lisa was also working a lot of overtime and in 1999 had fifty-two days off in lieu to take.

After Victoria's death in February 2000 (the eight-year-old had more than a hundred separate injuries, the result of torture by her aunt and her aunt's partner), Lisa was suspended and placed on the Protection of Children Act List (a database of people who are regarded as unsuitable to work with children) before being fired in 2002. Distraught at being made a scapegoat and traumatised by what had happened to Victoria, Lisa ended up in psychiatric care.

During Lord Laming's inquiry into the case in January 2003, it emerged that Lisa had not been properly supervised and had been 'badly let down' by managers.[1] In February 2010, ten years after Victoria's death, the General Social Care Council granted Lisa permission to work as a social worker again.

The joint area review of Haringey's children's services ordered by the Children's Minister, Ed Balls, after the death of Baby Peter and published in December 2009 found 'heavy caseloads' remained a significant issue at the council.

Nothing had changed in a decade. This is unacceptable.

When I met Mike I thought here was exactly the kind of young man we needed in social work: a graduate, desperate to help and fearless to boot. He reminded me of myself when I first joined the police. We hit it off straight away and Mike was quick to get to the root of child protection woes.

'There's too much pressure on our managers,' he told me. 'Cases have to be allocated come what may if the work comes in, but there simply aren't enough social workers on the team and that's why the cases pile up so quickly.'

He said that he'd never come across any caseload management tools. 'We get so many Section 47s that I can't write them up quickly enough.'

After a teacher, doctor or concerned relative contacts social services to raise concerns about the well-being of a child, a social worker will decide whether the case comes under Section 47 of the Children Act (1989). This is the key legislative document for children and families. It places a duty on local authorities to safeguard children, and Section 47 states that a 'Local Authority has a duty to investigate when there is reasonable cause to suspect that a child is suffering, or is likely to suffer, significant harm'.

Once a Section 47 is launched then we get involved and, along with all the relevant agencies, we look at the evidence and a child protection conference is held to decide whether or not the child is placed on the child protection register. This confidential list is only available to professionals, indicating that the child is at risk of significant harm and there is a plan in place to address the harm. A core group, formed by various agencies, decides the plan of action and follow-up conferences then take place at three-month, then six-month, intervals to review the progress.

'It's a nightmarish merry-go-round that never stops,' Mike continued. 'I never thought that overload could affect your memory and emotional state, but it does. It's scary. You get what you are given and in the three years since I've started I've never said "I can't do that" but I think it all the time. It keeps coming; somehow I keep working but I feel like I could fall apart at any time. This makes it all too easy for our bosses to blame over-worked individuals like me when things go wrong – which only adds to the pressure.'

When Jack's case came in, Mike's office was full of cake and fizzy drinks in preparation for someone's leaving do that night. 'They weren't much older than me,' he told me later, 'but the relief, joy even, was writ large all over their face. All I could think was that another one had bitten the dust and we had no one to replace them. I also wondered if that was going to be me in a few years' time. I left the office feeling scared and anxious about my future, that maybe all the training and all my hopes about this job had been misspent.'

Checks on Jack's family revealed that the police had been called to numerous domestic incidents at the house. This required a home visit. Mike gave the OK to the school to let Jack go home before alerting us to the fact that he would visit the family that night.

Helen picked up Mike's referral and agreed that a home visit was required to find out whether Jack was safe. They knocked at 5 p.m.

Jack's father swung back the net curtain and glared at Helen and Mike. He pulled the front of his vest angrily to indicate he was going to put a shirt on and bounded up the stairs. That was when Jack got his verbal warning that left him terrified, shaking, unsure what to do.

Even though he was eighteen stone, unshaven and muscle-bound, Jack's dad, who was about thirty, was the model of peaceful politeness as he welcomed the detective and the social worker in. They sat on a sofa facing him.

'Now, what's all this about then?' he asked.

'Could you turn off the TV, please?' Helen asked. The bottom of the range 42-inch monster that hung on the small living-room wall was blaring out the latest pop hits.

'Sorry, yeah.'

Jack was sat at the top of the stairs, listening.

'It's hard, you know, being on incapacity benefits,' his dad said. 'Hardly pays anything.'

Mike and Helen were both thinking exactly the same thing at this point. Jack's dad was six feet tall and had the physique of someone who liked lifting weights but also loved the booze. While his heavily tattooed arms were well muscled, a substantial beer belly hid any signs of a six-pack.

'Panic attacks,' he explained. 'I used to drive a bus but had a crash and since then I haven't been able to get behind a wheel. It's not easy with a young family, you know. I need more support.'

'We're not here to talk about you,' Helen said firmly, wresting the initiative away from this selfish giant, 'we're here about Jack.'

'Yes,' Mike added, 'Jack told his teacher that you hit him at the weekend.'

'Oh that. Right.'

'You admit hitting Jack then?' Helen asked.

'Oh no! Nothing like that. Jack is a good lad but every now and again he can get very naughty. Like most kids I suppose. On this occasion he'd been very rude to his mum. I'd taken his hand to smack it but I accidentally clipped his face. I told him sorry and Jack promised to be good in future.'

'Can I see Jack, alone?' Mike asked.

Jack's father waved him upstairs. 'Help yourself.'

Helen stayed with the dad. She'd seen straight through Jack's father, but that's not evidence.

Mike tapped quietly on Jack's bedroom door and went in. Jack was sat on his bed, hands in his lap.

'May I come in?'

Jack nodded, probably thinking 'Please take me out of here' over and over in his mind. But of course that's not what came out.

'Are you a social worker?'

'Yes I am, I'm here to help you.'

They chatted for five minutes and Jack denied his father had hit him. He said he loved his mum and dad and was happy at home. Every word defied his true situation.

Mike went back downstairs and they rounded up the visit. Helen had got nothing further from the dad. During their hall-way conflab, they quickly reached the conclusion that no further action would be required from them that night – but Mike said he would visit again, just to be certain, and they would make sure that Mrs Williams looked out for Mike. Hopefully, the knowledge that we'd been alerted would be enough of a warning for the father.

Tragically it wasn't.

When they'd interviewed Jack his mother hadn't been there; we think now she was hiding at a friend's place, or just keeping out of the way because her injuries would have been a bit of a giveaway.

Just a week later, Jack's dad hit his mum with enough force to send her front teeth deep into her lower lip – so deep that they had to be surgically removed. Jack's dad was a cowardly, lazy man, a leech that sucked money from the benefits system to pay for his alcohol dependency and to keep him from having to work for an honest day's pay. There are many more like him still out there, pathetic failures who, when fuelled by alcohol, take out their petty frustrations on those weaker than themselves.

Mum was now in a coma, the dad was on his way to prison and young Jack was quickly whisked away to a foster home. Jack was first taken to the social services' office where Mike had rung his way through the list of foster carers who were on call 24/7 until he found someone who was available. Handing Jack over to an emergency foster carer in these circumstances was a heart-breaking experience for Mike.

In this case, everybody had done the right thing and there was nothing anyone could have done differently. This was the worst possible outcome and Mike was going to have to find a way to live with that fact.

Looking at him then, as Mike left the station, I didn't rate his chances. Ironically, the only thing that might have saved him was his impossible workload, which would either force him to get back in the saddle and plough on, or would break him in two.

The fax machine whirred. Clara picked it up and brought it over to me.

A boy had been beaten by his family's lodger.

'Chin up, Harry,' Clara said, in her most comforting voice, 'I know you've had a couple of nasty falls today. But you need to keep getting back on that saddle.'

CHAPTER SIX

THE SLAP

'That's quite a knock you've got there,' Brenda said in a soft southern Irish accent.

'I hadn't noticed,' I replied. 'Is it too much?'

Brenda was one of the best social workers I'd ever met and I was always glad to see she was attached to one of my cases. Despite the fact she was tiny, she feared no client, no matter what their appearance or past history, and was equally prepared to voice her opinions with the police.

We didn't always see eye to eye and although our arguments sometimes got pretty intense, I much preferred dealing with Brenda than some of the more timid social workers we occasionally came across. She had more than ten years' experience and had seen it all.

'I guess all policemen knock on the door like that,' Brenda said. 'Some social workers I know have a special knock-and-run approach in these estates, where they brush the door with their knuckle, wait five seconds and then run, leaving the visit to someone else.'

Social workers often have to visit some pretty intimidating places and this was no exception. In fact, I wouldn't have blamed them for using the knock-and-run approach here. We were fifteen storeys up a particularly notorious tower block. The views of East London, which on that blustery spring day looked so grey it could have been black and white, were spectacular.

The wind whipped through the window and down the narrow corridor, forcing Brenda to wrap her long dark brown hair into a knot. I noticed it had flashes of red as she pinned it to the back of her head with a large hairclip. Despite the 360-degree panorama I felt extremely claustrophobic inside this thin building. There were just four flats on each floor separated by a short, narrow cross-shaped corridor. I'd had to stoop my head in the metallic lift, which only held a maximum of four people.

This is no way to live, I thought as I looked down through the narrow side window at the end of the hallway. The building's isolation only enhanced my claustrophobia. The tower was surrounded by a wide patch of unplayed-on grass; a Hackney version of no-man's-land, a scary place that no resident – law-abiding or otherwise – felt safe crossing after dark.

This patch of land had been built on time and time again; first late-Victorian tenements, then one of several zigzagging H-blocks scattered throughout Hackney, before this was replaced by the tower. People had been calling for its demolition for years; practically since the day it welcomed its first tenants. Why was it that the town planners didn't seem to ever get it right? Did they really succumb that easily to the skilful, optimistic pitches of 'visions of the future' sold to them by the architects?

I knocked again.

Footsteps approached the door. 'Who is it?' a woman said in a nervous, soft African voice.

'Detective Sergeant Harry Keeble from Hackney Police Child Protection Team. I'm here with Brenda from Hackney Social Services,' I explained calmly in my friendly copper voice, 'I believe you're expecting us.'

The door opened and we entered the flat. The woman, in her twenties, was wearing bright-coloured African dress. A flicker of recognition lit her eyes.

Where had I seen her before? It took me a few seconds as I started to run through a never-ending stream of possibilities. Of course! The illegal crèche I'd closed a few weeks ago, she was one of the young mothers. I didn't say anything; we hadn't come about that. The woman, whose name was Asanda, quickly welcomed us in.

The first thing that hit me as we entered the flat was the overpowering odour of strong perfume mixed with the potent smell of a meat casserole. A set of small wooden African elephants lined the hallway. African masks hung on the wall, giving the flat a flavour of the savannah.

Asanda led us down the corridor and into the lounge, where the lodger and her husband were waiting. The husband, whose name was Obi, was sat on an armchair. He was about thirty and wearing a security guard's uniform. His collar was undone and a cold drink sat on a coaster on the side table next to him. Their twenty-year-old student lodger, Raymond, was wearing shirt and jeans. They had taken him on to help with babysitting Jumu and the extra rent proved to be a real bonus for the family.

Asanda, who worked in the canteen of a large central London hospital, sat between them on the large cream sofa as we introduced ourselves and explained why we were there.

'Where's Jumu?' I asked.

'In his bedroom,' Asanda said. 'Shall I get him?'

'No, that's OK, I can speak to him there.'

Earlier that day Jumu had told his teacher that Raymond had hit him. The teacher had rung social services, but as there was – as usual – a shortage of workers for the many cases that had arrived that day, the response wasn't quick enough and so the teacher felt obliged to let Jumu go home after school had finished.

That's where I came in; I needed to judge if a crime had been committed and if so how serious. We couldn't let cases like this wait overnight because, as far as we were concerned, a child had told us that they were in danger, so they needed our help. If we failed to respond quickly then at best we had sowed the seed of distrust in the child as far as our abilities to act went. At worst we could have ended up facing a terrible tragedy.

'I'm sorry,' Raymond explained. 'Jumu was rude to me and I slapped him across the face. Not hard. With my fingers more than my palm, really.'

That he'd admitted it was a good sign.

'Has this happened before?' Brenda asked.

'No, never.'

'I think Jumu is jealous of Raymond,' Asanda said. 'We needed the money and we know Raymond's family, so this worked out well for us but Jumu doesn't like having another young man around.'

'Jumu can be a bit fresh, you know?' the husband said with a slight smile. 'We asked Raymond to apologise to Jumu and to promise not to do it again and he did.'

Leaving Brenda to talk them through their story a couple more times, I got up, left the room and knocked on the little boy's door.

'Come in.'

I slowly pushed open the door. Jumu was sat on the sheetless bed, staring at me wide-eyed. He shared the bed with his older sister who was in the kitchen, setting the table and singing to herself. There were clothes piled everywhere, but it was reasonably clean. On the wall was a Manchester United poster.

'Hi, Jumu, I'm a police officer and my name is Harry. I've come to check on you.'

'OK,' he said quietly. He maintained good eye contact. So far so good.

'Is that your poster?' He nodded silently and looked at it.

'May I?' I said, wanting to sit down next to him. He gestured with his hand for me to sit down, which I did.

This humble and happy little boy had the same hopes and dreams as many across the country at the age of ten. Although he deserved them as much as anyone else, I knew that he would be more unlikely than most to see them come true.

One of the things that never ceases to impress me about kids is that they are naturally modest and unassuming; Jumu was no exception. Social services already had a file on this family and so I knew their sad secret. I wondered if Jumu even knew he was HIV-positive. Once he was told and he understood what it meant, would he ever learn to live with it? Would he ever have a worry-free day? I felt quite sad for this little boy; the cards were heavily stacked against him.

His mum and dad had contracted HIV before they'd fled Zimbabwe, escaping the persecution of President Robert Mugabe's government. Obi had been a senior member of the Movement for Democratic Change. Now he was a security guard on near minimum wage and his son was being brought up in the urban jungle of a Hackney estate. I couldn't help but think that thanks to his illness Jumu's life would be made up of knockbacks, disappointment and sadness.

'I think they will win the FA Cup this year,' he said proudly, looking at the poster.

'Are you sure?' I replied.

'Yes, Raymond and I want to see them play one day, for real.'

This was a great hook for me, and I took it. 'How do you get on with Raymond?'

'He's OK.' He looked at the floor.

'What happened?'

'I was rude, I got angry and he hit me, but not hard. Please don't do anything.'

'Where did he hit you?'

Jumu showed me the left side of his face, but I could see no mark.

'Does it hurt?'

He shook his head.

'Does Raymond lose his temper with you?'

'No, never. He looks after me when Mum and Dad are at work sometimes. He sometimes lets me stay up and watch football on the telly with him. He takes me to school, too.'

I imagined what it would be like for Jumu at school if the other kids ever discovered he was HIV. A mixture of fear, sympathy and bullying, I suspected.

Kids often don't realise the power they have to make other children so desperately unhappy. Cruelty in the playground can permanently cripple a child's confidence. It was heartbreaking to think that this little boy, who asked for so little from life, had this threat hanging over him. As I looked into his face, I could see worry and uncertainty in his features – worry about what I was going to do.

'Do you feel safe here?' I asked. He nodded.

'You sure?'

'I'm sure.'

OK, judgement time. Jumu had no injuries; it was clear from what he was saying and from his body language that he was generally happy, wasn't frightened and didn't want me to intervene.

Of course, you can never be sure. All we can do is ask all the right questions, check for injury and record everything, for what we hope will never be the next time.

One of the unnerving things was that I could never really know for certain that after a visit once I'd turned the ignition key in my police car that the victim was not having the living daylights beaten out of them for 'telling tales'. The dread of receiving the call that proved you wrong was something we all had to learn to live with. On the plus side, it made certain that you would never leave someone's home without having asked all the questions you needed to and that you checked the place as thoroughly as possible for any clues of abuse.

I told Jumu I was going back to the lounge. Brenda was still in full flow and the discussion had moved on to the family's wider well-being, the reasons why they were already on the social services' radar.

'I got a job working for an international charity in Harare,' Asanda was saying as I entered the room. 'Part of the application process involved having an HIV test. I did it without thinking. Of course I wasn't HIV, I thought, I'd only had one partner, my husband. When I got the results I made them do it again.'

She paused. Obi shifted uncomfortably on his chair and stared at his drink.

'Being diagnosed HIV was like being given a death sentence,' Asanda continued. 'I felt angry, confused. The sense of hopelessness was unbearable. I thought my life was over and that all I could do now was wait for the slow and painful death I'd seen so many others go through. That was nothing, mind you, compared with how I felt when I realised my children had it too.'

'Yes, I gave it to her,' Obi said. 'At that time I had no idea I had it but I still feel like a murderer.'

Although I knew it was bad I had no real sense of the scale of the HIV–AIDS problem in Zimbabwe. According to the World Health Organisation, 25 per cent of adults between the ages of nineteen and forty-nine are infected with HIV – that's about 1.5 million people. Five hundred people become infected every single day.[1] I could only imagine the hysteria that would abound if anything like that were happening in the UK.

'There's next to no treatment in Zimbabwe,' Asanda said. 'I watched so many parents waste away and die, knowing that there was no one left to take care of their kids. I couldn't let that happen to us. I've seen street children covered in rashes, feverish with pneumonia or coughing with tuberculosis.'

In most rural areas of Zimbabwe, children with HIV are generally considered a lost cause. It's harder to treat kids. Their medication, which is up to three times more expensive, needs constant adjustment. In Zimbabwe most untreated HIV-positive babies die before the age of two. Out of the 1.3 million AIDS orphans, 100,000 are homeless.[2]

'The worst thing about the disease back home was the reaction when other people found out. Our landlord evicted tenants who had HIV. Other parents tell you not to let your kids play with their kids. It doesn't help that the church preaches that God has punished the "infected ones" for their sins. What sins have my little babies ever committed?'

Zimbabwe didn't have nearly enough drugs. Even though the number of people in need has risen from 350,000 to 570,000, only about 200,000 get the drugs they need.[3]

'We get the right treatment and support here and we can even work and pay taxes to help pay for it,' Obi said. 'But in Zimbabwe? Forget it. Kids are dying unnecessarily every day. I don't understand it. How can lust for money possibly outweigh a single baby's life?'

That was a question none of us were qualified to answer. Brenda steered us back to the matter in hand.

'I'd just like to ask Raymond what it was that Jumu did to make him so angry?'

'He was just being rude to me, disrespectful,' Raymond said earnestly. 'Most of the time we get on fine but the other night Jumu didn't want to go to bed and when I insisted, he started screaming at me.'

Brenda's response was firm, calm and clear. 'First off, you cannot hit children, Raymond, is that understood? Any hitting that causes bruising, swelling, cuts, grazes or scratches is punishable with up to five years in prison. Detective Sergeant Keeble here will have you in a prison cell in a flash, OK?'

Raymond nodded. He looked frightened. Message received and understood.

'I understand that it can be frustrating and that you are a young man with no experience of parenting. People use physical punishment simply because no one has ever taught them better ways to control children. It's very ineffective. You might be surprised to hear that it actually encourages violence and often has the effect of teaching the child to behave in exactly the opposite way from the way you want. The child assumes that once they've been punished that there's no need for them to feel any guilt any more.

'Keep that sort of thing up and you end up with children who are either frightened and intimidated or rebellious and defiant – or a mixture of both. Now I know Jumu's parents don't want that and I'm certain that you don't want that, do you, Raymond?'

'No.'

'Shouting is no good either, you have to show Jumu patience and respect. If you'd taken the time to look Jumu in the eye and if you'd spoken to him seriously and calmly he would have listened to you, wouldn't he?'

Raymond nodded.

'Well, that's what I want you to do in future, OK?'

'Yes.'

'Good. I'd like to have a quick word with Detective Sergeant Keeble in private before we leave.'

We retired to the hallway for a quick conflab.

'They're fine, good parents and Raymond is OK,' Brenda said.

'Well the environment might not be ideal,' I said, 'three adults and two children in this small three-bedroom flat, but it's warm and comfortable and Jumu seems to like Raymond.'

'I agree, there's no way we're removing him but I just want to see Jumu with Raymond before we go, just to check their body language.'

Brenda wanted to allay the dread of being proved wrong as well; to make sure she'd done all she could to remove the thought that Jumu was standing there as were leaving, silently screaming 'Don't go, please don't go, I am scared.'

'Fair enough.'

It was soon clear to us that Raymond and Jumu were the best of friends again. Asanda smiled proudly and told Jumu and his sister that she loved them both very much.

A well-respected and very experienced Hackney doctor once told me: 'If you have children, Harry, tell them that you love them and hug them every day. This will go a long way to providing them with all the well-being and stability that will stand them in good stead later in life.'

Looking at Jumu, I was certain he wasn't short of love and hugs. As I waved goodbye to him I said, 'Man U for the Cup!' I got a broad toothy smile in return. That smile was worth a lot and I banked it. As Brenda and I stepped into the small claustrophobic corridor high above Hackney, I felt a surge of optimism. The door closed behind us and I thought, Have a good life, Jumu.

Somehow, despite everything, something in his expression made me think he will.

CHAPTER SEVEN

THE CAGE

I was with Dev and I'd been banging on the door of the ground-floor flat for a few minutes. Dev waited patiently, smiling gently. It wasn't necessarily that the people inside were hiding from us, but from the after-dark activities of the local dealers, teen gangs and addicts. Although doorstep robberies were rare, the knowledge that they had happened was enough to add another layer of fear to those living on the estate.

This was the sort of neighbourhood where, if you were of a certain age or disposition, you only took your rubbish out in daylight. For some people, living on this estate was like being in prison. Dev and I had arrived just after 'lock-up', just as the night had taken hold. The metal security gate protecting the front door and the grilles on the windows only reinforced this feeling. I reached through the metal bars and knocked loudly again.

Three flats in the block across the road from where I was standing had been raided a few weeks ago. Two were crack houses, the other a brothel, all run by a husband-and-wife double act. They'd been victims of their own success: the flats had become so full of punters that they'd moved their business out into the stairwell and it was this that had drawn the attention of Hackney's overworked drugs squad.

Still no answer.

'They are most certainly in there,' Dev said quietly.

'What makes you so sure?' I asked. 'I can see a light on but anyone living here might leave the lights on to deter burglars.'

Dev smiled. 'That is easy, Harry. There are wet marks on the doorstep. They walked through that puddle and rubbed their feet to dry them. It hasn't dried so they can't have returned all that long ago.'

'How come you're so observant, Dev?'

'Even though my family left Mumbai when I was six I learned a lot while I was there. A city of fourteen million people, with less than half as much space as here, you've got to get streetwise very early on to survive. We lived in a rough neighbourhood and I learned to notice things, warning signs of danger, you know?'

Finally, after a few more of my 'I'm not going away' knocks, the door cracked open and a woman stared hard at me with fear in her eyes.

'Police,' I said, showing my ID. 'Can we come in?'

The door opened wide and we stepped into the hallway. Inside, the flat was pleasantly furnished, clean and tidy. Of course, the 42-inch plasma TV was on the wall of the lounge, as seemed to be the case in almost every council flat I visited. A window to another, better, world.

A large man entered the room. 'What's going on?' he asked casually in a West African accent.

What he didn't know was that a marked police van with five uniformed officers waiting patiently inside was parked just around the corner. The man had a history with the police and I wanted to make sure we had back-up in case things turned nasty.

'It's about your children. You have two boys, yes? One six, the other four?'

The man looked blank.

Dev chipped in. 'There seems to be no record of their existence with social services or Educational Welfare.'

This was very odd; normally children can be traced through various records, from child benefit to school meal allowance.

'We're just concerned about the well-being of the boys,' Dev said.

At this the man broke eye contact and started waving his arms, talking about nosy neighbours, money problems and long nights at work. A classic distraction technique, I don't know why they bother; Dev and I were both experienced enough to let it all wash over us.

'We're not concerned about that,' I said. 'I want to see the kids' bedroom.'

'What the hell is this? I want to see warrants,' the man demanded before continuing his rant. Again I let it blow over me. Section 17 of PACE (Police and Criminal Evidence Act) allows us entry to save life or limb. I turned and started walking down the hall.

'Are you coming?' I asked. Both the man and woman stayed put and sat down where they were. I reached the first bedroom, clearly that of the couple. A tidy room with several neatly arranged shoeboxes and a nicely made bed.

'You would think we are in the wrong place, would you not?' Dev said behind me. I had to admit, I was starting to wonder.

I walked a couple of paces down the hall and opened the door to the kids' bedroom.

Ah, no, we weren't …

'Oh dear, oh dear,' Dev said. 'I don't know about you, Harry, but this is a first for me.'

I almost didn't see them to start with. My attention was first drawn to the one uncovered, heavily stained mattress that sat near the door of the good-sized room. Beside it were two large and dirty plates surrounded by morsels of old food in various stages of decomposition. A couple of broken plastic toys sat next to the plates.

There was no other furniture, just a pile of dirty clothes in one corner. Huddled on top, camouflaged by their own filthy, soiled clothes that hung on them loosely, were two emaciated, ghostly boys. The room stank.

Quickly putting aside the anger, disgust, horror and pity (which wasn't easy) I wasted no time. 'Hello, my name's Harry.'

Nothing. Just wide, fearful eyes.

'What are your names?'

Still nothing.

'Harry, this is a cage,' Dev said, his voice barely above a whisper. 'They've been caged like animals.'

Dev was right. I couldn't say for certain but I expected that the last time these boys were outside was some months ago at best.

I'd seen children in conditions like this before but not with this contrast, not with the 'parents' (if indeed they were related) sitting in their comfy clean lounge, while two children were just about surviving down the hall, living in their own filth with no love, no stimulation, no toys, no school, no bathroom and probably leftovers for dinner. Parents who live in the same squalor as their children were less culpable than these two. It was beyond negligence, it smacked of the casual cruelty of a psychopath.

We arrested the parents, who gave in without a fuss, and removed the children from the flat. I took the older boy's hand and walked him down the hallway towards the front door. He gripped it tightly. A huge new chapter was about to open up for him and his brother. Their universe was about to expand to infinite proportions. God, I wondered, how on earth are they going to react to being outside? Just how long were they kept in that room? Have they ever been in a car?

Well, I was about to find out.

I opened the door. For once, probably thanks to the presence of the fully loaded police van, the estate was peaceful. It was a warm spring night. Heavy rain showers and thunderstorms had been coming and going all day and the wet estate glistened in the lamplight. It looked as if it had been freshly washed.

The boy pulled back on my hand as we crossed the threshold to the outdoors and I stopped. I looked down. He was standing on his toes looking left, then right, then away to the distance. He sniffed the air cautiously.

'It's OK,' I said. 'I'll take care of you, I'm going to take you somewhere nice.'

The boy nodded and looked behind him. Dev was there with his little brother.

'It's OK,' he said. The brother nodded and those brave little boys stepped with us quietly into the night.

Not long after we had the kids safely buckled up in the back of the police car, my job phone started ringing. It was Craig. 'Harry, you're on the Holly Street estate, aren't you?'

'Yeah,' I said cautiously, 'but I'm a bit busy. You're not going to believe what we've uncovered here.'

'Sorry, mate,' Craig said, 'you've got a job on and it can't wait.'

Damn, what now?

'A crack-addicted prostitute has just legged it from the Homerton with her newborn. She lives on that estate. Can you give her a knock?'

'It's OK, Harry,' Dev said, 'we're only going to put these kids to bed with the emergency foster carer now. Go.'

I jogged across the estate as thunder rumbled in the distance, found the door and gave it my best policeman's knock. No response. I bent down and called through the letterbox. 'Sharon, I know you're in there. Just open the door.'

You might as well, I thought, because I'm going to smash it down if I have to.

I stood back and surveyed the scene. The tiny front garden of this small terraced house was full of rubbish, a few beer cans, a broken bottle, some kids' clothing, a broken plastic toy and the obligatory rolled-up and rapidly composting rug. The dirty net curtains were drawn but I could see a soft light coming from the hallway.

Brenda arrived. 'Hello, Harry,' she said. 'This is a first for Sharon. All her other six were taken into care straight from the maternity ward.'

It's not possible to get a care order on a child while it's still in the womb, so social services have to wait until the child is born. Every once in a while, we would get a runner.

'Are you sure she's in there?'

'Very likely.' I pointed at the doorstep, which was spotted with a little blood.

It began to rain.

Brenda bent down and pushed open the letterbox. 'Come on, Sharon,' she called, 'we need to talk, we're not going to go away and you know it. Your baby needs help. You can't even feed her.'

No answer.

'I'll never forget meeting Sharon for the first time,' Brenda said as she stood up and opened her umbrella. Like me, Brenda had worked in Hackney for some years. 'She was hanging off the back of a parked motorbike whilst one of her mates and two guys were stood beside her, all talking at the tops of their voices. She was beautiful; Primark clothes and Dalston Market jewellery looked like they were worth a million on her. Her mum had got into a scrape with some local lads and they'd beaten her with a piece of wood. Sharon told me then that she wanted to get a gangster boyfriend, someone with money to buy her drugs, drink, clothes and to protect her.'

'Sound's like Hackney's equivalent of the American dream,' I said.

'She said she'd make him pay for everything. "Usually they fuck you and leave you," was what she said, "that's how come girls end up single mothers. But I'm lucky," she said, can you believe it? "I can look after myself."'

I banged on the door again. Silence. Right, that's it. Sod standing in the pouring rain while we wait for Sharon – who for all we knew was passed out on the floor. She'd just given birth after all. Or she may have been high. The birth had kept her away from the crack pipe for nearly twelve hours, supposing she had a stash at home?

Time to go in, Harry style. I stood back from the door and assessed it. A wooden Hackney council door painted brown. How many of these had I booted in over the years?

Just then the door clicked open. I gently pushed it wide and saw Sharon, still wrapped in a hospital blanket, walking down the corridor and into the lounge.

Brenda and I stepped out of the rain and followed, pausing at the entrance to the lounge. Sharon was on a street-scavenged sofa, sitting under a shadeless lamp, her silent baby cradled in her arms. She looked up and stared straight into my eyes. Her face was haggard, and like so many Hackney prostitutes, all of whom suffer violence at the hands of their clients, a front tooth was missing. Her shoulder-length brown hair was tangled but she didn't look too bad considering she'd given birth just a couple of hours earlier. She was wearing a dishevelled tracksuit under the blanket and the baby was swaddled in a white woollen shawl.

I sat down on a chair opposite her and said nothing.

Sharon looked up and stared at me for a moment. 'The social ain't taking her,' she said in a quiet but defiant voice.

'Sharon, we're just here to help,' I said. 'To do what's best for the baby.'

Sharon broke her gaze, looked down at her daughter and rearranged the blanket with shaking hands. Her addiction was starting to call. I knew she would give way, but not just yet, she needed time.

Sharon may have been an HIV-positive, crack-addicted prostitute but that didn't mean she didn't have feelings; that she couldn't love her child. But nothing, not even a newborn baby, could compete with her dependence on crack. As long as the drug held her in its euphoric grasp then she would never be a stable mother. Sharon's life was one of chaos, violence and broken promises. No matter how deep the feelings for her newly born daughter, nothing could compete with her addiction to crack, nothing.

It's essential to rescue babies from crack addicts for a number of reasons but most addicts don't realise how much damage smoking crack does to their baby; at the least they will end up with asthma, at the worst they will die from acute cocaine intoxication.

I'd heard of a case where a five-month-old baby born to a pair of crack dealers had died in their bed. They claimed they had accidentally smothered her but toxicology tests showed that the baby died of acute cocaine intoxication – from the crack smoke. Babies who are breast-fed by mothers with crack addiction also soon become addicts and can die from an overdose.

Sharon was cradling her child, looking deep into her eyes, rocking her slightly, the picture of a doting mother. Brenda and I knew better. In a few hours she would have to go in search of crack. She had no money, so all she could do was turn tricks.

As if reading my mind, she looked up. 'I'll give her up, I promise.'

I wasn't going to force her. This wasn't the time or place. For the moment, Sharon was enjoying some safe quality time with her daughter and I did not need to interfere.

Most mothers are prepared to do anything for their newborn children but Sharon would only ever go so far. She loved her daughter but her demons were far too strong. In other words, Sharon was prepared to do anything for crack, but not her daughter. She wouldn't stop the crack even though it was ruining her – in every sense. The drugs were destroying her mind and body. What I was seeing that evening was a rare moment of dignity; something Sharon gave no value in relation to her habit.

I saw this phenomenon time and time again in London and it is impossible to overstate the enormity of the social and financial impact. It's something I'll keep banging on about because it's such a massive problem. Thousands of teenage girls in the UK have sold their bodies, often having unprotected sex, in return for crack. As I'd already seen for myself on countless occasions, these girls give birth to countless numbers of 'crack babies'. In my experience, crack babies were two a penny. In one of the worst cases of its kind fourteen children born to the same mother were put into care one by one thanks to her crack addiction.

The majority of these kids were either fostered or lived in care homes, or were simply lost in the system, or never came to our attention. Apart from the terrible human cost, the bill to taxpayers to look after fourteen children was more than £2 million. It also cost an average of £25,000 to hear each case of care proceedings.

Many of these women were young prostitutes who had had unprotected sex to feed their addiction and kept getting pregnant. Incredibly, in some cases their pregnancy was naively encouraged by poorly trained social workers who thought a baby would set these women on the path to recovery. After all, what kind of woman puts her desire for crack cocaine above the love of her child? In one such case a woman had already lost three children because of neglect brought about by her addiction, but her history was ignored when considering her and her partner's ability to care for a new child. Instead, agencies were more focused on getting them to 'start again' – encouraging pregnancies when they should have been urging caution.

I hate saying it but Sharon wasn't a special case. Just ask Homerton's neonatal unit. The reason its maternity unit is so well equipped is thanks to the crack problem. If you give birth there any day of the year then you're more than likely to be sharing the ward with at least one crack-addicted prostitute.

Every night for years, Sharon had stood on the Brownswood Road from 11 p.m. to 3 a.m., a busy residential street, a rung on the ladder of roads that connects Hackney and Finsbury Park. As the cars pulled up she would stare through the windows and make an assessment of the punter's dangerousness. But what can you really tell from a quick look and a few words through a car window? Besides, Sharon would rarely decline any request by any punter, be they fat, thin, old, young, smelly, clean, perverted or shy and dull – no job was too small, too perverted or too disgusting.

Her fee was £20, in advance. For that, the punter could drive her to the industrial estate off the Seven Sisters Road. She was ready, nothing on underneath, lubricated with jelly, condom at the ready; she would drop the driver's seat back as far as possible and work quickly.

Then it was back to Brownswood Road for the next one. Three happy customers later, she would ring her pimp who would arrive in ten minutes and take the £60 in exchange for three good-sized rocks. Then Sharon was off to the crack house for a smoke and then more sex with buzzing punters prepared to share crumbs of crack in return for sexual favours.

Although Sharon was always clean-shaven to avoid crabs, she cared little for hygiene – crabs were just a nuisance that interfered with her work. Overall, STDs held little fear since she had contracted HIV – either through a split condom, one of the times she was raped or when she did it with a punter without protection for double the fee.

These thoughts ran through my head while I watched in horrified fascination as this woman, damaged beyond all imagining, acted the part of the mother, cuddling the baby she could not feed – her breast milk could kill her child, if it wasn't an addict already. We would find out soon enough – it had been cut off from its infected supply of nourishment for a few hours now. Soon it would be hungry for food. If it continued to scream after feeding, then it would be hungry for crack as well.

I looked at Brenda, who nodded understandingly. Just ten minutes more, then Sharon was going to have to hand her daughter over and say goodbye, probably for ever. It was always possible that she would turn up at the social and ask to see her but I doubted it. Crack addicts are terrible at keeping appointments. Their diary is ruled by addiction. Besides, Sharon hadn't asked to see any of the six that had gone before.

What future did that child have? Another member of Generation Crack, an army of half-brothers and half-sisters who would never know one another, who bounce around the care system through foster homes, care homes and the streets. Hopefully, Sharon's baby would be one of the lucky ones, quickly taken into foster care and maybe – if she wasn't already addicted to crack and already permanently damaged – she would achieve the holy grail of adoption by a loving family.

Although we were prepared to wait ten minutes, it only took Sharon five. She stood up without a word, walked across to Brenda and carefully passed her baby over, her last and best act as a mother, with great dignity. She may have run off with her baby, endangering her, but I certainly wasn't going to take any action. My only wish was to get the child back to safety without fuss or fighting and with Sharon's consent.

It was time to go. Treat her with respect, I thought, she's a human being and deserved it, no matter what her lifestyle. I looked her in the eye. 'Thanks, Sharon.' As we turned to leave, I added: 'Take care.'

'I always do,' she answered with a slight shiver of withdrawal. Her words were totally out of sync with her situation. The crack was coming to reclaim her soul. Soon she would be back on Brownswood Road, sleeping with the enemy, raising money for her master, making sure her crack pipe would never be empty.

I closed the door. Brenda and I stepped out into the rain and hurried to my car with a baby that would never know the drama that unfolded on her first night on earth.

The following morning, bleary-eyed and nursing a coffee I joined Dev for the memorandum interview of the two young boys who'd been caged in their bedroom.

It was one of the most heartbreaking things I've ever witnessed. The kids knew so little and their vocabulary was so limited that it was almost impossible for them to describe what they had endured. Drawings and toys were of little use. They stared at everything in wonder.

They had no concept that they had been through anything unusual. No idea that they were traumatised. For this reason, the interviews were far more stressful for the Child Protection Team than for them. We found it very hard to understand how they were feeling, what had happened to them and what the future held.

'I can't believe that in the twenty-first century we still have children just left in a room like gerbils,' I said to Dev. 'No one talking to them, reading them a story, playing with them. How was it possible for them to be so invisible?'

No one seemed to have an answer for that.

'I've read about child isolation cases,' Dev told me. 'There was another, even worse case than this one about twenty years ago.

The girl's mother was a deaf mute since childhood, the result of a car crash. Nobody knew who the father was and for some reason the mother's family decided to imprison both mother and child.

'From the day her daughter was born until she was a little over six years of age, mother and child spent their time together in a dark room with the blinds drawn, separated from the rest of the family. The parents of the mother did not permit her to leave the house alone. One day she escaped, carrying her child with her. Her daughter could barely walk or move and needed surgery to correct the malformation of the joints; she had the mental ability of a two-year-old and couldn't speak, just croaked when she wanted something.'

'What happened to them in the end?'

'I don't know about the mother but the studies I've read tell us that the girl learned human speech very quickly and reached normal intelligence by the age of eight, just two years later. She also demonstrated a very active imagination.'

Lucy had joined us. 'The most famous case I know of is thirteen-year-old Genie in California in the 1970s,' she told me. 'I studied psychology at university and Genie's story is part of the course about language development.'

Since the age of about twenty months Genie had been kept prisoner in a small room, naked and restrained to a kind of potty-chair by a harness her psychotic father had designed. She was fed a diet of milk and baby food and could only move her hands and feet. The father – who had let Genie's older sister die of pneumonia after putting her in the garage when she cried – forbade her almost blind mother to speak to Genie. The child was only discovered when the mother ran away from her husband and went to social services to claim welfare payments.

Genie couldn't speak; she walked awkwardly and displayed many of the characteristics of an animal. She did not know how to chew and could not control her bladder or bowels. According to the mother, Genie's father killed himself soon after Genie was found.

Over the next six years, Genie learned basic language, learning to speak at about the level of a two- or three-year-old, e.g. 'want milk', 'two hand'. She learned to use tools, to draw, and to connect cause and effect and acquired spatial memory. But she never improved beyond a certain level. She was studied by a group of scientists, the 'Genie Team', as they termed themselves. Unfortunately, after a few years their research funding was withdrawn and Genie entered a cycle of abusive foster homes, falling back into her world of silence.[1]

It was clear that these children were better off than Genie; they seemed to fit more closely with the example Dev had given. His analysis gave me hope that the kids would recover and go on to lead normal lives with little or no memory of their confinement.

The six-year-old's language was limited but he was able to tell us some things about his existence – that he was allowed to use the toilet, for example. There was precious little else. He wasn't allowed in the lounge and had never been to school. He was extremely withdrawn and found it difficult to interact, sometimes not even realising we were talking to him.

'Time would have gone by very slowly in that room,' Rob said. 'We have to keep the pace very slow. The greatest challenge for them will be in here,' he said, tapping his head. 'Adjusting to their new reality. They are going to need the best possible and most intensive foster care we can offer them.'

We kept human contact to a minimum, so that they only saw a limited number of friendly faces who gradually became familiar. That room had been their world but even so they had no questions about the new world. Just entering a new room was a big ordeal for them – like entering a new country. If it felt too unfamiliar they stopped. When they ate they tried to put their plates on the floor and used their hands.

They'd not been physically or sexually abused – as far as we were able to tell. Incredibly, it seemed as if the two boys had just been put to one side and completely ignored, apart from brief interactions at 'feeding time' and trips to the toilet.

What surprised me was the strength of the love as well as the patience and peace they had for one another. They did not fight or argue once and it seemed as though the elder child had developed a parental instinct to take care of his younger brother. I found this both fascinating and reassuring.

The scientists who studied Genie had been particularly interested in the idea that language might be innate, that there were language areas of the brain that simply had to be 'switched on' by the mother's voice. I think this case suggests that there might be some familial instinct that fosters love and protection; that the boys' terrible imprisonment had united them rather than leading to competition and violence.

Psychologists warned us not to separate them (not that the idea had occurred to us), explaining that the incredibly strong bond the two children shared would help with their treatment. It had certainly helped them to survive. Without each other they would have had no love, no hugs, no human touch. In other isolation cases where a child was found on their own, they were almost comatose or did not know what to do when they were hugged or shown affection. Thanks to each other they understood what love was.

As for the physical results of their confinement, their bodies had barely seen sunlight and had almost no exercise, which left their bones soft, their muscles weak and their eyes sensitive to strong light. They frequently 'oohed' and 'aaahed' in quiet whispers when they saw something new, particularly if it was brightly coloured, as if they found strong colours particularly pleasing.

As time went on the two boys became a little more confident. They were fascinated when adults tried to play with them or fooled around. They didn't get peek-a-boo at first but once they realised that playing and making noise was something they could do as well as us, and that we encouraged and rewarded them for it, they quickly got the hang of it, as well as the desire for company. That was the easy bit. They still had so much to learn about the outside world and human interaction – what the physical and behavioural limits were, for example. I wondered how they would react when they were punished for doing something wrong or if they were bullied at school. In some ways, I imagined that the older child was far more advanced than other kids in areas of responsibility because of caring for his little brother, something that he had handled superbly.

I thought that as long as they had each other then they would be OK in life, a sentiment that was reinforced sooner than I expected by another remarkable pair of children.

CHAPTER EIGHT

MEET THE CLEAVERS

Claire the social worker was standing at the top of the stairwell, in shock and shaking as Craig and I bounded up the stairs two at a time.

'Are you OK?' I asked.

She was hugging her clipboard to her chest. She nodded, her eyes wide, as if they were looking elsewhere, without saying anything.

'You don't look OK,' Craig said. 'Are you sure?'

She nodded again and looked back nervously towards the front door of the flat, the home she'd just visited a few minutes before.

Christ, what on earth had spooked Claire? She was one of the toughest social workers I knew, a true East Ender who thought nothing of putting angry fathers twice her size in their place for bad parenting. She was tall, attractive, in her early thirties and spoke with a soft Jamaican accent.

'It was just a routine visit, one of three I'd planned for today,' she said breathlessly, before briefing us on what had happened.

Anh, who was in her mid-twenties and had schizophrenia, had been struggling to raise her two children. Her schizophrenia was fairly mild and unlike many sufferers the prescribed drugs actually seemed to help. Social services had decided that the children, Ly who was thirteen and Qui who was eleven, were not in any danger, had never been harmed and coped very well.

'Cope' was something of an understatement. Like many other children I'd seen over the years, Ly and Qui were the carers, with Ly taking the lead. She would tidy up and take the rubbish out as well as make sure the electricity's key meter had been topped up and would ring the council to explain why all their letters went unanswered by her mum.

'I can't tell you how wonderful those girls are,' Claire said, clearly emotional. 'They really run the household together. They even balanced the family's very tight budget and know that they can't afford to join in any after-school activities. There's no time to play with friends, no money for clothes shopping. No, they have to rush home to make sure their mum is OK, that no one has taken advantage of her confused state of mind during the day.'

Schizophrenia is a disorder of thinking, feeling and behaviour. It usually starts between the ages of fifteen to thirty-five and affects about one in every hundred people.[1] It's been argued that schizophrenia is an umbrella term used to cover a wide range of psychological symptoms that may or may not be present. They include difficulty with thinking – finding it hard to concentrate, drifting from one idea to another, feeling controlled – feeling as though your thoughts are vanishing, that they're not your own, or that your body is being taken over and controlled by someone else; hallucinations – hearing, smelling, feeling or seeing something that isn't there. Hearing voices is the most common problem. The voices can seem utterly real. Although they may be pleasant, they're more often rude, critical, abusive or annoying.

Another symptom, known as a negative symptom, partly

because it's harder to treat, is loss of interest, energy and emotion. The sufferer doesn't bother to get up or go out of the house and feels uncomfortable with other people. Routine chores like washing and tidying go undone.

It seems as though schizophrenics are in some way hypersensitive, that they're unable to filter out information from what is around them. Most people have no trouble with this. For example, while buying a Supersaver day return ticket to Cambridge while in King's Cross station in rush hour, most people are able to filter out all the background noise of other people's conversations, tannoy announcements, footsteps, shouting, laughter, trains hissing and screeching and so on, so they can concentrate on getting the right ticket for the best possible price. Someone suffering from schizophrenia will find this almost impossible.

Anh sometimes became muddled if she encountered someone or something unfamiliar, like a door-to-door salesman, postman or a telesales call, and she often forgot to carry out household chores and pay the bills.

'Ly had told her teacher that her mum was getting worse,' Claire told me. 'I knew that Anh was well cared for by her daughters in the evenings but I was worried about how she coped when she was on her own during the day so I decided to do an unannounced visit to see how she was getting on. It turned out that an unannounced visit to a worsening schizophrenic wasn't such a smart idea.'

Claire wasn't a 'light knocker' of the sort Brenda had described to me. She'd knocked for five minutes, a very long time. Someone else might have marked the file 'No Reply' and walked away, but not Claire. She'd knocked for so long that a neighbour had stuck their head out to see what was going on. As soon as she saw the stranger on the landing, the neighbour instantly knew who Claire was and why she was there and had ducked back inside again.

Claire knew that Anh was in. She rarely went out. Claire was especially fond of the two girls and wanted to make sure that Anh's illness hadn't degenerated to the extent that they would be unable to cope or, worse, jeopardised their safety. She'd once seen a case where a schizophrenic's flat had been taken over by crack dealers.

All too often in the media we get to hear about the 'nightmare clients', the ones that we all love to hate; it's rare to hear about the ones the social workers are attached to in such a lovely way. Claire, who was a single mum, really cared for and was genuinely worried about Anh and her daughters.

When Anh finally answered the door, she'd beckoned Claire inside with a friendly smile, saying 'Please come in, come in, come in' in her thick Vietnamese accent, walking backwards as she did so, radiating friendliness.

Claire noticed that Anh's right arm was behind her back and realised something was wrong, but couldn't put her finger on it. She should have left at this point. Instincts in these sorts of situations are often all too right. It's always possible to come back later with reinforcements.

As Claire stepped into the kitchen, Anh lifted the meat cleaver she'd been holding. Claire didn't even scream, just turned and ran. Claire escaped the flat just in time and was extremely relieved not to be chased along the balcony. Anh had decided that her front door was the line that no one could cross.

I looked down as Claire told us this, and saw that she was wearing flat shoes. This may sound over the top but social workers need to think about what they wear to work. They have to be able to run. They may only need to do this once or twice in their career, but if they can't, then they might end up seriously injured, or worse.

Although Claire was still in shock, she emphasised time and again how happy the girls were. They were bright, intelligent and completely untroubled by the fact that they had no child-hood. They loved looking after their mum.

'One can't help but feel pity for them,' I said. 'It's hardly fair, is it?'

Claire looked at me crossly. 'Pity? You shouldn't pity these children, you should feel respect for them, for their determination and courage to get through each evening while all most kids have to worry about is whose turn it is on the Wii.'

I looked down the hall nervously. 'OK, Craig,' I said, sounding a lot more confident than I felt, 'let's take a look, see that Anh's all right. Hopefully she'll have calmed down a bit by now.'

'Er ... Are you sure, Harry?' Craig said. 'We might just spin her out like Claire did.'

Too late. I was already at the front door, which was still open. Anh was in the hallway, beckoning me forward, one hand behind her back.

'Come in, please. Come in, please.'

She was tiny, delicate and looked the very picture of calm politeness. I went inside. Being six foot five, and with Craig right behind me, I felt pretty confident that little Anh would see that she had no chance of scaring us off, and that I would be able to talk her round.

Needless to say, my expectations were hopelessly naive.

'Hello, Anh, my name's Harry. I'd just like to talk to you for a moment, to make sure that you're OK.'

'Come in. Come in, please.'

I followed her into the lounge. As I stepped through the doorway, Anh turned, her expression transformed into a look of righteous vengeance as the meat cleaver, which she had been holding behind her back, rose ready to swing at me.

'RUN!' I yelled at Craig who wisely did so; I was about to follow but changed my mind at the last moment. I didn't want to get tangled up in the hallway with Craig or trip over anything and end up with a cleaver in the back. Anh looked to me as if she would show no mercy.

As I reached the doorway to the lounge I stopped, turned and dropped, raising my left arm to block the blow from the meat cleaver that was already coming down hard. At the same time I stepped under her raised arm and threw out my right fist with as much force as I possibly could, punching Anh with a mighty crack, right in the middle of her face.

I'd never thrown such a hard punch so successfully in all my life. It lifted tiny Anh off her feet and over the sofa. I'd put so much of my weight behind it that I followed her over the sofa and we tumbled together on the floor.

I couldn't believe that she was still conscious, and still holding the meat cleaver. Her wild eyes glared at me murderously. I quickly rolled on top and sat astride her, pinning her arms, noticing that three of the knuckles on my right hand had been cut by the punch. I felt awful. If I'd done that to my hand, what had I done to poor Anh?

Sure enough, blood started to pour from Anh's mouth and nose, and her lip quickly began to swell. Oh God, I felt so terribly ashamed. I'd just whacked a mentally ill woman – who was half my size – in the face. My shame was matched only by the relief that her children weren't there to see it. I felt sick.

'Harry!' I looked back over my shoulder. Craig had run back in after me, fearing the worst. Claire was right behind him.

'It's OK,' I said, still panting from the adrenalin rush.

I caught Claire's eyes, and nodded a thank you. She needn't have come back in with Craig, but she did. Although the work was about more than the money, there was no way Claire was being paid enough for doing this kind of job, one of the most important in our society, looking out for those amongst us who needed help the most. Compared to a social worker, police officers are like premiership footballers. We're paid overtime (most of the time) and have excellent pension benefits (although we still pay for these, of course). After today's 'incident', Claire would be massively behind on her visits and couldn't expect to receive overtime as she desperately tried to catch up.

Anh stayed quiet and still. Tears had started to roll down her face, mixing with the blood.

'Let's get Anh restrained and treated,' Craig said, taking out his handcuffs. 'What are we going to do, Harry? She's attacked both you and Claire. At the very least it's assault, at worst it's attempted murder.'

'I don't think we should press any charges,' I replied, looking at Claire. My punch was perfectly justified, but I was really unhappy about it at the same time. Besides, Anh needed help, and charging her with assault wasn't going to do her or her daughters any favours.

Claire agreed. 'I can record the incident on her mental health file for future risk assessment. In the meantime, we need to get Anh to a secure unit.'

It's a little-known fact that many assaults on police go unreported; the most common of these is the drunken idiot in the town centre at 2 a.m. who whacks a cop and gets whacked (quite rightly) back. The penalty for assaulting police is so low that it's hardly worth the bother anyway – and a caution for drunk and disorderly is a lot easier on the paperwork. Those idiots arrested for D and D nearly always wake up with a hangover and shame-faced, head hung low, wrapped up in a blue police blanket, praying they won't lose their job while the custody officer gives them a dressing down.

In this instance, we were still left with a major question: what was going to happen to Ly and Qui? The answer, although straightforward enough, didn't go down that well with any of us. Even though they'd done an amazing job looking after their mum and household, there was no way they could be allowed to live on their own while their mum spent a month detained under the Mental Health Act for assessment.

'Even if she hadn't flipped during my visit,' Claire said, 'I think I would have had her assessed anyway. Goodness knows what Ly and Qui have been through with their mum as she's become worse. For all we know, the voices in her head might have commanded Anh to throw her daughters out onto the street in the middle of the night.'

As there were no other relatives that meant foster care. At least Claire would make sure that Ly and Qui would stay together. It was a harsh end to a difficult case, I thought, and I could only hope that because Anh was receiving the treatment she so desperately needed she would be able to live with her children again.

'I'm going to do all I can for Anh,' Claire said. 'You should take heart that the girls will be together and will still be able to see their mum, whatever happens.'

No matter how often I'd seen it, I was always amazed at the resilience and coping abilities of children placed in extraordinary circumstances, something that was soon reinforced when I came across a disturbing new phenomenon unique to Hackney.

CHAPTER NINE

THE LOST CHILDREN

I looked at my watch for the fifteenth time. Where was the bloody translator?

I'd been sat in our interview suite looking at the small Vietnamese child for the last fifteen minutes. A uniformed PC had stumbled across him, standing quietly alone amidst the chaos of Dalston Market. It seemed that the child, who looked to me to be about seven years old, spoke no English. We'd eventually managed to establish that he was Vietnamese by reading out phrases from a website. He nodded when we'd hit on the right one and answered 'Hang' when we tried to ask him his name using a phonetic online translation.

I was really puzzled. We had a reverse missing-child situation. No one had reported a missing child but we'd most definitely found one. What I didn't know was that Hang would be the first of many.

The chaotic atmosphere of Dalston Market in Ridley Road is unique. After walking around for a few minutes you start to feel as though it's possible to buy anything from anywhere on the planet (including anything illegal). There are more than a hundred stalls – many of which are brightly decorated and over-lit with naked light bulbs – with expert marketeers and entrepreneurs selling everything from designer wigs to witchcraft videos at rock-bottom prices: 'I'm cuttin' me own throat, madam,' was a popular refrain.

In Dalston, you can load your shopping bag with the finest African fruit and veg, fresh fish, fake fags, textiles, Korans, hundreds upon hundreds of Nollywood (Nigerian) movies and Vietnamese children.

Yes, that's right: Vietnamese children. Except you don't have to pay for the kids, they're literally a giveaway. It's easy to miss them in the chaos of the market, one or two tiny lost and lonely souls standing quietly amongst the hubbub while East End fruit and veg boys yell over the booming voices of the West African wig sellers, who in turn compete with the house music coming from the stall selling so-called 'legal' highs.

Hackney has a large and thriving Vietnamese community about 4,000 strong. The first settled here as refugees after fleeing Vietnam in 1975. This was at the end of the disastrous war with America when thousands of men, women and children, fearing persecution from the victorious Communist forces, climbed on anything that would float and set sail for the stormy South China Seas, hoping a passing ship would save them.

Many were picked up by British ships and good old Hackney, the most cosmopolitan borough in our cosmopolitan city, welcomed them with open arms. One of the first Vietnamese refugee centres in the world was founded in Hackney, a kind of decompression chamber where the newly arrived could be contained as they acclimatised to a very different kind of life in the UK. They were taught English, trained in the ways of English business and helped with accommodation. The Vietnamese community centre, An Viet ('Well Settled') House in Englefield Road, is still going strong. Its canteen serves some of the finest Vietnamese food in London.

The new arrivals quickly proved to be valuable additions to Hackney's unique mix. They became known for their hard work, self-reliance and enterprising nature as they rapidly launched dozens of successful restaurants, factories, off-licences and, more recently, the nail parlours that seem to be on almost every street corner these days.

The fact that there is such a large and thriving Vietnamese community has led to a new, very peculiar and as yet unexplained phenomenon: the dumping of young Vietnamese children (usually under the age of ten) in Dalston Market. As far as we were able to tell, whoever takes them there simply tells them to look for a Vietnamese family to take them in.

Although this is more within the remit of the Immigration Service, we were called more than once a week to collect these children, so often in fact that after about the first ten cases Rob decided to allocate them all to one person, Patrick, one of our most experienced officers. By interviewing the children with an interpreter, Patrick was, over time, able to build up a detailed picture of the people-smuggling operations while liaising closely with the Immigration Service.

It soon became a standing joke in the office. All sorts of people would ring us up, whether uniformed police officers, members of the public, social services and so on. They'd start to say, 'I've found a Vietnamese child and it's a bit strange because—'

And we'd finish the sentence for them: 'You found them in Dalston Market.'

'Yes, how did you know?'

'Well, because it's the third one this week.'

We soon found local families who were quite happy to tell us about the day a child tugged on their sleeve and asked them quietly for help. They'd taken them in and raised them as if they were their own. Many just walked into Downham Road Social Services to tell them about their new arrival while others no doubt simply decided to live below the radar and remain unknown to the authorities.

These were the happier stories we heard about. It's still early days but it wouldn't surprise me if we discover that the less fortunate kids are turned into virtual slaves, working long hours in restaurant kitchens or in a Dalston sweatshop.

Unbelievably there are plenty of sweatshops in the UK. Although foreign sweatshops that manufacture goods for well-known international companies have received wide coverage, UK-based sweatshops receive scant publicity. In September 2009 for example, twenty-six workers from China, Turkey and Vietnam were found to be working illegally in a sweatshop in Dalston, producing clothes for a famous high street clothing store.[1]

I suspect that some sweatshop owners kept a wary eye open for the lost children dumped in Dalston and quickly swept them up to be used for slave labour. Some reports suggest that the youngest children are being put to work in some nail bars and that others are being exploited by their 'owners' in other ways, possibly sexually.[2] As these children don't officially exist they easily bypass all the usual checks in society that are supposed to help keep them safe and they live as part of Hackney's uncounted population – that surprisingly large section of the community that never makes it onto any census.

This type of trafficking, where kids are simply dumped after being smuggled into Britain, is known as 'better life trafficking'. Parents think that smuggling their children here is the best thing they can do for their family. Of course it isn't. The family back home find they end up paying off the transportation costs to ruthless gangs for many years. And the traffickers have an unpleasant use in mind for the older children once they arrive.

Back in 2000, when I was running my little drugs squad in the London Borough of Haringey, we raided a house after one of my officers said he could smell the cannabis from the street. When we charged through the front door, it was as if we'd just crashed into the Amazon. Everywhere we looked, floor to ceiling, the whole place was covered in green.

The first two reception rooms on the ground floor were full of plants. Above them a gentle whirring sound revealed that lights on timed electric rollers made sure every single plant was fed exactly the right amount of light. An automatic hydroponics system took care of water and food. A huge water barrel sat at the top of the stairs alongside a massive main junction box, the source of the factory's electrics. Upstairs was the drying room with dozens of enormous plants draped over ordinary clothes dryers. Every other available space was crammed with growing plants.

The meter had of course been hot-wired. It whirred like mad, its numbers spun in a blur, a result of the massive amount of power this place was consuming. We shut it off and carted off the cannabis – it took us three days and three skiploads, each packed to their absolute limit. Police officers were photographed by the press staggering down the stairs with bin liner after bin liner packed full of the super-strong weed.

We found documents that took us to £365,000 in cash hidden in a safety deposit box in Knightsbridge. We then recovered more safety deposit keys from our suspects and got hold of another £750,000. Other paperwork revealed accounts in Luxembourg and another £1 million or so – this had all been earned from the produce of just two houses.

This was still in the days before hydroponics had really caught on in terms of growing weed; it was one of the very first such marijuana 'factories' of its kind that we found.

It soon caught on, however.

Between 2004 and 2006, 1,500 cannabis farms were shut down in London alone. The London Fire Brigade stumbled across fifty cannabis factories over the same period because of house fires caused by faulty lights or dodgy wiring. Presently across the UK, the police raid at least three cannabis farms every single day.[3] Part of the reason for the surge in factories is that growing marijuana is much cheaper and safer than smuggling smelly buds and/or heavy blocks of resin. The Vietnamese have the best-established high-volume production methods after refining them with great success in Australia and Canada before colonising the UK, starting with Hackney and North London and then moving to the Home Counties and most recently to the north of England.

We now know that about three-quarters of UK cannabis farms are run by Vietnamese gangs. Teenagers that have been smuggled are hired to water, feed and light the plants; they're cheaper and more reliable than automated systems. Those smuggled Vietnamese who are old enough to cope with the management of the marijuana factories are employed by the gangs, while those that are too young are simply dumped on the street. Judges sometimes complain of having to deal with so many Vietnamese cases in one day, stating that it quickly becomes impossible to tell them apart. It doesn't help that when the Vietnamese teenagers end up being arrested, they nearly always give the same surname: Nguyen, the Vietnamese equivalent of Smith.

Some rescued children have described – usually through translators – horrendous journeys spent hungry, thirsty and locked up in containers for days at a time. Their long journey follows a path through the North Vietnamese border into China as far as Beijing, and then on the Trans-Siberian Express through Russia. From Russia, all sorts of methods involving boats, lorries and trains are used to transport the children the rest of the way to the UK. Traffickers smuggling Chinese children are now using the same routes.

The conditions in cannabis homes are cramped and dangerous. Drugs squads have found workers living in cupboards and lofts to maximise space for plants. Fire or electrocution is a real hazard. The labour needed for the daily care of the plants is not intense, however, and two or three people can easily look after one house that might produce a £750,000 annual tax-free profit.

Unfortunately these kids often find themselves victims twice over – both at the hands of the criminal gangs who brought them to this country, forcing them to work in cramped, dangerous conditions – and again when they find themselves treated as criminals. Once they're arrested, some of these teenagers are charged with drugs offences, which can carry a maximum sentence of fourteen years. In one case, a boy said he was fifteen but as he could produce no documentation to support this, magistrates ruled he should stand trial in an adult court.[4]

Many young people who smoke weed grown in the UK believe that large-scale cannabis cultivation is a 'victimless crime' but the reality is that vulnerable young people are being exploited by ruthless operators who couldn't care less about their 'helpers'.

I wish people who smoke cannabis would think about that the next time they spark one up. Drugs are illegal for a number of reasons, not just because they're bad for you. It's an ethical issue too. Millions of people suffer across the world, from Argentina to Afghanistan, exploited by the traffickers, and as usual when it comes to drugs, none suffer more than the children, whether forced to work for the dealers or turned into addicts by them.

As far as the question of legalisation goes I'd be happy to see cannabis available on prescription for sufferers of multiple sclerosis but legalising it is a complex issue that may cause more problems than it solves. (Who's going to produce it? Private companies? Would they be able to compete in terms of price with the illegal growers? What strength should be allowed?

What taxes should be levied?) Besides, no politician in his right mind and who wants to keep his parliamentary seat will dare suggest the idea, as some elements of the media would quickly and mercilessly crucify them.

For now, the best we can hope for is to educate the young about the dangers and ethics of drug production to try to discourage them, and to ease the burden on police by making possession of small amounts punishable with on-the-spot fines and cautions. Anyone caught with anything over a set amount should be prosecuted for intent to supply (at the moment proving intent is a real pain).

As time went on and knowledge about Patrick's work spread through the Vietnamese community, whole families rolled up to say they'd taken in a child weeks, months or even a year or two before. Whenever we finished interviewing these children, looking for evidence, to try to find out more about the techniques of the traffickers, we asked them what they wanted. They would nearly always tell us that they wished to stay with their 'family'. So that's exactly what we did, with just about all of them. Although I'm certain we did the right thing, I hope history will prove us right.

CHAPTER TEN

LIFE ON MARS

I was pissed off, stood outside the same house for the third time this week in the pouring summer rain, getting no reply to my door-rattling knock. A teacher had reported the daughter as being 'worryingly thin' and she hadn't been to school all of last week. The mother, Nadifa, was known to social services but the file was thin. An aristocratic and fatherless family from Somalia, Nadifa and her daughter came from a nomadic people, refugees from the civil war.

There are so many civil wars going on around the world that it's impossible to keep up. People from the globe's trouble spots end up here, in the comparative safety of Hackney: Algeria, Yemen, Angola, Cambodia, Afghanistan, Iraq, Congo, Chechnya, Sudan, Uganda, Rwanda, Ivory Coast and Haiti were just the tip of the iceberg.

Nadifa also had a history of not answering the door. If I could be certain they were in, then I'd knock until the door fell down. A bit overdramatic perhaps? No. I was worried. This was the sort of family that every police and social services worker dreads. Not because they were in immediate danger, but there was an ominous sense of the unknown. Frankly, they scared the pants off me.

I normally didn't like to disturb the people next door – nobody likes a neighbour that brings the police to their street, a family that is distrusted for no good reason other than the fact that they are different may be further stigmatised; ammunition for the gossips. In this case, I felt as if I had no choice.

It was a good street. Large Victorian semis, mostly broken up into flats, although a few still remained intact. This property had been bought by a housing association many years ago, when local house prices hadn't yet reached incredulous levels, and had been converted into flats.

I tried neighbour number one. An old man answered. Bored, with nothing to do, he tried to keep me talking. A local boy, his family had been there since the end of the war, when half the street was 'giant potholes' as he called them, bomb craters. You could tell where the bombs hadn't fallen by the century-old trees that stood untouched.

'And what about the neighbour? A woman and her daughter. Do you know anything about them?'

'That's about all I know, guv,' he said. 'She almost never goes out and I can't really see her that much to be honest. She's covered head to toe, walks with her head down. She's tall. Maybe Asian, maybe African. Your guess is as good as mine. We've got neighbours from all over the world and I know a bit about most of them but bugger all about . . .'

I was already halfway down the pathway. 'Thanks very much,' I called over my shoulder.

'Sorry not to be more help. What's she done anyway?'

It was the same up and down the street; even though her neighbours were chatty – an Iranian black cab driver, a famous photographer and a stay-at-home mum – they all knew as much as each other, which was nothing.

'She may be Somali,' the photographer said. 'She's very tall, slender and definitely black.'

I asked them all if they'd ever spoken to her. 'Never,' was the universal reply.

Even in London this was strange. There's usually some glimmer of information, even if it's just about their shopping habits, or if Royal Mail had brought any post, or if strange noises emanated from open windows, or if there were visitors, but no, here there was nothing.

I was worried. My instinct was telling me not to go away, that there was something inside that house that I needed to see. I stared up at the grey sky, and wondered how many times I was going to have to come back before I got through their front door. All the neighbours now knew that the police wanted to speak to the occupants, so perhaps they would see something. I left my card and asked them all to call if they did.

I started back to my car, passing by the place one last time. The curtain twitched. I snapped my head round; for less than a second, a young girl's face – maybe twelve years old and gaunt, wearing a headscarf – appeared at the window, before she was yanked back.

Now I knew they were in I wasn't going anywhere and if they still didn't answer, I'd have that door off its hinges if necessary. I started by rattling the letterbox. I wasn't able to call through it, it was sealed; plenty of people in Hackney are fed up with fireworks and dog faeces flying through, an endless source of amusement for young troublemakers for more years than I care to remember.

My fist went to the door. This time, my firm regular thudding had an effect. The door slowly opened, finally.

It was the mum. Just as the photographer said, she was tall, close to six feet, but she was beyond slender, more like skeletal. She was in Somali dress; a long dark wrap enclosed her body. Her large eyes looked out at me over her hollow cheeks – they were full of contempt.

'Hello, I'm Detective Sergeant Harry Keeble,' I said, introducing myself as gently as possible, trying to play down the word 'police' and definitely not mentioning 'child abuse'. Not yet, anyway, it was too early.

'May I come in?' I asked gently.

This tall woman, head held high, shook her head with all the aloofness of a queen.

I wasn't asking for her permission, it was an attempt to empower her, to give her the feeling that I wasn't simply pushing my way in. I wasn't about to turn around now. My bluff called, I gently pushed the door open with my right hand to signify that I was coming in no matter what. The woman got the message and stood aside. I breathed a sigh of relief.

'It's Nadifa, isn't it?'

She said nothing and simply walked ahead of me to the lounge.

The hallway was bare; the lounge was almost empty. No 50-inch plasma, PlayStation or Wii. I could see no reason for the austerity. They'd been living here for some months.

'We're just concerned that your daughter hasn't been at school for two weeks,' I said, hoping this might get an answer. Neither Educational Welfare nor social services had ever managed to get a response, despite repeated visits.

Nadifa sat down on a plain brown sofa and looked up at me. She unnerved me. I broke her stare by looking around the room. There were some small, framed pages of Arabic writing on the wall.

'What are these?' I asked.

Nadifa didn't take her eyes off me but said nothing. I could feel her suspicion, her anger. I don't believe in ghosts but I felt as if I were in a haunted house. These sorts of homes frighten even the hardiest of social workers. I'd normally bound confidently from room to room throwing doors open without hesitation. Not here. I moved slowly, bracing myself for whatever I might find, while Nadifa's eyes bored into me, as if seeing right through to my soul.

I'd also normally chat and question my suspects quite happily as I searched but as Nadifa ignored my every comment I quickly fell silent. She did not deem me worthy of communication. I was the enemy, a threat. I felt that deeply.

'May I see the kitchen?'

No answer.

I entered the kitchen. It was bare, save for a pan simmering quietly on the gas ring. A pasta-vegetable mix of some kind. I opened the fridge door, slowly. Sometimes, in abusive and neglectful families, food is left to rot. The stink can be like a slap in the face, and the nausea can hang round for a good few minutes.

Not here. The fridge was spotless and empty, save for a jug of milk. Nothing in the little freezer. I checked the cupboards. All clean, all empty, save for one which contained a bag of rice and a bag of pasta.

This family was living on the barest minimum – milk, rice, pasta and a few boiled vegetables. A lack of nutrients for a growing child perhaps but I had to admit that it made a change from so many of the poor family homes I saw, overflowing with empty buckets of fried chicken and empty cigarette packets.

I went back into the lounge, where Nadifa was waiting. 'I need to speak to the kids,' I told her.

Silence. Just the stare.

'Is that OK?'

No response.

'I'm going upstairs.'

Silence.

Bloody hell. At least you knew where you were when dealing with an aggressive seventeen-stone, shaven-headed thug. I slowly climbed the stairs. Although I really had no idea what to expect, I guessed I'd find a frightened child, bewildered by this strange man in their bedroom. I prepared myself by plastering a calm and friendly expression on my face.

As I reached the top of the stairs, I saw a bedroom to my right. A girl was sitting on the bed looking out of the window. She turned her head to look at me.

'Aisha?' I asked, radiating friendliness.

Wide-eyed and alert, her pupils were dilated. She was wearing the same style of clothes as her mother. I tried to gauge her thoughts, what would be the worst thing going through her mind right now? 'This man is coming to get me. He is evil. My mum told me one day, bad people would come for us.' At least if I started off thinking this then I couldn't get it any more wrong. How does a forty-year-old white male cop communicate with a thirteen-year-old Somali girl brought up in a war-torn country?

There were no undersheets on the bed, just a bare mattress and duvet. Not soiled, it just looked 'used'. The room had no other furniture. Her eyes were full of mistrust and fear, while mine were full of uncertainty. I stayed in the doorway and leaned on its frame, doing my best to appear relaxed and friendly.

'Aisha, I'm just here to make sure you and your family are OK.'

She nodded. Great.

'So how's school?'

I rambled on, hopelessly trying to get her to engage. All the time, Aisha – who was desperately thin – stared at me anxiously. I made no progress, just like her schoolteachers. I was way out of my depth here, there was a huge, impenetrable barrier between us and I needed help; I wondered if we had access to a social worker from the Somali community.

I recalled the news reports about a famine in Somalia less than a decade earlier, when a million people had died. I wondered if the frugality stemmed from there. Nadifa had lived through it after all, and I suspected that would leave psychological scars, possibly mental illness.

I had to stop here and now, my sensitivity was getting me nowhere. In most other cases it was simple: a six-year-old boy with lacerations tells you he has been whipped, you take him; a five-year-old girl tells you her dad has put 'white stuff' over her, you take her. It's a whole different ball game when dealing with an entire family, all of whom have withdrawn from mainstream society. They scream out concern in their manner and appearance, but trying to put these feelings on paper is incredibly difficult. They didn't want to talk, they were thin but had some food, the house was clean; her daughter seemed uninjured, there was no evidence of physical abuse, although they were too afraid of me to talk.

Justifying any further action was extremely difficult. These are the children who fall through the gaps, not by incompetence, but by the inability to translate our concerns into actionable evidence. It was extremely frustrating but I wasn't going to give up on Nadifa and her family. It wasn't going to be easy; on the surface their difficulties seemed to be minor and they were more than likely to lose out in the battle for the limited resources of Hackney's Social Services to more dramatic-sounding cases.

I was definitely going to return. For now though, twelve investigations of varying urgency needed my attention and my phone had been vibrating with quiet insistence in my jacket pocket. As soon as Nadifa had slammed the door behind me, I answered.

It was Rob. 'It's a nasty one, can you take it?'

CHAPTER ELEVEN

BLOW-BY-BLOW

Two minutes later I was stuck in a good old Hackney traffic jam, drumming my fingers impatiently on the steering wheel as the sunshine heated my little tin-can car to boiling point. A drunk staggered past, Special Brew in hand, walking like the pavement wasn't strong enough to hold him.

A 'police incident' the local radio said.

That'll be a shooting then, I thought. Sure enough, I spotted crime scene tape fluttering across the junction with a side street about fifty metres ahead.

'Sod it. I've no time to muck about.' Causing a few honks, I heaved the unmarked car through a three-point turn. I had no blues and twos, so I proceeded with caution, turning against a 'no right turn' sign to get into the road I wanted, and started to flow with the traffic to the address.

All too often, I found myself at my desk, fifteen crimes in front of me, trying to decide which of the hundred important things I should do next. Get a call like this and that all melts away and a long line of clear decisions quickly follows.

The child was already in police protection in Homerton Hospital's Starlight Ward with his mum and dad, who had split up a year or so earlier. The suspect, the mum's new boyfriend, was at Stoke Newington police station and the scene was under police guard.

The cogs in my brain started to whirr. I was at the start of what the police call 'the golden hour'. Evidence and memories were still fresh, crime scenes and the surrounding areas undisturbed, victim and suspect yet to undergo a forensic examination. The golden hour starts with the platinum ten minutes. I needed a photographer, Scene of Crime Officers (SOCOs), a full forensic medical of the little victim and samples from the suspect. All of my actions would be documented in a decision log.

The little boy was three. Although the youth of the child makes the crime seem even more shocking, it was possible to put a positive spin on this. He wouldn't understand what had happened to him and it wouldn't be long before any memories of the event were pushed to the very back of his mind, buried out of harm's way.

His future carers would have to decide whether to tell him or not later in life. It must be hard enough telling someone that they're adopted or that 'Dad' isn't 'Dad', but that they were raped as a child? They may decide never to tell but then there's always the risk that a neighbour or another family member may unintentionally reveal all. Then there's their social services file, which they'll be given access to as an adult, should they wish.

My plan was to drive to the scene of the crime first, then to the hospital. In the meantime I called the custody officer on the hands-free and gave him precise instructions as to what to do with my suspect.

'Stand him on a white sheet, strip him, bag his clothes in breathable paper bags. Then package the sheet and give him a white paper suit [this suit has an unfortunate name, a 'rape suit']. I want non-intimate samples, by force if necessary, and a penile swab. Tell the arresting officer that he is not to let the suspect out of his sight until all that has been done. On no circumstances should he be left alone for a second.'

I was extremely pleased to hear that the custody officer had noticed a damp patch on my suspect's pants as he was searched and had already had the foresight to have a PC stand over him until I called to outline the forensic strategy, after which his clothes could be removed.

Next, I rang the Starlight Ward and asked the doctor to prepare for a full paediatric forensic medical.

The scene of the crime, a terraced council house, looked exactly as one would expect, wholly unremarkable. I signed the crime scene log and entered. I noted a child's drawings on the wall of the lounge and, as usual, the giant twenty-first-century plasma in the middle of a wall covered in late-twentieth-century wallpaper. I made my way to the first-floor bathroom. I looked in, studying the scene, staying just outside the doorway, leaving the room clean for the scene of crime team, our very own CSI.

Nothing jumped out at me. It was just a smallish bathroom, clean, sink, loo; bath with showerhead fixed to the taps, two adult toothbrushes; one child's in a plastic pink cup.

I went back downstairs and spoke to the officers on the scene. A uniformed constable in his forties briefed me on the story so far. Mature constables, officers that have 'seen it all', are worth their weight in gold. Young, eager PCs sometimes make basic mistakes, which is totally understandable.

'The suspect is the mum's new boyfriend,' he said. 'He took the little boy to the bathroom and that's where the incident happened. Mum found out this morning, when he complained about the injury at playgroup. She didn't call the police, but the boy's father. He came straight round and detained the suspect at the flat until the police arrived.'

I start to ask: 'When you say detained ...'

'No violence.'

'Thank God for that,' I said. Dad had sensibly realised that we'd need the suspect to be taken intact – he was going to be treated as a crime scene. If the dad had laid into him this would have become a very complex investigation and chances of getting accurate forensics could be drastically reduced – especially if the suspect had ended up being hospitalised.

'The suspect didn't even try to run,' the officer continued. 'Just sat and waited until we arrived.'

Paralysed by shame and fear, no doubt. Running would have forced Dad to intervene, giving him more reason for his anger to explode through fist and boot; there would be no outrunning or overpowering. We could easily have finished up dealing with a murder by reason of temporary insanity.

How can we know how we would react if the unthinkable had happened to our child and we were in range of the suspect in an empty flat? I know that many men would proudly boast that they would 'rip the bastard to shreds', but in my experience people who have been unlucky enough to find themselves in that position rarely feel the urge to commit violence.

'Mum hit the nines once she knew Dad was with the suspect,' the officer told me.

In a few seconds sirens were fired up in different parts of Hackney and the cuffs were snapped around his wrists minutes later, probably much to his relief.

I quickly made a few phone calls, getting the scene under way. The snapper was the first to arrive, just minutes later.

'That was quick,' I said, pleased.

'SCD5 Command says you're high priority,' he said with a shrug. 'So I dropped everything. Bermondsey CID will have to wait. Child rape is it?' he asked with an ill-concealed expression of disgust.

He was an old hand, he'd photographed it all: the grisly

murders, victims with gunshot and machete wounds, but like all specialists who are called in to work on the occasional child protection case, he had little stomach for jobs involving the sexual abuse of children. He wanted this over with quickly, so he could get back to photographing murders and drug busts.

Moments like these brought it home to me that something inside you has to make you want to do this type of investigation, something that makes you overcome your disgust and distress to pursue justice on behalf of the little victims.

Next, the scenes of crime officer turned up, a businesslike woman in her mid-thirties. She donned a whole white suit while we discussed strategy.

'I'm looking for blood and semen,' I told her, 'footprints, fingerprints, hand smudges that might tell us something about positions. There's nothing obviously visible to the naked eye that I can see from the doorway.'

I wanted her to find me something that would reveal that normal-looking bathroom's terrible secret.

'The outcome of this case is going to depend almost entirely on the forensics,' I said, 'the victim is three years old, not an ideal age to cope with the trauma of a memorandum interview.'

I was fairly certain the boy would escape having to relive the day in an interview but this wasn't just because of his age; if a rape had indeed happened then the extent of his injuries would tell the story for him.

As the SOCO got to work, Craig and Lucy rocked up. I asked them to start searching the suspect's bedroom.

'I want his laptop,' I said. 'Don't forget we're looking for the golden prize of any child sex investigation: the stash.'

Paedophiles like trophies. These days, they tend to be secret files buried on their laptop under an innocuous name. However, some perverts like to take physical mementos, usually an item of clothing hidden in a loft, shed or wardrobe, but you never quite know what you're going to find, whether it is a soft toy or a family photo torn from an album.

Certain that the scene was under control and under proper examination, I left them to it and rushed over to the Homerton. I strode into the familiar surroundings of the Starlight Ward and knocked on the door of the private room. On the other side of that door, a family sat in shock, trying to come to terms with the unthinkable. This is where the case takes on a human face – where I become acquainted with Mum, Dad and the little boy.

I waited a second before entering, took a deep breath and opened the door.

The first thing I noticed, much to my surprise, was that the little boy was actually running around and playing.

'I'm Detective Sergeant Harry Keeble,' I said quietly, introducing myself to the mum and dad, holding out my hand.

The mum was in her late twenties, with long dark hair, red eyes and nose. Her husband, about the same age, his hands stained with black engine oil, fiddled with a biro, the consent form for the forensic examination on the table in front of them. His face was full of worry. I could feel the division between the two: guilt from the mum, anger from the dad.

I briefly explained the details of the operation so far.

'Just make sure he burns in hell,' the dad said quietly.

I explained what was going to happen next and that doctors needed to perform a forensic examination their child.

The mother wept as I did so.

'Shall I stop?' I asked.

'No. It's OK.'

The father reached out an arm and put it on her shoulder. 'It's OK, I don't blame you. How could you know that …' He stopped himself just in time, the little boy was building a tower of wooden bricks in the corner of the room. 'You couldn't know that he was – that he was a …'

With a little difficulty, I interrupted them and carried on explaining the procedure.

They had no questions. All the mother could do was go over and over in her head: 'Where were the signs? Where were the signs?'

There aren't usually many. Paedophiles are often expert predators who rely on the camouflage of fake love and friendship seemingly above and beyond what's usual.

I excused myself and kickstarted the PFE (paediatric forensic examination) strategy discussion. A PFE is a huge job with many challenges. Like me, the doctor would have had a lot of cases on that day but now a member of the hospital's on-call team had taken them on. This child was the priority. What we found during the PFE would determine the outcome of the case.

While I was of course extremely keen to get a result, our number one concern was the health of the child. An examination like this is complex on many levels. Apart from the necessary medical knowledge and the skill to take and package forensic samples, the doctor has to be able to use camera equipment (including a colposcope to record internal injuries), to communicate comfortably with possibly traumatised children and their upset parents about very sensitive issues, such as testing the child for sexually transmitted diseases, or explaining that although the photos they'll take will never be seen by any jury out of respect for the victim, the defence team might request copies to show their own expert witnesses.

They also need to understand, and be sensitive to, the child's developmental, social and emotional needs and intellectual level. And then months later, they have to be prepared to stand up and explain the child's injuries to a courtroom, often under cross-examination. It's so important to get these sorts of examinations exactly right but at the same time we have to remember that we're dealing with a scared little boy who may not want to cooperate. If the child doesn't want us to go on then we will stop, it's that simple.

Our conversations were clinical, the only way such horrors can be dealt with; we were all professionals clear in our determination to achieve the highest standards of forensic evidence and medical care. Whether the case stood or fell depended on us. If we could get the results we needed here, then in all likelihood the evidence would be incontrovertible and we'd be able to avoid putting the family through a trial.

Back at Stoke Newington, the suspect played the non-com card but at least he was charged, in custody and in deep trouble. Good.

It was dark when my desk phone rang. It was Claire the social worker. 'I've got someone from Somalia who can help with the case of the mysterious princess,' she said, 'shall we try again tomorrow?'

CHAPTER TWELVE

THE AFRICAN RIPPER

'People are crazy about their dogs. I envy dogs round here. They get better treatment than people,' Aisha said. Aisha was tall for her age, thin and beautiful.

Now I knew why Nadifa behaved the way she did. Good God, I'd heard some stories in my time but this was almost too much to bear. It turned out that Aisha was indeed only thirteen, that she simply looked a lot older. The proof of this was the terrible event she had been subjected to.

I was with Claire and Cecilia, a representative from a Somali community centre based in North London. I realised straight away from Cecilia's booming, no-nonsense voice and bone-crushing handshake that she was a force to be reckoned with. In her forties, she had been in the UK for over twenty years. She was quick to warn me that she was often 'painfully honest': 'I don't have the luxury of mucking about,' she said, 'I tell it like it is.'

I liked her.

'There is a large but nearly invisible Somali population in London today,' she said, 'and little is known about the problems they face here. I shout till I'm blue in the face but it's taken for ever to get the government to listen to anything I've got to say.'

There were over 15,000 Somali people living in the neighbouring Central London borough of Tower Hamlets, where they were the second largest minority ethnic community. About 5,000 more lived in Hackney, where 10 per cent of the Muslim youth were from Somalia.

'In Hackney 60 per cent are single-parent families,' Cecilia said as we travelled to Nadifa's home. 'That's thanks to the death or detention of the husbands back in Somalia. There tends to be lots of children, so over half the Somali people in the UK are nineteen or under. That's a great resource for us to have in this country and we should be grateful.'

'Why do we have so many in East London?' I asked.

'Somali people arrived here before the First World War, they even fought on the British side against the Germans. They used to work as merchant seamen and many settled near the docks and found work locally. They were known as the Fortune Men,' Cecilia said with a smile, 'because they sent a large part of their pay packets home to their families. So since then Somali people have travelled to the East End because that's where they thought there were fortunes to be made.'

I nodded. Although I had a good idea as to the answer to my next question, I asked it anyway: 'Why have so many arrived now?'

'Conflict. The troubles back home have kicked off again since a new government was formed in 2002. Always fighting, fighting. Except now of course, instead of trained seamen looking for work, it's mainly young and poorly educated mothers who are unlikely to find work. Many of them are nomadic and illiterate, so adjusting to life in the UK is very difficult for them. That is why about 90 per cent of Somalis don't work – they're either children or uneducated women who don't speak English.'

She went on: 'Many of these families don't even know what help is available to them. Research in Hackney has shown us that a quarter of Somali families have no or little furniture, one fifth do not have sufficient kitchen equipment, while almost a third of children do not have sufficient clothes, two in every five children do not have a warm waterproof coat and one in five do not have new, properly fitted shoes.

'You and I can survive in Hackney because we know how this borough works. You've got to be tough and streetwise. Somali women are anything but. They're soft targets for cowardly criminals. In almost one in five Somali households someone has been mugged, a similar number have been victims of vandalism, and one in ten have fallen victim to violent attacks.

'It's crazy because although there's so many Somalis here, many of them feel totally alone and don't feel as though there's any sense of community. There are Somali community centres in London but they can only do so much. The isolation of these young women, combined with the trauma of the experiences in Somalia, means that some develop mental illness, which carries high levels of stigma and is likely to go unreported or misunderstood. It's not all bad by any means. I have high hopes for the young generation who are receiving a British education. Of course, this can create a cultural divide between mother and children, which may cause problems in the future if we don't watch out.'

We arrived at the house. I was about to knock in my traditional manner when Cecilia stepped in front of me and said, 'Allow me.' She rapped her fist on the door and leaned right up close to the letterbox and in her booming voice called out something in Somali.

Aisha opened the door a minute later. Amazed, I glanced at Claire who simply shrugged. I realised that Aisha had let us in against her mum's wishes as they spent the next five minutes arguing in the hallway before Cecilia managed to get things under control. Aisha's facial features were strikingly flawless, although her cheeks looked hollow. In contrast with her mum, her English was near perfect.

I told her that I was worried about their frugal living conditions and the fact that they looked so malnourished.

'Mum doesn't like owning things you can't carry,' she said quickly, 'and we come from a nomadic family where the diet is simple. We live on pasta and vegetables. Italy used to be the colonial power in the south, so spaghetti is a national dish. Mum doesn't like other food. Don't worry about our diet; we're like a pair of fatties compared with other people from Somalia.'

Then Aisha asked me about ten times to promise that what she was about to tell us wouldn't leave the room.

'I'm sorry, I can't,' I kept saying. 'I have to take action if it involves a crime.'

'You have to tell us, my dear,' Cecilia said, 'so we can help. That's all we're going to do. Help.'

Aisha gave in. She had no choice.

Aisha's story wasn't about their escape from Somalia – far from it. It was an equally terrible danger that they faced here, where they'd fled to be safe.

'We used to be friends with other people from Somalia,' Aisha said. 'Life was going well. School was frightening at first but I got used to it. Mum had some Somali friends and during the school holidays we were invited to a dinner party at their flat. I knew their daughter from school. She was lovely, my best friend.

'When we arrived, we were told it was a special day; when my friend and I would become women. I did not understand.'

Aisha paused for a moment.

'But we soon did.'

Nadifa was sat next to her daughter on the sofa, rigid with tension. She was on high alert, in full protection mode.

'There was a Somali woman there who spoke no English,'

Aisha continued. 'She looked like she'd just got off the plane. I had no idea she was a "cutter" from Mogadishu.'

'A what?' I asked, alarmed at the term.

'Let her finish,' Claire said grimly, 'she'll explain soon enough.'

'They said I had to have it done. That if we didn't we would never get married. I started to panic. Get what done? My mum started to shout but they made her be quiet.

'My friend . . .' Aisha said, tears already streaming down her face.

'It's OK,' Cecilia said kindly, 'you can tell us, Aisha.'

Aisha nodded and took a deep, shaky breath through the tears. The next part of her story was delivered in a stream, to get it over with as fast as possible.

'There were a lot of people there. They grabbed her in the lounge; they pushed her to the floor. The strange woman lifted a big handbag full of metallic . . . things. It was heavy. She put it on the floor. They held my friend down and the woman took out a knife and began cutting – between her legs. My friend screamed and screamed, so hard. I was screaming too, my mum just grabbed me by the arm and we ran from the flat together, down the stairs, through the streets. I cried and cried. Mum said she would protect me, keep me safe from this evil woman. I wanted to know what had happened to my friend. I thought they were killing her.'

Aisha stopped. Nadifa had one arm round her shoulder while the other one held her left hand. Her knuckles were white with tension.

I felt light-headed, dizzy, as though the floor was about to give way below me. Although I'd seen and heard so many horror stories, I never grew used to them, never grew immune to the suffering of children.

So many crimes had been committed here I hardly knew where to start.

Aisha looked up; anger was on her face. 'They'd done it in the school holidays to give her time to recover, in case there were any problems. Mum doesn't want me to go back to school in case they come for me there. We were thinking of running away but where? We don't know the UK. We don't know where to go. My school is here and we just got this great home.'

She carried on: 'We can't trust anyone to help us. One man whom we thought was a friend said girls like us should get their *kintirs* [Somali for clitoris] cut off if they can't control themselves. That was when mum turned our home into a prison.'

The inhuman practice of female genital mutilation (FGM) is a lot more prevalent in the UK than most people realise. It involves removing part or all of the clitoris, the surrounding labia (the outer part of the vagina) and sometimes the sewing up of the vagina, leaving only a small opening for urine and menstrual blood. Cutting often results in life-threatening complications such as septicaemia, haemorrhaging or cysts. Sex is painful for the rest of the victim's life. FGM reduces the chances of becoming pregnant and those women who do are usually forced to opt for a caesarean section.[1]

Now I understood Nadifa's position. I'd feel exactly the same way. They had escaped war and famine in Somalia only to find they had to hide from the cutter in Hackney. She didn't want her kids put through that barbaric nightmare that prematurely ended childhood and blighted adulthood. Perhaps it had happened to Nadifa.

Although I'd heard of FGM, I'd never encountered any victim of it directly. It is carried out for a variety of cultural reasons, all of which are complete bullshit. Some people say the practice is to increase the sexual pleasure of the man. It is also done to demonstrate a wife's virginity on her wedding night; and because 'uncut' girls with the ability to enjoy lovemaking are considered more likely to be promiscuous, unhygienic, and prone to diseases such as AIDS.

Attempts are also made to justify it on religious grounds. Some hard-line Muslims insist that women must undergo genital cutting to remain faithful to the purest teachings of Islam but it's not even mentioned in the Koran, and only ambiguously in the Hadith (a collection of oral traditions about the life of the prophet Mohammed). To me it smacked of the usual reason for much of the abuse carried out against young women – it was about control.

It's still a taboo topic today; many people refuse to accept that it can be so prevalent in the UK. But it is. More than you can possibly imagine. By conservative estimates, 86,000 women and girls living in Britain have been forcibly mutilated.[2] That we know this at all is thanks to a study carried out by the Foundation for Women's Health, Research and Development (Forward) in 2002. They also found that more than 7,000 girls in the UK were at a high risk of genital mutilation.

Some families club together to fly professional 'cutters' from Africa to Britain. These women perform the crude operation for a fee, usually in someone's home, without anaesthetic and using dirty household instruments.

We needed to talk about this. Cecilia, Claire and I adjourned to the kitchen where Cecilia filled us in with some of the details. 'I know it sounds impossible,' she said, 'but some people argue that the freedom to carry out FGM is a fundamental principle of our multicultural society.'

'Screw that,' I said bitterly. 'Anyone who thinks so doesn't deserve to have a say in what happens in our society.'

'Well, I've been trying to bring it to the attention of people for a while now and several London councils declined to publish my research – for fear of offending.'

'Stuff whether the community's happy,' I said angrily, 'I'm only interested in the rights of the child.'

'Well, I suppose the Met has been upsetting communities for decades now,' Claire said, 'so there's nothing new there.'

'Very funny.' I grinned slightly. 'But you and I know there is only one rule in child protection: the child's well-being is paramount.'

We decided that the family was safe for now. I would start an investigation into the mutilation of Aisha's friend while Claire and Cecilia would work on getting safe local community support for Nadifa and Aisha.

That decided, we said our goodbyes. I thanked Aisha and Nadifa for their incredible bravery in telling us and apologised for scaring them on my earlier visit.

'It's OK,' Aisha said, 'I think you can help us now.'

As soon as I got back to the office I found Rob.

'What do you know about female circumcision?' I asked.

As usual, Rob got straight to the point. 'What you're referring to isn't circumcision, Harry. Boys who are circumcised go on to lead a long and healthy life of erotic pleasure. For girls, "female circumcision" is a violent amputation that removes the clitoris, the main, and for most women the most satisfying, physical source of pleasure. It is emphatically not circumcision, nor simply "genital mutilation". The physical, sensual and emotional scars that remain are profoundly distinct from those of male circumcision. We should name this horrific practice for what it is – clitoral amputation.'

Fair enough, I thought, I won't ever make that mistake again.

'FGM was outlawed way back in 1985,' Rob said. 'Here we are, nearly twenty years later and the problem is even worse. "Cutting" is even stronger here than in Somalia. Here, it seems, some people feel the need to keep their traditions going. The

2003 Female Genital Mutilation Act means that those involved can be jailed for fourteen years.

'Over many years our impotent hand-wringing has condemned countless girls to a lifetime of pain and infection and possible infertility. Would we tolerate it if white women were circumcised before their wedding night? How would the public feel if some monster was prowling the city, cutting girls' genitals? People don't seem to understand that this barbaric act is being carried out here in the UK, on our little girls.'

Rob told me about the French, who were way ahead of us. Back in 1999, an African woman was sent down for eight years for cutting forty-eight children. These days all French children of African background are checked by social workers and doctors during infancy. Any abnormal behaviour or prolonged absence from school is immediately investigated. The usual patient confidentiality rules go out the window if a doctor discovers a mutilated child.

Even today, in 2010, we've still got miles to go. The Met has a special task force to deal with FGM but they've yet to secure their first conviction. The Well Woman Clinic at St Thomas's Hospital in South London has performed a number of successful operations to reverse genital mutilation – sadly this is possible only in less severe cases. They try to help about 500 young women every year. Hopefully, a scheme is about to be launched in East London where teachers will be trained to detect victims of female circumcision, and to identify pupils at risk.

We tried to find Aisha's friend but – perhaps thanks to Nadifa's reaction – they realised that trouble could be ahead, and so her family had vanished without telling anyone where they were going. We were unable to trace them. The cutter was no doubt back in Africa. All we could do was stay vigilant and try to raise awareness. We'd taken too long getting to grips with this horrendous problem.

As Cecilia said: 'Female genital mutilation has nothing to do with tradition, religion or culture. It is the most cynical form of child abuse and a crime that has to be punished.'

This is all too common with so many types of child abuse we saw in Hackney, perhaps none more so than the very next case.

'Another one for you, Harry,' Rob said as he handed me the fax.

'What is it?'

'Endurance punishment.'

CHAPTER THIRTEEN

HEART OF DALSTON

'You've got half an hour before the strategy meeting,' Rob said. 'Good luck.'

I hadn't eaten all day, so I grabbed a coffee and some toast from the canteen, sat with my feet up on the desk and opened the file.

Ten-year-old Sefu, and his sister, twelve-year-old Tanesha, had both been born in the UK to parents who'd sought asylum from Sierra Leone. The family lived in one of Hackney's high-rises; like so many it had long been scheduled for demolition.

Their parents believed in 'endurance punishment', a practice completely alien to most people but something I'd seen used often in Hackney – the use of a stress position to punish a child. Whenever Sefu or Tanesha were naughty their father would not only make them stand in the corner, he'd force them to hold a hardback Bible straight above their heads or to hold their arms straight out in front of them.

Bearing in mind that it is lawful to hit a child in the pursuance of moderate protection, this in itself was not serious enough for us to get involved. However, the report said that social services were worried that something far worse was going on and wanted our help.

I checked my watch. Time to go. I drove down to Hackney
Social Services at Morning Lane, bluffed my way through the
security gate and squeezed into the tiny car park. I suppose those
that had acquired the building had been told that few social
workers would be able to afford the luxury of a car, let alone have
one provided for them.

It's such a shame the social services aren't set up properly for
an emergency response. Like us they should have duty cars and
job-mobile phones. I can only imagine it's because they're run by
councils who won't allow their budgets to stretch to buying cars.
I've lost count of the number of times I've waited for a social
worker to get a bus to a home visit. I soon learned that it was far
easier to just pick them up on my way to the job – the police taxi
service. This was of course useless when you were already in
someone's home, waiting for social services to arrive. As for job-
mobiles, most social workers simply use their personal mobiles
and foot the bill themselves.

Brenda was in reception, armed with a large bag of papers and
the family's file; although it was a lovely cool summer's evening
she was nevertheless swaddled in hat, scarf and giant coat. She
blamed her attire on a 'summer cold'.

'Sorry to drag you out on this one, Harry,' she snuffled, 'but
I'm the sort of person who trusts their gut and my gut says there's
something not right with this family.'

Lamps cast long shadows behind us as we stood at the bottom
of yet another one of Hackney's tower blocks, one of those crazy
utopian dreams that turned into a dystopian nightmare. It was
dark, and the windows of the tall building were dotted with
lights. The glares of many televisions flickered; the sounds of distant house music thumped from a high-up open window and
bounced around the estate as if telegraphing our arrival. As I
looked up I imagined there were enough dramas going on in
there to rival the complete works of Shakespeare.

Entering these tower blocks reminded me of visiting a prison. The walk through 'no-man's-land', the loud buzzers that released the fire doors, the uniform doorways that lined concrete corridors, the protective grilles that covered the entrances to each small flat, made up of an interconnected set of small cells.

The hallway and lifts stank of stale urine and bleach. Someone had tried to cover up a terrible human smell with an even worse artificial one, creating an eye-watering pong that burned the nostrils.

We stepped into the lift. 'This is ridiculous, it's even worse in here,' I said to Brenda with a cough. 'Let's take the stairs.'

'No bloody way. It's on the twelfth floor.' She punched the button and the doors ground together. 'Don't be such a baby. Just do what I do and hold your nose.'

I did my best to ignore the smell and tried to distract myself by taking in the words of wisdom scrawled, scratched and sprayed on the lift walls. Apparently, Baz was very free with his promises and mobile phone number while 'The Hackney Boyz Rooled [sic]' and were going to do something very unpleasant to the Tottenham Man Dem.

I leapt out of the lift as soon as the doors opened. It smelled better up here. A cold breeze rushed through the slits in the hall windows. Glancing out through them I could see the monoliths of the City, many of which were surrounded by cranes.

'Great view,' I said.

'Yeah,' Brenda replied. 'Shame about the neighbourhood though.'

The dad, who was called Matabe, opened the door straight away. He was a short man in his early thirties, fit-looking and friendly. His voice came out in a dry rasp, as if he had a permanent frog in his throat, and he spoke with a strong West African accent.

The house, which was simply and plainly furnished, had been

freshly cleaned in preparation for our visit. Portraits of religious
icons lined the hallway; a row of solemn-looking saints who'd
given their lives in the service of God. A large flat brass religious
cross was hung on the lounge wall above the 42-inch flat-screen
TV.

Brenda had already spoken to Matabe on the phone but I still
explained why I was there, that we were worried about his children and wanted to make sure everything was all right at home.

'I'm sorry for this, the inconvenience,' Matabe said, suddenly
looking and sounding like he was about to cry. 'They are good
children but my wife and I find them difficult to control. I did
not think my methods of discipline were wrong. They are in my
background.'

Crikey, this was a good sign. A babbling confession and I'd
barely said a word. He wanted to explain, to justify his actions
and so we let him, making sure I paid close attention, as I would
have to write it up in my report as soon as I was back in the
office. It would go in the family file and we would keep it for
seven years after the youngest child reached eighteen.

'Have you been to Africa, Detective?'

'I have.'

'Really? Where?'

'Ghana. Work took me there.'

'Ah, Ghana. OK. Well, the west coast of Africa, the part that
I'm from, is a beautiful part of the world but there is much trouble there. I was a soldier; I fought with the British against the
rebels, the Revolutionary United Front, you know? Before the
British came, I fought street by street with my unit in Freetown
when it was invaded by the rebels.'

Here we go, I thought. I'd heard so many sob stories, many of
which were obviously fake, vain attempts to win sympathy.
Freetown, which sits amid lush rice paddies and rolling green
hills, was established in 1787 as a home for freed slaves. The

British cut off the slaves' shackles on a block in front of a tree that's still standing today. But Sierra Leone is no paradise: the UN recently ranked it the least-developed nation on earth. The life expectancy of the average male is thirty-four.

Sierra Leone's descent into madness began on 25 May 1997, when a group of rebel soldiers led a *coup d'état*, replaced democratically elected President Ahmed Tejan Kabbah with Major Johnny Paul Koroma, and allied themselves with the RUF, the rebel movement that had fought a brutal civil war earlier in the 1990s.

'After two weeks of street-by-street fighting,' Matabe told us, 'there were so many burning buildings you could barely see the sky. The dead were everywhere, on the street, on the sandy beach and floating in the sea. The port and airport were smoking ruins as well. The rebels had swept in from the jungles to the east of the city. They dug up weapons that had been buried in churchyards. I had seen many bad things as a soldier. I had killed men. Shot them point-blank in battle, you know.'

Matabe paused for a moment. 'But until then I had never fought a child. Do you know that the city had been invaded by an army entirely made up of children?'

I had to admit that I didn't.

'Five thousand children,' Matabe held up an open palm to emphasise the number, 'most about fifteen to sixteen years old. They carried AK-47s and ambushed us by running out from alleyways, shooting from the hip, screaming as they did, spraying bullets everywhere, forcing us to dive for cover. It seemed as though it was like a game to them. Some would laugh. We also carried AK-47s so you can imagine the amount of bullets flying through the air. Every now and again a child would find itself out of the game, permanently.

He went on: 'At night the children would set buildings on fire to light the city, so that they wouldn't have to sit in the dark.

They drank, took herbs that made them see things, that turned them crazy, that ate their fear so they could attack us. They were bad kids. They did terrible things to our people. We heard nightmare stories about babies being cut from the womb of pregnant mothers, about limbs being cut off, really terrible stuff, you know?

'Well, our rations soon ran out and we were living off pig feed, so one day I was sent with my unit to see what we could find to eat in the city. We found some rice in one house and as we were leaving a rebel soldier, a teenage boy, appeared in the doorway, blocking our exit. I had my gun ready, I could have fired. But he was so young. He was a child. I could not fire. I could not do it. It was impossible.'

Matabe paused and looked up at the cross on the wall: 'Yes, there are too many bad things happening.'

'What happened?' I asked, now keen to hear the rest of Matabe's story.

Matabe looked surprised. 'He shot me of course!' He lifted his shirt. 'I don't know how I survived.'

I saw a set of three jagged pink and white semicircular scars in the shape of cutlasses across his stomach. Each one was at least six inches long. These scars, combined with the marks left by brutal, deep and impossibly thick-looking stitches, looked like barbed wire.

'Someone else in my unit shot the boy. Killed him. "Why didn't you shoot?" they asked me after. I told them it was because he was a child. They said I was stupid. They had no problem killing anyone who was trying to kill them, even if that person was a child.

'When I got better, many months later I rejoined my unit to find the British had come to help us. Just the knowledge that they were in Freetown was enough to stop the rebels from trying to launch another assault. The presence of your disciplined forces changed everything straight away. That's where I learned about discipline. From you, from the British.

'In battle, we used to find a sheltered spot and just fire our machine guns from there. We'd be pinned down for hours. Nobody even thought of trying to change position under covering fire. Nobody wanted to "stick their neck out", as you say. The British soldiers showed us how it was done and how to actually push forward and drive the enemy back. They taught us to fire rifles accurately rather than spray everything with machine guns. They taught us that the soldier's greatest weapon is to be patient, remain calm while under fire, no matter how many mortars were exploding around you, and carry out your orders. One carefully fired bullet could change a battle, they told us.

'They made us strong, we ate more, we exercised more and when we did something wrong we had to exercise again, to run, to do press-ups or dig a hole. That's how I learned to follow orders. Before the British came we would get away with ignoring dangerous orders, especially if we were in the bush, but with the British I would have to think twice otherwise I'd be digging a ditch for a week.

'Getting drunk on palm liquor used to be encouraged by our officers but the British punished us for it. More ditch-digging and I stopped drinking. I was a better, stronger soldier. I wanted to defend my country and my friends. I shot teenagers after that. I saved the lives of my friends by doing so. It was thanks to discipline. With the right kind of discipline you can achieve anything.'

'But this isn't the right kind,' I said, referring to his children. 'Your children were upset enough by it to tell their teacher.'

'I am sorry for that,' Matabe said. 'Kids who were not disciplined in Sierra Leone disobeyed their parents and went out into the streets where they ended up dead, chopped, or were kidnapped by the rebels and turned into soldiers. I can still see the six-year-old daughter of a friend who had her arm hacked off at the elbow. That is what the rebels called a "short sleeve amputation", you know? She showed her arm to me and asked: "When will my fingers grow back?"'

'That's not going to happen here,' Brenda said.

'Have you seen this neighbourhood at night?' Matabe asked.

I had to admit he had a point. Although it wasn't exactly Sierra Leone, there were plenty of blades that flashed through the air on most nights somewhere in Hackney.

'Tanesha is a wilful girl,' Matabe said. 'She refuses to come home at the times I tell her to. I have to show her discipline. You have to be certain they will obey otherwise they will die on the streets. It is the same here. But yes, I am sorry. I did not want to hurt or frighten my children.'

Brenda said that we needed to speak to Tanesha and Sefu.

'That is no problem at all,' Matabe said. 'They are good children. They will answer your questions honestly and clearly, I can assure you.'

We spoke to Tanesha next. She was short for her age and really nervous. The first thing she asked us was: 'What's going to happen to my dad?'

This set off a small alarm bell. We were here to talk about holding Bibles, weren't we? Why did she think we were going to send her dad to prison? She could have just been scared by our presence perhaps but I wasn't sure.

Still, her concern for her father was really touching. I wanted to tell her that nothing would happen to him, as I was reasonably certain this would be the outcome, but it also depended on whether she revealed anything new to us now.

'We need you to tell us everything,' I said quietly, 'and then we will talk to your dad, but try not to worry, what you think should happen is really important to us. Our job is to fix families, not ruin them.'

After easing Tanesha into the chat, we spoke about what happened when her father punished her. She told us about holding the Bible, about standing with her arms outstretched, but like Brenda I got the feeling that there was something she wasn't telling us about.

'You've been great, Tanesha,' Brenda said, 'you've been really honest and open with us and we're very grateful for that. But is there anything else you want to tell us?'

Tanesha looked down and studied her shoes for a moment.

'He does do something else sometimes. Only if we've been really, *really* bad though.'

I looked up. 'What is it, Tanesha?'

'It's a bit embarrassing.'

'It's OK, you can tell us.'

'The first time he made me take off my skirt and my underwear.'

Oh no, here we go, I thought. When a child starts to tell you this type of thing draw in a deep breath and mentally prepare yourself for something nasty. It's like waiting at the top of a rollercoaster, preparing yourself for the inevitable drop.

Tanesha shifted uncomfortably and looked at the floor as she continued. She was back there now, reliving this traumatic experience. My heart went out to her but I kept my mouth shut, letting her explain at her own pace and in her own way. In my mind I was urging her, 'Come on, come on, spill the beans, just do it, just come out with it.'

'He went to the kitchen. When he came back he had some green chillies. He rubbed them in me.'

'Where did he rub them?' Brenda asked.

'Between my legs. Inside.'

She looked up blinking, tears rimming her eyelids. 'It hurt but we'd been bad. Don't do anything to my dad, will you?'

'What did he do to Sefu?'

'He rubbed them in his eyes.'

This was torture, not the short sharp pain of a smack but a long-lasting and agonising burn – they must have felt like they were on fire. I'd suffered the effects of CS gas, which felt like someone had pounded both of my eyes with their fists and thrown acid in my face.

That was bad enough, but I couldn't begin to imagine the agonies that Tanesha must have gone through; first the humiliation of her father rubbing the chillies then the searing, burning pain that must have lasted for some hours. Children are amazingly brave and unselfish creatures. Even after telling us about this appalling crime, Tanesha was more concerned about her father than anything else. Both Brenda and I were deeply touched and we felt her worry strongly.

We always try to keep what the child wants at the top of our list of things to achieve but Tanesha had to trust us to make the right decisions that would help her life, not destroy it. She wanted to be at home with her family and be happy. Of course, so did we, but this would depend on her father.

We spoke to little Sefu as well. It was very hard for him, but at least he didn't seem to feel any humiliation when he told us about the chillies and it was a much easier conversation as the chillies were only rubbed in his eyes. He was nervous about 'telling on his dad', but bravely got through it. I felt for him so much; he must have rubbed his eyes to try and stop the pain, but this would have just made it worse. They would have been red and raw, running with tears and stinging like hell.

This was clearly a job for the police; the question was whether we prosecuted or 're-educated'. This type of endurance punishment was both physical assault and emotional abuse but usually the best result for children is not to split the family – it's a last resort. Entering the world of state-sponsored care is fraught with risks for children and can often be the start of a downward spiral.

Although I bought the father's story and I understood the stresses of living in H-Block Hackney, there were no excuses for rubbing his daughter's vagina with chilli peppers.

Sorry, old boy, you're damn well getting nicked, I thought.

I hoped that by arresting him we'd be able to re-educate him, provide a good strong warning that we not only took this sort of thing very seriously but that he would end up going to jail if he did it again.

'I'm not sure we need to take the kids into care,' I said to Brenda, 'but I do want to arrest the father.'

'Hang on, Harry. This isn't a case of a quick arrest, lecture, walk away and tick the box marked "job done". Sefu and Tanesha need to go on the child protection register. I'm going to have to monitor them and that means I'll need to build a relationship with the family. It's a process of education and protection. If you go in and slap the cuffs on Dad, then our relationship is off to a rocky start.'

I wasn't so sure; the dad needed a strong wake-up call.

In the end we reached a compromise. The children would get a full medical, memorandum interview and then I'd arrest Dad. If at any point he didn't 'play the game', then I'd charge him. That would mean splitting the family; victim and suspect can't live in the same house. This was the last resort. Everything hung on whether Dad said the right thing, that he realised what he'd done was wrong, that he now wanted to change and cooperated with us fully.

All being well, I would arrest and caution the father, the family would stay on the register, give us no more cause for concern and then they would gradually be set free as new and urgent cases steadily squeezed them out of the system. It was crucial that we got this right; we were counting on being able to trust the family that there weren't any more dark secrets. As long as we felt the family was being straight with us then a framework would be in place to protect Sefu and Tanesha.

Matabe accepted his arrest without question and expressed his willingness to deal with us, a really good sign. It seemed clear to me that he was prepared to be a part of the process that would see his family stay together.

In his interview the following day, Matabe told us what we already knew. He accepted he was wrong and cried when we put to him the humiliation element of what he had done. These could have been crocodile tears but I felt as though they were born of genuine emotion, especially when he faced the fact that he had humiliated his daughter in a truly appalling way. This was the beginning of what we hoped would be that rare thing: a straightforward success story. Our intervention had worked and we'd created a foundation to build upon. Of course careful monitoring would follow and in the end only time would tell.

Matabe had told us that he wanted Tanesha to obey him because he was afraid of what would happen to her, that something like what he had seen happen to the children of Sierra Leone would happen to her here, in London. Although I was appalled by Matabe's behaviour and I wanted him to be punished for what he'd done to his son and daughter, I could understand where his warped idea of 'discipline' had come from – thanks perhaps to the glimpses I've been given into inner London society of the last twenty years or so.

I believe that all kids start out wonderful but there are many evil things in our inner cities that turn them into monsters: a sense of hopelessness reinforced by the poverty trap and a weak support system for the poorest and most vulnerable members of society, which made drugs, crack houses, gangs and violence appealing options. It's those poorly supervised kids who end up hanging out on the estate after dark and being absorbed into gangs, where all too often honour and respect, those two most precious commodities for those who have nothing else, are decided by the spilling of blood.

Crack cocaine is like a recruiter for the local militia, new addicts join an army that forces them to do unspeakable horrors, to give their bodies away to strangers or to rob and kill for money. There is plenty out there for parents to worry about and there is plenty we still have to do as a nation, to repair our damaged societies to protect our children. All Matabe had done was to try (albeit very badly indeed) to protect his kids.

CHAPTER FOURTEEN

IT'S A LONG WAY

The door flew open. The smile fell from the young woman's pretty face.

'Sally Wilson?'

'Yes.'

Lucy and I showed our warrant cards. 'May we come in?'

'Oh, sorry,' she said, 'you're a bit early, I was expecting someone else.'

Sally, who was twenty-four and a public-relations officer for a large company based in Birmingham, ushered us to the sofa in the lounge and went to put the kettle on.

'Nice place,' Lucy said, 'I think I chose the wrong career.'

It was indeed a beautiful apartment. Framed photographs from several expensive-looking skiing holidays sat on bookshelves and on the large Moroccan-style coffee table.

'Our wedding photos have just been delivered,' Sally said, coming back into the room with a pair of steaming mugs. She pointed at a large book with a cream cover. 'And I thought you were my husband. I can't wait for him to see them.'

Even after all she'd been through this beautiful young woman had found the perfect life far from London and its dark memories.

Sally set the mugs on the table in front of us. 'Now what's so important that it can't be discussed on the phone?'

I could have just come out with it but as Rob told me, it's usually best to start at the beginning. Be clear, be brief and get to the point quickly.

'Thanks for seeing us today, Sally, we very much wanted to talk to you in person.'

Sally nodded. Her expression had changed; she was now clearly braced for something; she suspected.

'We want to talk to you about something that happened in your past.'

I paused. I'd confirmed her fear.

'Are you OK for me to continue?'

She sat, leaning forward slightly, with her elbows on her knees and her hands clasped.

'It's fine,' she said, almost professionally.

'Do you remember when you were nine, something serious happened to you?'

Sally drew in a deep breath, closing her eyes as she did so. So he was back in her life. Vivid, horrific images that had been pushed to the back of her mind raced forward. She caught her breath in the rush of emotion.

'Yes,' she said, the last of her happy confidence evaporating.

'I think I should tell you what I know to avoid any confusion,' I said.

Sally nodded shakily. 'OK.'

'We investigated an allegation that your parents' lodger, Andrew McIntosh, raped you on at least three occasions fifteen years ago.'

She sat back, practically reeling. Tears welled as the painful memories of long-repressed sights, smells, sounds piled in hard and fast. Sally trembled slightly and I sensed her heart racing, the nausea and trauma at disturbed feelings of betrayal and powerlessness. When she finally spoke, the words came in a whisper.

'Go on.'

'We interviewed you in 1990, but McIntosh got wind of the investigation, changed his name and fled. He's never been seen since. Are you aware of this?'

Sally nodded.

'Sally,' I said, making sure I had eye contact. 'We got him last night. He's in custody.'

She burst into tears. After a few moments, she managed to speak again.

'They never forgave themselves, my parents, I mean. They're both dead now; both were heavy smokers but I always felt as if – "he" were somehow to blame.'

Neither of her parents had any clue about their lodger's paedophilia but the guilt at their failure to protect their daughter, the fact that the man responsible had escaped and was living a life of freedom, possibly preying on others, had weighed heavily on them.

'Oh God, I feel so alone,' she sobbed.

'What about your husband?' Lucy asked.

'He doesn't know,' Sally said. 'I want to tell him but I find it so difficult, like something's holding me back. It's not been easy. I can hardly bring myself to talk to my father-in-law because he reminds me of the man who attacked me. Even now the smell of alcohol and cigarette smoke on someone's breath makes me sick; I have a fear of entering bedrooms that remind me of the one I was attacked in. I go out of my way to avoid kissing older men in greeting; it was almost all I could think about on my wedding day, all those elderly male relatives.'

She paused. 'I can't believe that my parents are dead and that bastard's still alive.'

*

Andrew McIntosh's undoing was his credit card. He was one of many thousands who paid for their perversions online. His details were eventually picked up by Operation Inkerman, the team of officers tracking paedophiles through their online purchases, and we had an address soon after.

The 7 a.m. boot-the-door-in raid revealed a dark, dank and mouldy bedsit, hairy food in the yellowing fridge, unwashed and heavily stained grey sheets, grimy windows, one shiny new laptop and a very frightened-looking little old man sitting bolt upright in bed.

The cops in ballistic vests stared at him with barely concealed hatred.

'Mark Jones, also known as Andrew McIntosh, we have a warrant to search this premises for indecent images of children and you are under arrest for a serious sexual assault.'

His laptop was password-protected but we had a specialist department to deal with that.

'I thought you'd come for the bloke up the hall,' he said as I sat before him in the interview room. 'He was dealing drugs, you know.'

McIntosh was in his sixties and looked every inch the paedophile; a tight, pinched mouth, rodent-like teeth and tiny, almost entirely black eyes. His thinning hair was stained with nicotine, as were the ends of his dry, cracked fingers. He did his best to look innocent, but his faltering denials to the arresting officers had already helped convince me that we had our man.

Although we had him bang to rights for the online pornography, as far as Sally's case was concerned, as the rapes had been reported after her wounds had healed, it was the victim's word against his. There was no DNA. I didn't rate our chances that highly.

Rob, however, was more optimistic. 'Don't ever forget, Harry,' he said, pushing his glasses back on his head as he spoke, 'the way you interview a suspect like this can make all the difference.'

He was right, of course, but this skill isn't easily learned.

Studies have shown us that most paedophiles have a distinctive ability to rationalise their perversion. This is often described as 'distorted cognitive reasoning'. In interviews, some paedophiles paint a picture of the world where children share similar sexual desires to themselves; that they want to have sex as much as the paedophile does. This way, they're minimising the seriousness of the abuse to themselves.

For example, in one study, researchers interviewed ninety-four convicted paedophiles, asking them to explain why they were in prison. Eleven per cent of the sample denied the allegations, 12 per cent admitted the reasons why, while the remaining 77 per cent admitted but attempted to minimise the extent of their offending, often piling blame on the victim for 'leading them on'.[1] The 77 per cent spoke about adult sexual behaviour with children in positive terms. By describing children as willing partners and emphasising the sexual rights of children, they were trying to deny responsibility and make their actions seem more palatable or even acceptable.

Some attempted to mitigate their actions by claiming they were under financial stress, or were drunk, depressed or, more commonly, had themselves been abused when they were young. If that was true, then why the hell would you inflict it on someone else? People sexually abuse children because they're paedophiles, not because they're victims. The 'cycle of violence' theory – that abuse leads to abuse by the abused – has a lot to answer for. In fact, people who are sexually abused as children are no more likely to become child abusers in the future than the next person.

People stuck to the 'cycle of violence' theory for so long because abusers who were caught used it as an excuse: 'Show

mercy, I was a victim too', and people fell for it. The vast majority of convicted adult sex offenders have told researchers that
they were not sexually abused as children. More recent longitu-
dinal research – studying children who have suffered sexual
abuse over time to determine what percentage become adult
offenders – has also gone a long way to disproving the 'cycle of
violence' theory.[2]

It's possible to use paedophiles' warped beliefs against them in
the interview room but it really isn't easy. As a policeman, you're
used to doing interviews in a certain way. There's a need to obtain
explicit, institutionally preferred, precisely worded accounts.
For example, an officer will write up his notes like this (I'm exaggerating slightly to make the point):

'I was proceeding down the highway in a south-westerly direction.'

As opposed to:

'I was walking down the road.'

This formal, over-elaborate vocabulary is used to try to avoid
misinterpretation by the criminal justice system. The traditional
interview method relies on the victim's witness statement, where
the police officer uses it as a basis to describe the offence. It's
adapted into institutionally preferred legal terms and sexually
explicit vocabulary. This approach doesn't go down well with
paedophiles, however, who tend to clam up when confronted
with formal descriptions of their crimes.

Talk about their hideous acts in more emotional terms then
sometimes, just sometimes, they can't help themselves and let
slip little details, and admit things without realising, helping us
to send them away for a very long time.

Words like 'love', 'friendship' and 'affection' are more likely to
get them talking than graphic physical references to sexual activity and bodily contact, such as 'vagina', 'penetration' and
'intercourse', which is more likely to make them clam up.

It's difficult when you've spent most of your career trying not to use emotional language in the interview room, making sure there's no room for misinterpretation, but if you get the questions right, it's amazing how quickly some paedophiles open up. Often, they can't help themselves, they want to share; they want to show off; to relive the memory of their triumphant conquest with someone else. They genuinely think they've done nothing wrong, that the children wanted them, that they were brave enough to achieve what other men can only dream of.

Another important aspect is to try to let the suspect hold the floor as much as possible, giving them the chance to slip up, to make mistakes that can be seized upon, or to use strangely worded phrases or expressions which we can in turn use to build the interview on. Again, this is easier said than done when you're in the middle of an extremely stressful interview that will very likely determine the future of all concerned.

On top of this, to interview a paedophile successfully, you have to think like them, to get them to like you; worst of all, it helps if you can turn them on. As I said, it's not easy and it's not for every police officer.

As far as our records told us, apart from the online pornography, McIntosh had behaved himself since Sally, but there was always the chance he had committed other as yet undiscovered sexual crimes between then and now.

'He may even think we've pulled him in for something else, a more recent assault,' Lucy suggested.

I started by talking about his online use, which he admitted to straight away.

'Did seeing the images online make you want to see if you could be with a child?'

'For real?'

'Yes.'

'I drove around a bit, but didn't do anything.'

Christ, this man was a walking timebomb. The temptations of seeing images of children on top of the abuse he had enjoyed with Sally were impossible to ignore. He'd never taken a child because he'd never stumbled on that million to one chance. That's what it would have taken – an opportunity on a plate.

The fear parents have of their children being abducted is not matched by the reality. Child kidnapping is extremely rare. But of course this is no consolation to the parents of Sarah Payne or Madeleine McCann.

I was certain there must have been other children in the fifteen years since Sally. The many thousands of files on his laptop dated back to 1999. What about the four years before he discovered the Internet?

We danced around this topic for some time but McIntosh revealed nothing, so I brought up the fact that he'd been a lodger with Sally's parents.

I saw a brief twinge of pleasure in his face at the memory; such was the depth of his perversion. He quickly overcame this micro expression, however, and adopted an innocent look but admitted that he'd been on good terms with Sally and they'd spent time alone together.

'What sort of situation would allow you to be with Sally?'

'Just whether she wanted to come out for a walk with me.'

'Once this had started, when you first started talking to her and you got to know the family, what were your feelings towards Sally?'

'She was a charming little girl. She was interested in music and nature and I started showing her around the woods nearby.'

'How did your relationship develop to the point where it brings us to where we are today?'

'Uhm. Well, it was a long time ago you understand. Er ... There was one time when I opened my drawer while she was in my room and she saw some er ... magazines in there. She was inquisitive, like all little girls.'

'Mmmm.'

I wasn't about to agree but at the same time I had to be non-committal. We were already on our way. Although the interview seemed like harmless, ambiguous chat, the way McIntosh talked about Sally, it was as if they'd had an adult relationship.

He'd created an image of an intelligent child, giving her maturity and curiosity, something he encouraged. The child's supposed interest is a common justification by paedophiles for sexual acts with children, hence the story of the 'magazines' (obviously pornographic); the accidental discovery is designed to make the beginning of their intimate 'relationship' look as innocent as possible, with Sally's natural 'inquisitiveness' about the magazines leading them on to the next stage.

He'd already mentioned his 'feelings', which could be perceived as either innocent or sexual, yet the question I'd asked allowed what seemed to him to be an innocent response. He'd also failed to react in the obvious manner to 'the point where it brings us to where we are today.' This in itself was highly significant. The use of ambiguous language allowed McIntosh to tell his story whilst avoiding any explicit reference to sexual and criminal behaviour. In his mind he thought he was safe but the reality was far different.

McIntosh echoed my 'Mmmm' and then added: 'Yes, well, that's when our relationship began to develop.'

I chose my words carefully. The trick is not to ask: 'Was Sally attracted to you?' This is a closed question, just asking for a straightforward denial. I needed something more open; another step forward on his path to prison.

'Were you flattered by how this much younger person responded to you in the way you described?'

This question is potentially incriminating; I'd used the term 'much younger' as opposed to younger.

'Absolutely.'

Admitting flattery is also incriminating. A fifty-something male would normally react with concern to a nine-year-old who was showing romantic or sexual interest. The jury would not like that.

'How did you view your relationship with Sally as it developed?'

'Well, we might not *do* anything. But Sally quite enjoyed uh, erm, it when we did things together.'

Saying 'we might not do anything' in an attempt to downplay their relationship implies that he sometimes could 'do' something. I took it up a notch.

'Right, you mean these sexual sessions.'

'You must understand. She wanted me; *she* tried to seduce *me*. She was always teasing me. She was always walking into my room unannounced, hoping . . .'

Got him. Even better than I hoped. I'd used the word sexual and McIntosh hadn't blinked. Worry now started to crease his face.

'But even that's no excuse,' he continued.

I kept quiet. He was only making it worse, and I hoped he would end up digging a deeper hole for himself. McIntosh was trying to portray Sally as if she were actively seeking a sexual encounter. Whatever he thought in his twisted little mind, as far as I was concerned he'd admitted his guilt.

His solicitor, who was still staring straight ahead, stayed silent. Good man. Like many where child abuse was concerned, he'd given me a free hand to question his client without interruption.

'I know,' McIntosh said, looking down at his hands, 'it shouldn't have happened.'

This was typical paedophile language, treating children like adults, and as if they had consented, while seemingly unaware of their own twisted psychology.

'She said it was the other way round,' I said quietly. 'That you wanted her.'

'That's rubbish!'

Too late, McIntosh.

'OK then. What was it like, living in the house with, as you say, Sally trying to seduce you?'

'It was difficult. I'm a man. I er . . . I mean I was embarrassed.'

Damn, not quite the answer I needed.

I eased off, steering him back inside the house. I wanted him to get to the incident that Sally had told us about all those years ago. If he could corroborate anything Sally had told us, then we were really on our way.

'What was it like when you were both in the house alone together?'

'She would just walk into my room without knocking and we'd start talking.'

'What would you talk about?'

'Everything under the sun. She was a very curious girl.'

Aha. We were back on track again.

'Can you remember any of the subjects?'

'No, not offhand. It was a long time ago.'

I risked a leading question. 'Did she ever come into the bathroom unannounced while you were in there?'

'Yes! Yes, she did, you're right, that's exactly the sort of thing she'd do.'

This was where the rape had happened. I could see in his mind he was back there now, reliving the 'pleasure'. His eager expression told me he wanted to talk about it but in his own twisted way. Fine by me.

'What happened in the bathroom?'

'I was in the shower and she came in. She said she wanted a bath so I finished and ran one for her.'

'And then?'

'She got in the bath.'

'And then?'

'I helped wash her. It was nothing, entirely innocent.'

Got you again. I had him now. How far could I push him?

'And then?'

A long pause.

'You remember, don't you, Andrew? You were in the bathroom, helping Sally wash.'

'She wanted me to.'

'To ...?'

Silence.

'Sally said you held her wrists together ...'

McIntosh's eyes widened. He seemed genuinely shocked. 'Liar! She's lying!'

'And that you washed her in the bath afterwards, telling her it was your secret; that Sally's parents wouldn't understand.'

'Who does? Who does understand?'

Now it was time to put Sarah's description of what he'd done to her. His stress levels soon hit the roof as he pathetically tried to deny rape. Finally, his solicitor looked me in the eye and coughed.

OK, I had enough. Time to terminate the interview and get the wheels of justice in motion.

A common assertion in police interviewing research is that officers are typically unable to persuade criminals to admit guilt. But as Rob was always keen to point out, the use of this open interviewing style can sometimes work wonders. If we can interrogate suspects effectively then we can make a difference in the interview room. I could never know of course, but a more formalised interview of McIntosh may have led to a straightforward non-com, instead of a gradual growing leak of information and corroboration.

We bailed him out and the CPS authorised the charge of child rape. Sally's testimony back in 1990 had been strong, now she would have her day in court. But, thankfully, she was spared as McIntosh pleaded guilty. He was locked up for a long time; so long that he'll be lucky to get out alive. That's the beauty of some child protection investigations. If you 'win' the sentence is often excellent, you feel as though children are protected and the criminal has received the strongest punishment possible under our justice system.

I was delighted. We'd worked long and hard to get to this stage; I'd failed in many other interviews to crack the paedophile's shell but in this one I'd managed to split him wide open.

Sally was also pleased. Everyone has the right to tell the truth about his or her life. The problem is that most survivors have been taught to keep their abuse a secret by their torturer, but of course continuing this silence is only in the interest of the abuser.

Sally had done the right thing and had spoken out at the time, telling her parents, and they had called the police. Warning us that there are children still at risk is difficult but also an incredibly brave step. Some devious perverts are one-man crime waves (one study concluded that a paedophile can have as many as 200 attempted, aborted and actual victims).[3] I have heard countless times from survivors who didn't think that their abuser would hurt anyone else but had then found that not only had he abused other children but also their own young relatives.

If we had never known about McIntosh then he could still be out there, unable to control his twisted urges, waiting until one day he found a little victim alone on a quiet pathway.

*

Although Sally had told her parents and the police, she felt as though she could never tell her husband. Us finding McIntosh had brought this unwelcome issue crashing back into her life.

'It was awful,' Sally said when we met after McIntosh had been jailed. 'I'd wanted to tell Steve for years but something was always holding me back; I felt afraid, confused, I wasn't sure how he would react and I didn't want to burden him. What helped was that the police believed me. They had done everything they could to establish the facts and to preserve for me an accurate memory of what had happened.'

Of course, there is no right or wrong way to tell others what has happened to you but it is important to be clear that whatever you do, you are doing it for yourself.

'It felt as though by telling Steve that I was fulfilling my marital commitment and now, in return, Steve provided me with all the love, understanding and support that he was able to. It was wonderful. Up until then, I had this feeling that anything I said or did could blow our perfect world apart. But of course, talking about it wasn't going to break the bonds I had with my husband.

'When I sat him down and said I had something to tell him, I thought he was going to faint, he went so white. He was terrified that I was dying of some terrible disease or that I was somehow in very deep trouble. All he said when I told him was: "I'm so sorry." He just held me. His desire to protect was purely instinctive. All I could think was: "Why didn't I tell him sooner?"

'Steve wanted to destroy McIntosh, tear him limb from limb. I know I shouldn't say this to a police officer but it was great, I loved it. Lucky for McIntosh, he's already in prison, hopefully for the rest of his life.'

Sally smiled. Finding and eventually convicting McIntosh

had closed an old, dark chapter in her life and had opened a new bright one that looked forward to the future with great optimism and strength.

Don't give up. Once you've told us your story we never will.

CHAPTER FIFTEEN

INNOCENCE TWICE LOST

Craig tapped me on the shoulder. 'You're going to want to see this one,' he said. 'Dev's waiting for you in the interview suite.'

I stopped what I was doing, headed down to the suite. Dev was on the sofa.

'Hello, Harry,' he said. 'I believe you and Anna have already met, have you not?'

A teenage girl and her thirty-something mother, Karen, were sat next to him. The girl smiled shyly.

'Anna?' I said.

She nodded.

'What happened?'

Karen scowled at me as she answered for Anna in her strong cockney accent. 'I walked in on them doing it, didn't I?'

Anna looked at me and shrugged, a gesture of helplessness.

To make things worse, Karen had confided in the wrong people and now the community was up in arms and out for our suspect's blood, never a good thing. To save his skin, David, Karen's boyfriend, had gone on the run.

All I could do was hope we found him before he struck again.

'I'm ready to talk now,' Anna said quietly.

I was certain that inside Anna had wanted to tell someone about this for a long time but knew that her mum and older sister, Sue, loved David and would just say she was jealous, that she was making up the incident to make it seem as though David was just as interested in her.

'A week after you interviewed me, I was home with David. He was babysitting me while Mum and Sue went to a party together. It was a nice evening and I was relaxed as I got ready for bed.

'He came for me later that night.'

Her eyes shone with fear as she relived that night for us step by step. At first, when Anna awoke and saw David's silhouette at the door, she thought she was having a nightmare.

He was watching her, standing perfectly still. It was as if he were just watching her sleep as many fathers do, myself included, especially when the working days are long and precious child time is short. But this was anything but the case here. Anna began to shake with terror as David began to creep across the room, like some nightmarish monster.

'I hoped I would wake up, that this was some bad dream. But it wasn't.'

Anna froze and shut her eyes, pretending not to have seen him. Perhaps if she stayed still for long enough he would go away. When she opened them again David was in the dark room and the door had fallen closed behind him.

He moved nearer the bed, a terrifying sight beyond any young girl's imagining. Past the poster of Five, past the wobbly dresser covered in make-up and mirrors, past the pile of clothes and cuddly toys. Anna had nowhere to run and lay silently, shaking as he leaned over the bed and through beer breath he whispered something, something Anna refused to hear. Then he leaned his head closer and closer until, finally, his lips touched her neck and he climbed into her bed.

What could she do? Mum and Sue were out. Mum loved

David. Sue loved David too. She didn't want to be the one responsible – as she saw it – for tearing her family apart, for making enemies of the ones she loved by destroying the only good thing that had happened to them in years. Sue was always going on about how David was 'not like other men'.

'She didn't know how right she was,' Anna told me.

From that day on, there was no one to rescue Anna. If she complained David turned nasty. He was too strong, too clever. If Anna did nothing then at least it was over quickly. She would try to pretend it wasn't happening; she squeezed her eyes shut, tensed her body and tried to pretend she was somewhere else.

'After we came here, David was extra nice to me. He read the same magazines as me and started talking about love and doing romantic stuff. He told me I was beautiful. He even talked about white weddings. I let him decide everything about my life; he bought my clothes, even bras and make-up, and gave me a lot of pocket money. He decided when I was allowed out; he didn't like me hanging out with friends after school and kept taking me on special trips, like the cinema and stuff, in the evening, 'like father and daughter' he said. But then he kept touching me, more and more until, well, until this happened. I felt so alone, so confused. There was no way I could tell Mum, no way.'

David had had it all. He had successfully placed himself deep within a family and created a complex set of control mechanisms so that he had strong support from the victim and her family – all so that he could sexually abuse one young girl. For me, he was the definition of evil; he had spun a web in which Anna was trapped and had exploited her delicate teenage emotional balance to confuse, frighten and oppress her. Getting over this ordeal would not just be a recovery from the sexual abuse, but also from the virtual indoctrination he had put her through.

David had hoped to rely on Sue; that the bond he had created with her would be enough to split the two sisters apart, should Anna suddenly let fly with an accusation. While he had been grooming Anna, he had been exploiting every opportunity with Sue to attack Anna's character, painting her as a needy, inarticulate girl whose imagination sometimes ran away with her. Sue had been taken in – as had Karen. David was handsome, charming and had brightened up her otherwise dull life with love, sex and attention. Through it all, his only motivation had been to get Anna into bed.

It's impossible to imagine the strength of the perverted force that drove David. His twisted desire dominated his every waking moment. And he was not that uncommon. Every now and again Rob would order us out to warn vulnerable mothers on Hackney estates about sexual predators who would choose carefully, picking on single mums with lots of children by different dads, especially where there was already a history of abuse. There were quite a few families like this in Hackney. These lowlifes usually stay rent free, contributing nothing, except lies to the mother and, amid all the chaos, abuse.

'There's one more thing you need to know,' Anna said. She paused for a moment. 'I'm pregnant.'

Damn. Although the cop in me knew that this was great evidence.

'I haven't told Mum yet.'

'We can do that together if you like.'

'Yes please. She's going to freak out.'

I could well imagine.

I can only speculate but I suspect that the realisation of his desire had run away with David and he had lost control. His plan, I suspected, might have been to get Anna pregnant once she turned sixteen, trapping her for life. He'd place the blame at the feet of an anonymous local boy and he would win further praise for trying to track this fictional character down.

I could have cried. We're supposed to be protecting children but sometimes all we can do is pick up the pieces.

At that moment, I was due to crack another hopeless case, so as Craig launched the hunt for our predator and Anna's family began to agonise over what to do about her pregnancy, I headed for Paddington. I had a train to catch.

A few hours later, I was sat in front of a paedophile in his lounge, my eyes locked on his. I'd put the allegation to him as clearly and as simply as possible and the silence was working, gnawing away at him.

We were on the Welsh coast, near Cardiff, and I could hear waves crashing on the stony shore, only fifty metres or so from his front door.

Please, please, please don't let the phone or doorbell go, I thought.

I didn't have a clue whether he was about to deny or confess.

I saw the beads of sweat on his brow multiply. His eyes were wide; he started to wring his hands.

Another wave rolled in. Still silence.

Christ, this is killing me, I thought.

I maintained eye contact, pressure, pressure, pressure.

When I'd set off for Wales that morning, I'd left London thinking that this job was a waste of time; that we just had to go through the motions.

Thirteen-year-old Ellen had already led a life full of trouble; she'd been in and out of care and her mother, who seemed to show little interest in her daughter, had a string of boyfriends, one of whom had abused Ellen when she was twelve. Ellen's statement was simple: 'He came into my room and put his fingers inside me. He'd do it whenever he was staying over with Mum and I was there.'

Ellen, who'd previously been the victim of rape and physical assault, did not place the repeated abuse she'd suffered at the hands of her mum's latest fling on the same scale of seriousness that most other people would.

'I don't want 'im done,' she told us matter-of-factly.

For many crimes, if the victim doesn't want to press charges then this would be the end of the matter. Not so in Child Protection. We plough on until every avenue of investigation is exhausted. For a start, I wanted to know if anyone else was at risk.

Ellen was smart; wise even. Her cruel real-world education had taught her much about life. She'd had so many interactions with social workers that she was almost one of them and knew exactly what we were looking for. Even though she didn't want to press charges Ellen knew we would still look for this man, and that we would do all we could to make sure he wouldn't harm anyone else. She was even OK with us talking about the specifics of her allegation with him, understanding that this was essential if we were going to have a chance of getting any kind of admission.

'I don't want no trouble,' she told me. 'I know my mum's going to kick off when she finds out. But that's OK though.'

I had to keep reminding myself that Ellen was just thirteen. There were no tears, just an acknowledgement of the facts combined with, well, as I saw it, a professional approach. Ellen also knew that children like her, kids who have been in and out of care, are usually stigmatised as unreliable witnesses and troublesome attention-seekers. She also knew that the odds were against us getting anywhere in a 'his word vs her word' case.

This is one of the reasons why child protection has such a poor clear-up rate. She'd simply done all she could to help us and for that I was extremely grateful. However, she wasn't prepared to testify in a court of law, she didn't want to face the humiliation of a cross-examination.

By the time I'd finished interviewing her I was in awe. Even though she'd been cruelly violated, she'd been able to articulate her wishes and see that others were protected while understanding the risks. There are a lot of grown-up kids in Hackney and Ellen was one of them.

It took a while but I eventually found my suspect's address in Cardiff. I rang ahead to tell him I wanted a 'chat' and that I'd be there by lunchtime.

He invited me in. He was a well-spoken and well-dressed black man. He had a fantastic seafront flat with sea views. There were pictures of a woman and her kids in a mantelpiece photo. Had he found a new family?

'Can I get you some tea?' he offered.

'No, thank you.'

I sat down on a new white sofa. He took the armchair opposite. I could see he was nervous. After all, cops don't travel down to Cardiff from London for nothing.

He leaned forwards, gently wringing his hands. Yes, he was definitely stressed. This was a good start. I was fairly certain that he wasn't going to try to get rid of me with a straightforward denial.

'Earlier this morning I spoke to a girl called Ellen.'

Recognition flashed across his face followed by a brief look of fear.

'Do you know her?'

'Yes, she's the daughter of an old girlfriend. Well, I say old, we've just split up. She was a troubled child, difficult to control I'd say.'

Although I said nothing, I immediately picked up on his strategy. He was not going to be angry at Ellen's allegation, he was simply going to spout sympathy about her difficulties and behaviour, stating how he did his best, before blaming her troubled nature for her 'lies' about being abused. He was already outlining the case for the defence.

Many paedophiles have leapt on the stigma associated with care home children and do their best to destroy a child's evidence by blaming their 'turbulent upbringing'. To the child it's a second punishment. They've already suffered trauma to end up in a care home, then this distressing time in their life is used against them by the men who abuse them, adding infinitely to their unhappiness.

Bastard.

I decided, as he was already nervous, to take the blunt approach.

'OK. Well, Ellen has alleged that on repeated occasions, when she was alone in her bedroom, that you entered her room with a towel. You asked her to undress and lie on the towel. You then placed your fingers inside her. Afterwards you told her not to tell anyone otherwise she would get into trouble.'

His hand wringing intensified as I spoke. Once I'd finished talking I didn't ask any questions, just sat there in the silence.

He opened his mouth to speak, but no words came.

Many cops will tell you that this is the moment when you have to let the silence do its work to get the suspect to talk. That's usually when your colleague, who is on the wrong wavelength, opens their big mouth and relieves the tension for the suspect.

Come on, you bastard, I thought, tell me what I want to hear. Tell me what I want to hear.

Finally, after such a long silence that even I was starting to feel the temptation to break it, he started to talk.

'I need to word this carefully,' he said, and paused again.

This was unusual and a very good sign. He'd let the silence last so long that it was now impossible for him to make a straightforward denial. He was going to try to sell me a story. I wondered how good it would be.

'Ellen told me she was uncomfortable down below, and I wanted to help. I asked her to lie on the towel and she did so. I got some KY and gave her a very gentle massage inside.' He paused for a moment as I sat there silently. 'I was very gentle.'

I sat for a moment, frozen. I was dumbfounded.

As the realisation of what he'd said sank in, I wanted to shout out loud as the adrenalin of victory surged through me. I had no idea what possessed him to come up with such a terrible cover story. This was as good as it got in terms of an admission.

I was delighted for Ellen. She would be reassured by his admission. She wouldn't face a battle and a serious counter-allegation. We'd taken her allegations seriously and they'd turned out to be true, validating her honesty. Her abuser should have been in deep trouble, but unless Ellen wanted to press charges then he was heading for a caution. He would soon be on the sex offenders' register, however, and would never return to the family home where his new stepdaughters lived.

I stood up: 'You are under arrest for sexually assaulting a minor. You do not have to say anything, etc. etc.'

He repeated his 'cover story' in the interview and I bailed him. Ellen didn't change her mind about pressing charges and we accepted her view without argument. It was her body that had been violated and although I would dearly have loved to have heard the cell door slam behind her abuser, it was not to be. So a caution it was.

Not just a bastard, but a lucky one too.

As I travelled back to London on the train, I mulled over the case. I still didn't know what had made the suspect open up in such a strange way. An odd feeling of gratitude towards Ellen's abuser came over me. It sounds strange, I know, but it was so rare to see a case like this, a case that at first glance seems to be totally hopeless, end up going so well, it was so unexpected. I was grateful to him for having confessed. If only they were all like that; if only they all felt compelled to admit what they'd done when confronted by their innocent victims. Sadly, as I was about to be reminded, these were definitely in the minority.

CHAPTER SIXTEEN

COURTROOM SCANDAL

I was sat in the back row of a large courtroom and I was furious. Georgie, seven years old, was undergoing cross-examination and the barrister had quickly torn her story to bits.

'Do you remember watching the film with Jerry? You said before that it's bad if people don't tell the truth, didn't you?'

Georgie's image was on the courtroom monitors and I watched as she shifted nervously in her wheelchair. She stayed silent.

She didn't fail to answer the question because she didn't want to but because she didn't understand.

'One question at time, Ms Bradley-Jones, if you please.'

'Yes, ma'am.' She then leapt ahead to another, traumatic part of little Georgie's story.

'OK. Now, are you sure a light wasn't on in the hall?'

'Yes.'

'You said that [the accused] came into your room, didn't you? Now, would I be right in saying that you weren't able to tell who it was because it was too dark?

Silence.

'I am suggesting that you simply couldn't tell if it was him. All you were able to see in your room was a dark figure. Isn't that so?'

Silence.

'I would suggest that you don't really know if it was him? All you could see was a figure coming into the room, that's right, isn't it?'

Silence.

The under-sevens are particularly vulnerable to cross-examination once they're in the courtroom.[1] I tend to talk about justice a great deal when dealing with child protection cases because it's something that's very difficult to achieve. Even though all sides work desperately hard to end up with the best possible result for the child, it sometimes feels as if the odds are stacked against us. A barrister is tasked with defending their client against the charges but is it still justice when they defend them, perhaps suspecting their client to be guilty? When you've been with the child witness for months in the lead-up to the case, from the moment of rescue to the day in court, it's easy to rage and snap at the barristers who take them apart on the stand. Although the courtroom is full of it, it often seems as though justice has little room for emotion.

Back in the mid-eighties, children were treated as second-class citizens in the eyes of the law because they made such poor witnesses. Police questioning was not geared towards children's differing cognitive and linguistic abilities and children could not cope with the traditional method we applied to criminals and witnesses – and many hardened officers were not capable of allowing children any concessions in the interview room. Not surprisingly, as often it's the child's word against the suspect's, only a small proportion of offenders who sexually abused children were successfully prosecuted at this time.

This started to change in the early nineties and, thankfully, it's now accepted that a child can be a reliable witness as long as they receive appropriate questioning and legal procedures take into account their age and vulnerability. But that doesn't make it any easier of course. Children are often very tricky to interview. They think, for example, that adults know everything and that only children ask questions. Very young children often assume that because one adult knows what took place, other adults must already know the whole story. Many children are warned not to speak to strangers and children are generally told not to talk about certain topics, sex in particular. When these facts are combined with the all too common threats made by the attacker at the time of the abuse as to what would happen to them if they told anyone, then the task of interviewing a child in instances of alleged sexual abuse is, to say the least, extremely challenging.

The police realised, albeit belatedly, that what was needed was training. As I've already mentioned, there's a strategy we use to put the child at ease and to maximise the usefulness of their testimony. The idea is to build rapport at the start of the interview (making it clear to the child that they have done nothing wrong) and to give the child the opportunity to give a free narrative account – to tell their story, perhaps prompted by open questions, e.g. 'What happened next?' followed by more closed questions, e.g. 'Which room were you in?' to fill in missing information before closing the interview. At this point, the child has the chance to ask us questions and we explain what's going to happen next.

The Crown Prosecution Service then decides whether the video will stand a chance of becoming the evidence in chief at the trial. And that's where the problems start: in the courtroom. Unfortunately, police officers trained to interview young children can give those children false expectations of what to expect during a trial where they are treated quite differently.

Things have improved in recent years. Until 1992, the child had to appear live for cross-examination, although they could be hidden behind a screen or in an adjoining room using a Livelink video (this has since been extended to include vulnerable or intimidated adults). Now they can give evidence in a recorded interview. Other special measures have been also introduced, including the removal of wigs and gowns to make the judges and barristers appear less intimidating.

The main problem in the courtroom is that the defence barrister will do everything they can to avoid open-ended questions. They will be structured in such a way as to require a straightforward yes–no answer so that they are fully in control of the interview. Lawyers employ a number of strategies to get the answers they want, including the use of silence and body language, topic maintenance, question form and timing, the use of repetition and intonation and so on. None of these things are forbidden during the cross-examination of children.

Therefore, what a child might experience in the initial interview and under cross-examination is drastically different. For a start, there's no attempt to build rapport. Of course, there may have been pre-trial visits to the court and, most likely, the judge will have introduced him- or herself to the child, in the presence of the barristers, before the case begins. However, when the cross-examination starts, there are no pleasantries, the defence lawyer jumps straight into direct questioning.

The child – who is already in an unfamiliar environment (often a small link room) and who has to sit still in front of the camera – is thrown in right at the deep end. This can be an intimidating experience, even for the most competent child witness.

In the courtroom there is no chance for a child to tell their story at their own pace and in their own words. The child is quickly confronted by a professional interviewer who uses a series of closed questions, often asked in rapid succession, sometimes not even waiting for an answer before asking the next question, creating a sensation for the jury that the child is uncertain and may have imagined or made up the whole thing. Police interviews are slow and carefully controlled to allow for the child's age and ability.

There's no winding down in the court either. In a police interview the child is given the chance to ask questions. For example:

Interviewer: 'OK, that's lovely. There's nothing else I want to talk to you about. Is there anything you'd like to say?'

Child responds.

Interviewer: 'You've done very well remembering everything and you've been very good coming to see me. It's not easy with people you haven't met before, is it?'

And then some other chat about whatever takes the child's interest will follow.

In the courtroom, Georgie's questioning finished like this:

'You didn't even speak to him about smacking your bottom?'

'No.'

'Thank you.'

Georgie left the courtroom confused, upset and worried. This man thought she was lying and she hadn't been given a chance to explain. She had no idea what question was coming next and had been unable to question her cross-examiner. This was also the last exchange that the jury heard, another sucker punch that was intended to expose the supposed weakness of the victim, when in fact Georgie was a clever girl who had very clear and accurate memories about what had happened to her.

Children can easily be turned into unreliable witnesses when being questioned. For example, when they feel intimidated, kids won't always want to play ball – especially if they're being asked to talk about unpleasant things.

There are so many things to think about in an interview, children's abilities to answer questions varies with age, so that young children will answer what, where and who questions easier than when, how and why.

So the barrister asked Georgie simple questions in the most difficult way:

'When did he tickle you?'

Silence.

'How did he do it?'

Silence.

'Why did he touch that part of your body?'

'Don't know.'

She would probably (of course I can't say for certain) have answered differently if she'd been asked:

'Who tickled you?'

'My uncle.'

'Where did he tickle you?'

'Between my legs.'

'How did he tickle you?'

'He put his fingers inside.'

In police interviews we try to avoid why questions and we need to use yes–no questions with care as young children often answer 'yes' because that's what they think we want to hear, or what they think they should say.

For example, in one interview I asked:

'Can you remember my name?'

'Yes I can.'

'What is it?'

Silence.

So the same thing could happen in the courtroom, where the child doesn't know the answer but answers 'yes' anyway. The barrister won't necessarily double-check it, he or she will quickly move on to the next question.

As far as I know, this is done in all innocence. Police officers working in Child Protection are taught these strategies but those serving the court are not. Studies have shown that the police take more time to elicit the child's story spontaneously, to overcome issues such as the child's reluctance to speak, and that they ask more questions to check the credibility of some stereotypical responses.

In court, the children's responses are much more controlled in cross-examination by the use of closed questions, limiting the child's answer to 'yes' or 'no'. This potentially makes the child more vulnerable to suggestion and less convincing to the jury. During cross-examination the barrister is able to determine exactly what the jury hears. The under-sevens are particularly vulnerable to closed questioning. Many children are simply not given time enough to respond and although an adult might be able to cope with three questions at once, a child will not.

For example:

'You are not sure where you were touched, who did it and when this happened, are you?'

The trend in most cross-examinations of children by the defence barrister is to present a series of statements without the child having any opportunity to respond. At the end of the series the child is asked to agree or disagree, something the child may find impossible to do. The jury is also led by the barrister's questioning. Much of the time the child has no opportunity to speak and when she or he does it is a simple yes–no response.

This is a genuine and extremely serious problem in child protection. Children don't get the chance to tell their story as they did when we interviewed them. When you listen to a child spontaneously describing the abuse they suffered – with almost no prompting – it is impossible not to believe them. In court, it feels as though the opposite is true; unlike the police officer, the barrister dominates the interview.

This negates all other efforts made by the court to make trials involving children as fair and as non-intimidating a process as possible. Something needs to be done; this really is a disgrace of the highest order. I can't believe that the courts are twenty years behind the police when it comes to dealing with child witnesses.

Judges and prosecution lawyers are told to make sure the language stays simple and for the most part it does; but a far more important factor is the way in which language is used and this has not yet been acknowledged. The best solution – in the short term at least – is for judges to take on a more controlling role with regard to the form of questions if children are to function effectively as witnesses. In the long term, there need to be strict guidelines in place.

I watched Georgie's abuser, who happened to be a former Catholic priest, as he smarmed his way through the evidence. He had been well groomed when it came to answering the prosecution's questions, and he walked away from that court a free man, smiling as he descended the steps. He climbed into a black cab and disappeared into the teeming streets of London, while the family waited for me to explain what the hell had just happened to their case, a case that had dominated their lives for so many months.

CHAPTER SEVENTEEN

GANGS OF TOWER HAMLETS

I swallowed a yawn. Why do people think it's a good idea to have two-hour conferences in stuffy meeting rooms just after lunch? I never normally felt tired in my working day; I was kept on my feet running from one job to another, even the paperwork flew by in a cyclone of ticks, crosses, signatures and statements, simply because so much of it had to be done so quickly. I had calluses on the inside of my forefinger from where the biro rubbed – one of the many side-effects of modern policing.

I'd had no choice. Rob had ordered me, pushing me jokingly out the office door; such was my reluctance to attend. I had about five minutes' worth of input into this child protection conference and then I could have gone but no, I had to stay to the end and look interested as teachers from different schools, health visitors, GPs and social workers offered their input. It wasn't because the case was uninteresting or unimportant. I simply felt that as my input to the meeting was minimal my time could have been better spent getting to grips with new cases.

As soon as the interminable meeting ground to a halt, I leapt to my feet a little too eagerly and said my thanks, adding quickly:

'Must dash back to work, heavy caseload, I'm sure you all under-stand,' and indeed, everybody did very kindly understand. I rattled down the stairs and left the building almost at a jog, Claire the social worker hot on my heels complaining that with travelling time it had cost her half a day and at least two home visits.

As we emerged onto the street in the late summer sunshine we began talking about some of the recent cases we'd worked on together and I was grateful for the rare chance to get updates on some of the children. As we stepped into the street I was so absorbed that my normally sensitive trouble-radar took a while to pick up on the fact that something wasn't quite right.

I slowed and looked around me. We were in a Whitechapel side street, a row of short squat workers cottages, a couple of pubs and a post office. The busy chaos of the Whitechapel Market was about fifty metres away. In front of us were some fifteen Asian men, one of whom was wielding a machete. I looked behind me and saw another group pouring out of one of the pubs.

Claire and I were right in the middle.

Oh fuck.

I turned to Claire and handed her the bundle of paperwork I'd been given at the conference. 'Right,' I said in a businesslike voice. 'I'll deal with this. Off you go, stay out of the way and call the police if it all kicks off, OK?'

'Are you mad?' Claire asked.

'Go, Claire. I'm a cop, it's fine, I'll deal with this.'

I had to admit I sounded a lot more confident than I felt.

Claire obediently walked away. The gang let her pass without so much as a second glance. Once she was behind them she stopped, turned and looked back over her shoulder. She was holding her phone.

OK, a plan of action, I thought. First, neutralise the threat.

I looked for the man with the machete. He looked angry and was panting slightly. The ball was obviously in his court and all eyes were on him. He would determine how this played out.

Going against everything they tell you at police school, I put my hands in my pockets as I walked up to him, noting he had the muscular, lithe physique of a martial artist. Hands in pockets is a terrible defence position but I wanted to make sure he didn't see me as a threat and so introduce me to his little friend, Mr Machete.

I walked up as bold as I could manage, until I was about three metres away.

'I'm Old Bill, mate.'

'What the fuck do you want?' he said, pointing the machete at me and moving it in a small circular motion.

I didn't show my warrant card but he seemed to believe me. Who else would be so stupid? I started to feel a bit more confident. In the Met, support is everywhere and I suspected it wouldn't be long before more on-duty officers would arrive.

'We've got to sort this out,' I said. 'Don't move.'

'What?'

'Stay right there. Don't move an inch.'

I was already walking towards the other gang. The leader of this bunch was swaggering towards me in extremely baggy pants. It was a walk that would have made a cowboy proud. Either that or he had elephantiasis of the scrotum.

'Who the fuck are you?'

'I'm Old Bill.'

'Old fucking who?'

'Police. I'm a cop. We're going to sort this out, OK?'

He froze in amazement and turned to look at his mates, his face a picture of incredulity and anger. Who was this gangly idiot?

I then walked back to machete man, but addressed the whole

gang. Stealing a line from the end of *The Italian Job*, I said: 'Listen, lads, I've got a great idea. Why don't you get rid of the machete and fuck off home before you start getting nicked?'

'Huh?' the man with the machete said.

I had to admit that this was a very risky style of policing, not the sort you read about in any manual, but I think that any front-line cop would probably do the same. We can't help ourselves, if we see trouble we're instinctively drawn in to try to sort it out.

Slowly and firmly, I repeated myself.

To my relief and amazement, the man passed the machete back into the gang and it vanished.

I walked back to the other gang.

'Listen, lads, I've told them all to fuck off before people start getting nicked. I suggest you do the same, OK?'

About twenty young men looked back at me open-mouthed as their rivals disappeared into the side streets. They must have wondered what on earth I'd said to make them walk away. Seeing there was no one left to fight, they turned their backs on me and headed off in the opposite direction.

'I called 999,' a voice said from behind me. I turned to see Claire, who was still standing a little way up the road holding all of our papers. 'They're going to think it was a hoax. I've never seen anything like that before. You've just told about thirty blokes to fuck off and they did what you told them! What's your secret?'

I grinned at her. 'Communication? Truthfully, I have no idea. It could have gone a lot differently!'*

Cops break up fights all the time. By speaking to combatants in their language and by using the right language (even if it does involve swearing) people will generally respond.

* Unless you're an experienced cop, don't try this at home!

Moments later my phone rang. It was Rob. 'Harry, where the hell are you? That meeting finished ages ago.'

'I ran into a er ... little incident afterwards.'

'Fair enough but we've got a job on and I need you on it straight away.'

'Right, where is it?'

'Glasgow.'

'They call this part of town Legoland you know,' Heather said, looking out of the window at the infamous twenty-five-storey tower blocks that made up Glasgow's Red Road estate, 'and that's just how it was assembled, except it was stuck together using asbestos. That was where we were living when it happened.'

Heather paused. She was forty-one years old and lived in a very pleasant council house on what seemed to me to be a far superior estate to the likes of those I saw in Hackney.

'They have large balconies. On a clear day, which I admit isn't often, you can see the Forth sparkling away from the top and that's forty miles away. For a while I liked it up there. The flats were never damp, never noisy. Everyone had a job, carpenters, plumbers, shipbuilders, seamen, railwaymen.

'We all knew each other and it was amazing to watch everyone streaming out of the block from 7 a.m. every morning. Bit different now, of course. Now it's a ghetto, used to dump families of asylum seekers until the council gets round to demolishing it ...'

Heather stopped for a moment, her happy memories fading as she recalled why we were there. 'Yeah, for a while my memories there were happy ones.'

Lucy and I were sat in her lounge, cradling cups of tea. I saw a framed picture of Heather as a young girl on a side table with, I presumed, her sister. They looked out at us innocently from the 1970s. I wondered if that had been taken before or after.

'I can't believe you've come all this way to see me.'

This was a typical statement from victims of historical abuse, something that humbles all police officers. We travel wherever the case takes us, without question or hesitation.

'It was over thirty years ago now, you know.'

'We know,' I said, 'just let it out, as fast or as slow as you like. We've all the time in the world.'

'That's not what I meant,' she said with a steely glint in her eyes, 'I know exactly what happened and I can tell you in as much detail as you can take, as fast or as slow as you like. I remember everything, how it felt, the odours, my emotions. And I can talk about it. I've been through hell to get to a place where I can talk about it. Now I can tell you exactly.

'For years I wanted to speak out. I felt as if I had to but whenever I tried to I felt frightened and confused. Joining a group for abused women proved to be my salvation. First of all, it was easy to tell a small group of strangers who had been through something similar. I realised that I had to speak out not only for myself and for my own self-respect but for other children who have been abused.

'Problem is,' Heather added with a ironic smile, 'no one can shut me up now.'

Lucy and I smiled awkwardly.

'I want validation that these things actually happened, from my sister who was abused and saw our father abuse me too. I want to get my memory straight. I want my father and my mother to know what this has done to me. I want to see that bastard suffer. I want to warn others that other children in the family were at risk. God knows I hope not, but there may be more.'

'If there are,' Lucy said, 'then we will do all we can to protect them and make him pay for what he's done.'

Heather nodded. 'I appreciate that. The most important thing to me is that you're taking this seriously.'

'What do the rest of your family think about you coming forward?' Lucy asked.

'I told Mum first. It took me for ever to bring myself to do it. I was afraid that it would kill her and I had to decide whether I could live with that. The answer was that if she got sick and died then it was her choice. It was not my responsibility; I was the victim after all. Of course, this didn't stop it from being extremely distressing.

'She said she'd been worried about me, she knew I'd been depressed. I'd been avoiding the family and she asked me what was wrong. Something in me just clicked and I thought I should just do it now and get it over with. I just said: "Dad sexually abused me when I was a child." I regretted it almost immediately. She didn't say anything, I just heard the line click, leaving me hanging alone, listening to the dialling tone.

'When I did speak to her next, she took it seriously all right, but not in the way I expected her to. She said: "These are very serious charges, you'd better have some facts to support your accusations."'

I nodded sympathetically. 'You're not responsible for proving that you were abused. Did anyone believe you outright?'

'No. Not at first. I then tried writing to my mother, explaining everything that happened and then she wrote back to me, saying that she now believed me – to a degree – and although it was hard she forgave me for having sex with my father! What was I supposed to do with that? I now know that when you start something like this, you have to be ready for the unexpected and to be able to cope with anything, from attacks, to surprising responses. It really helped to have friends from the support group who were there for me. And now I have you, of course,' she said with sudden brightness, smiling pleasantly.

She was right. We will always take these kinds of actions seriously, we will listen to everything a victim has to say and we will act on it. Although I spent much of my time in Child Protection completely appalled by what I uncovered, my faith in humanity was always restored by the dignity, honesty and courage of victims who came forward years after the abuse.

Heather's mum's extreme defensive reactions may seem strange, yet they are surprisingly common. Family members often find exposure of these dark secrets so threatening that they turn the victim into a scapegoat, either disbelieving her, accusing her of exaggerating or, as in this case, blaming her for leading her father on.

'I told her again what he did to me the first time. He put his hand down my trousers and rubbed me. He then pulled out his hand, spat on it and put it back down there, talking to me the whole time. I was speechless. Then the door slammed and he whipped out his hand and turned all aggressive, warning me to keep my mouth shut or I'd be in real trouble.

'It was Mum who'd come in. I couldn't tell her, I was too frightened and I didn't know how. I think now, looking back from the expression on her face, sometimes I think she knew but she did nothing and that's what haunts her now. It kind of makes sense. If she didn't protect me from my father when he abused me, then it's unlikely that she'll want to start talking about it. Perhaps she's still readying herself for that moment, to tell me there was nothing she could do.

'The next time it was my worst nightmare, one I hadn't even realised possible. I couldn't breathe, scream or move. He penetrated me, then forced his penis, which was covered in my blood, into my mouth. I choked and threw up afterwards.'

Heather paused. 'I'm sorry. This can't be easy for you.'

Again, Lucy and I were humbled by Heather's consideration for us.

'We're fine to keep talking if you are,' I said.

Heather nodded. 'My sister wouldn't talk about it. Still won't.

I don't blame her. At first I was angry. I thought she'd feel the same compulsion to talk as I did. Perhaps she had managed to bury it better than I had. She's older so perhaps that helped. I just didn't understand what had happened. I was eight. I knew nothing about sex.'

In some ways, Heather's story was typical. It's essential that victims approach any confrontation like this focused on their own needs rather than anyone else's as everyone is different and will react differently. People who you think should support you may well turn out not to. It's important to be ready for defensive and aggressive reactions. As a child you were innocent, defenceless and had no way of protecting yourself from the godlike figures of your parents. You don't have to be so vulnerable as an adult.

'I hoped for a more positive response from my mum at least. I was expecting to get everything I never got as a child: her help, her sympathy and her unconditional love.'

Reality is often very different from the scenarios we play out in our minds. In my experience people are often surprised to find that loved ones will support them and they find that their bonds grow stronger than ever, while others find the reverse. When victims come out and tell the truth about abuse that happened in their family, they are destroying illusions, trying to force the real picture of the abuser into the open. It's a shock to many to learn that their family might have known about the abuse and did nothing and therefore never had the victim's best interests at heart.

'I expected the world to stop spinning when I came out with it but everything just carried on,' Heather said. 'It was as if everyone just shrugged and got on with their lives. What made it worse for me was that Mum and Dad were divorced. I thought maybe this might at least explain why, that she suspected something and couldn't stand to be with him any more. But no.

'After I told Mum, I looked up Dad in the phone book. When I saw it, everything came flooding back. I could taste the blood, smell him, felt nauseous and threw up. I'd left home as soon as I was able, when I was sixteen. Never looked back when I left Red Road. Now I look at those buildings every day and recall my own personal horror that took place there.'

Heather paused. 'But I can handle it now, mainly thanks to my friends at the support group. They're pretty hard core, you know. Some of them have no fear about telling anyone. They told me about one woman who told everyone at her grandad's funeral what he'd done to her. She was supposed to be reading a eulogy. Someone else told all the guests at her dad's wedding when he was getting remarried. Kind of ruined his big day, you might say.

'I was scared to even see my father again. Even though he was in London, I expected my mother to tell him about what I'd said and that I would open my door one day to find him standing on my doorstep, ready to kill me. I hadn't the slightest idea that the opposite was true, that I, little old me, could actually scare my father. When I was younger I used to have fantasies about killing him. He's an old man of eighty now and I could easily take him on.

'But don't worry,' Heather added quickly, 'I'm not about to do that, I don't want to end up being the one behind bars. The main thing I feel is a sense of relief. It felt awful before I did it, it felt awful while I was doing it, and I felt heartbroken and alone when it was over, but at least there's no longer a secret hanging in the air, over my head, blocking the sunlight, shrouding me in darkness. Now everyone knows why I can't have anything to do with my father, why I'm never there at Christmas, why the bastard never gets a bloody birthday card.

'Mum eventually told my father and can you believe it, he demanded proof too! He denied it and said he'd never touched me in all my life. I was terrified but I didn't change my story, I knew what was true and stuck to it. The girls in my group always told me that the freedom of telling the truth is really amazing and they were right. Now I wish I'd done it sooner.'

Of course Heather had done the right thing. It had been a very long and difficult journey for her, and it was one she was still on. You can't come forward until you're ready but child sexual abuse thrives in a climate where people try to lock the past away and hope for the best. As adults we all have a responsibility to children to confront abusers, to warn others about them. The key question in this situation is to ask yourself how immediate is the risk to other children? You can always call us anonymously through Crimestoppers to report abuse. You can also talk to teachers and the family doctor.

Heather was already on the way to achieving this when her sister called.

'My sister accepted that it had happened but quickly forgave him and buried the memory. I don't think that she really forgave him. I think she just couldn't bear to talk about it and this was the quick way to get herself free of the subject. She also didn't want to banish herself from the rest of the family.

'When she called that day, she mentioned, almost so casually that I missed it at first, that our half-sister was leaving her nine-year-old daughter with him. That was it. I called our half-sister and warned her. She took it very calmly and thanked us. It was scary and empowering at the same time. To have told his other family and to have protected that girl. That's when I called the police.

'I'm never going to forgive my father, it's impossible. Maybe if he'd come to me and apologised and said he would get help and never do it again but I don't know.'

Lucy was quick to jump in here. 'Although there is a need for you to make peace with your past and move on, whether or not this includes forgiveness is a personal matter. Not forgiving is fine, it's perfectly all right.'

'I realise that now. After all, he stole my innocence and, for a long time, ruined my life before I was able to build a new one for myself.'

Heather had been through so much, but she had managed to come to terms with what happened, the consequences of what her father had done and the effects of her decision to bring the story out into the open. I often think that it must be so hard for victims to tell us what has happened to them, without spitting hatred for the perpetrators. But it's extremely rare to see hatred in the eyes of the victims; most are like Heather, in that they show tremendous dignity and because they've thought about it for so long, they're almost professional in their approach when dealing with us.

When it was time for us to leave Heather, she told us that it didn't matter so much to her whether her father went to jail. 'What I want is for people to take me seriously and to hear what happened to me and accept it and you have done that. I can't ask for more.'

We flew back to London, Heather's words ringing in our ears. I had no idea what to expect when we sat down with her father but when George entered the interview room I was slightly taken aback. He couldn't have looked less like an abuser if he'd tried.

A pale eighty-year-old man stared back at me. His face was fairly wrinkle-free considering his age. He had a full head of white hair and was polite and friendly; his Glaswegian accent had softened since he'd come to live in London. He spoke slowly, carefully and politely. He was almost jovial as he sipped his tea. But soon the pleasantries were over. It was time to get down to business.

As Lucy joined me, I hit the record button on the tape deck and confirmed that our amicable chat had not been related to the case in question.

George nodded.

'You have to speak. For the recorder.'

'Oh yes,' he said with a soft chuckle. 'How silly of me.'

He gave his name on cue, his soft Scottish accent and baritone voice filling the small bare interview room. His solicitor followed suit.

We opened with a bit more chitchat, this time about his family life and upbringing. He was calm and he spoke about his family with affection. He seemed to me to be the perfect elderly gentleman. I was almost completely sucked in by the seemingly pleasant persona of this 'dear old chap'. But all I had to do to break the spell was look at the manila file on the table in front of me. Inside that file was a monster.

Sadly for me, the monster remained in the file throughout the interview and George made a firm denial, so all we could do was prepare for trial. I hoped Heather's new-found strength would last that long and survive the trauma that a courtroom would bring.

As usual Rob asked me how I got on.

'Not so great,' I said. 'I just hope Heather realises what she's letting herself in for.'

'Make sure she does,' Rob said. 'Don't try and dissuade her, just make sure she understands that the courts aren't as nice as we are.'

Craig entered the office. 'Are you free, Harry?'

I looked at Rob, who shrugged. I then looked at the mountain of paperwork that sat teetering on my desk.

'Free as a bird. What have you got?'

'A five-year-old girl with serious scalds is on her way here from the Homerton. I need someone in the monitor room.'

'Count me in.'

CHAPTER EIGHTEEN

HEARTBREAKER

Five-year-old Gemma, deep blue eyes and long light-brown hair, was sat on the sofa in our suite, cradling her bandaged left hand in her right, the result of a nasty scalding. As she'd spent most of the day being treated in Homerton Hospital's A&E department we'd decided to spare her the full medical until the following morning.

When we'd walked from the car to the suite Gemma had reached up and taken my hand, a wonderful sign of trust in me to keep her safe. I was taken aback however. This was the first time this had happened to me. The only physical contact cops usually have with people is when we shake hands or fight. It felt strange, holding the tiny hand of a five-year-old whom I'd only just met, but it brought it home to me that she needed love and reassurance, as she was still only part-way through her ordeal.

Gemma had been off school for most of the week with a tummy bug, but had returned on the Friday morning. Primary schools are supposed to be safe havens where kids can be kids until they enter the comprehensive battleground, which in Hackney can sometimes be like stepping into the Wild West. Fortunately, this was especially true of Gemma's school. She was a good pupil and like many others in her class she adored her young teacher, Bryony, a recent college graduate. Good teachers who develop strong bonds with their children are invaluable to both the police and the kids they teach.

So when Bryony asked Gemma about her hand, which was wrapped in a crude bandage, Gemma felt as though she could tell the truth – although her disarmingly frank reply stunned the young teacher: 'Mummy got cross and did it.'

We had Gemma in police protection within the hour. I love this aspect of our job: we face no barriers whatsoever when it comes to protecting children in cases like this. It's always a huge relief to know that we've managed to place an injured child in our care; then we can carry out a carefully reasoned investigation. If anyone tried to resist our efforts then we fought them with the full weight of the law behind us. Of course, although we have the powers, the trick is in successfully applying them in the right circumstances.

I was pleased to see that Claire was handling the case for Hackney Social Services. Before we got started I asked her about Anh, the Vietnamese lady with the meat cleaver a few weeks earlier.

One of the frustrating parts of this job is not knowing how all the cases turn out. We saw so many children that it was impossible to keep track of them as they passed through the system. Once the police aspect of any case was dealt with and social services took over, often we'd never get to find out the outcome. Every now and then, though, something wouldn't be shaken off.

'She's much better,' she replied with a soft smile. 'Ly and Qui have been able to see her in the secure unit and they're with a good family, but it's still early days. The best thing about it is that at least they've been able to have a rest from running the household for the first time in their lives and start enjoying more child-friendly things.'

After a pause, Claire smiled and added: 'Oh yes, I'm sure you'll be pleased to know that Anh's face has healed just fine.'

I grimaced and turned bright red.

Claire showed Gemma around the suite, putting her at ease. They quickly became friends. Gemma had a beautiful smile and she used it often. She was enjoying all the attention; everyone was so nice, so much fun. She asked lots of clever questions and it was hard to believe that this little girl in the bright pink coat had suffered at all.

Craig did the interview while Claire and a new girl, Alison, sat in the control room. Alison, who was in her early twenties, had joined us on attachment from uniformed police to experience what working in child protection was really like before deciding whether or not to join. Sitting in the control room was a good place to get a feel for the job. As I've said, interviewing abused children is one of our hardest tasks.

Craig started with all the usual build up. He chatted to Gemma about her interests, what she liked about school, her favourite games, TV programmes and so on. Gemma seemed totally normal; she was relaxed and chatted with Craig quite happily, causing those watching to smile. It wasn't long before Craig felt he could move on to the subject of her injury.

As Gemma seemed to be quite eloquent and chatty, with an amazing vocabulary for a five-year-old, Craig asked open-ended questions.

'Can you tell us what happened to your hand?'

'Mummy had a really bad week,' Gemma said matter-of-factly. 'She had a row with Daddy on the phone. He was supposed to give Mummy some money but he didn't. He was supposed to come and see me but he was busy and Mummy was upset.'

We already knew from the teacher that Gemma's parents had split up after a short tempestuous marriage.

'Mummy was on the phone to Dad, shouting at him. She was

making a cup of tea in the kitchen. James was in the kitchen.'

'Who's James?'

'My brother.'

'Is he younger than you or older than you?'

'Older. He's seven. He's such a baby. He drew on the wall with a crayon. Mum saw him and told him off. She was going to hit him but I was in the way.'

Gemma paused. All our smiles were long gone.

'And then what happened?'

'I was in the way. Mummy had the kettle in her hand and she put the water on my hand. It really hurt. I cried a lot. Afterwards Mummy said sorry but that I was naughty and that's what naughty people get.'

'Did you go to school afterwards?'

'No. Mummy said I was sick.'

'With what?'

'I wanted to go to school but Mummy said I had to wait.'

This was enough. We'd arrest Gemma's mum by appointment, interview her and charge her. The family would be split but Claire had already identified an aunt who would be a suitable carer. There are many fabulous foster carers but the extended family is often best.

Before he could end the interview, Craig had one more question.

'Has anything like this ever happened before?'

Gemma fidgeted a bit.

'It's OK, you can tell me. You won't get into trouble, you'll be helping.'

Gemma nodded, saying nothing. She stood up and took off her pink coat, placing it neatly on the sofa, just next to her. She then undid her cardigan and took it off. She reached across her body with her left hand and raised her T-shirt, exposing a section of her back.

I felt like I'd been hit with a sledgehammer. My head spun. Gemma's back was a mass of angry-looking scar tissue. Huge sections of her delicate skin had been all but destroyed. The burns must have caused her agony for days, if not weeks. They must have blistered and her nerves would have been permanently damaged.

Craig struggled to control his shock as he asked Gemma to put her cardigan back on and started to end the interview. It had hit him hard. He had a daughter the same age and Gemma was her spitting image. It was totally unexpected and horrific. I don't think any of us had ever seen a clearer demonstration of the innocence of an abused child. She'd been through so much, yet she seemed so delightful, so normal – better than normal in fact.

I looked across. In the control room there was no child to remain professional in front of. Tears were streaming down Claire's and Alison's faces. I defy anyone to tell me that social workers don't care. This was a typical reaction to the sort of abuse they saw every week.

Looking at Alison, I thought: And another one bites the dust. All too often officers who joined us on attachment decided, understandably, that working in this world was not for them and that they could be better employed in other parts of the Met. I had second thoughts on a couple of occasions, especially after seeing child pornography for the first time. I wasn't sure if I would be able to handle studying it day in and day out. I cannot begin to tell you just how revolting it is: everything you can imagine and much worse besides.

I commiserated with Alison afterwards.

'It's unbelievable,' she said. 'Gemma is so perfect, she's an absolutely wonderful child. I can't understand what's wrong with her mother. I don't think I could live with myself knowing that there are children like her out there being abused.'

'I know. I quite understand if this job isn't for you.'

'What do you mean?' she asked, obviously annoyed.

'It's OK,' I said, 'this line of work isn't for everyone.'

'No, Harry, you've got it the wrong way round. I want to do everything I can to see that the mother gets what she deserves! And Gemma has a brother who needs rescuing.'

All Alison wanted to know was how soon she could transfer. Seeing Gemma had only reinforced her desire to join our seemingly unwinnable war against child abuse. Maybe we can't stop all child abuse, but we can change many kids' lives for the better. How many lives we save, I'll never know, but it must be a significant amount. Having said that, even now, at the end of the first decade of the twenty-first century, two children die every week in the UK from abuse and neglect.

We still need a lot more Alisons.

CHAPTER NINETEEN

THE DAMAGE DONE

I was sat in the lounge of our suite. The young woman in front of me sobbed uncontrollably; Claire was sitting beside her, holding her hand. The woman, Justine, was innocent of any wrongdoing, but I had just given her some horrible news about her children.

Claire looked at me and nodded softly, her lips pressed tightly together. That look told me Claire realised this was going to be a tough case, but that we would get through it.

It had started that morning at a large Hackney primary school, when, during the morning break, six-year-old Joanne told her teacher, Miss Watts, that she was sore.

'Where are you sore, Jo?'

'Down here.'

Miss Watts wasn't too concerned as this was a fairly common complaint.

Then Joanne added: 'Dougie put his fingers in there.'

Miss Watts froze as her world started to spin. She was a young teacher and had never encountered a pupil that had been sexually abused before. Her first instinct was to comfort Jo and put her arm round her.

But what to do next?

This part was crucial. The rush of emotion that comes with a disclosure like this makes it hard to find the right words. All too often at this point teachers find their child protection training a distant memory.

First, Miss Watts made sure she had heard correctly. Yes, Jo said that Dougie put his fingers in there. OK. Now take action.

'Jo, try not to worry, we will get your mummy. It's class time now, are you OK to go back in?'

Jo nodded. Miss Watts ran off and found another member of staff to cover her class before she dashed over to the office of the deputy headmistress, the school's child protection officer. There, she wrote down the conversation, date and time and signed it. She had done everything perfectly.

Teachers play an absolutely vital role in child protection and are responsible for saving thousands of children from further sexual abuse and neglect but still, in my experience, many remain woefully uneducated in the way child protection works. They need to attend regular courses; one day at teacher training college just doesn't cut it.

At least two teachers need to be made child protection representatives. Schools also need to have a big child protection poster up on the school wall, which states that the duty of teachers is to report concerns. It must be made clear to parents that this is part of the teacher's responsibilities.

Sometimes, teachers are under the impression that parents must be told if a referral to social services is made. This is WRONG. I cannot stress this enough. If it's a case of the child being smelly or other minor examples of neglect, of course tell the parents. If it's a case of indecent assault or an explicit disclosure, then don't. Refer the matter to social services, but be clear that you have not told the parents. Ask for instructions as to what to do. Telling the parents of children who are being sexually abused would almost certainly lead to the loss of forensic evidence and would give the abuser time to influence their victim's testimony.

If you're not sure what's been said, just ask the child to say it again. Ask open questions without putting ideas in their heads. If you ask: 'So was it Uncle Billy who touched your privates?' then you've probably blown the prosecution and hampered a chance to make the child safe. Instead, just ask: 'What happened? What are you worried about?' Never, ever, suggest a name of an abuser or an act. Remember, children often use words to mean several different things; by using the word 'sex' they may mean kissing, for example. You can ask: 'What do you mean?' if it seems unclear.

Having said that, most mistakes made at the point of disclosure can be rectified and it's pointless getting angry and shouting if things haven't been done as they should, as invariably it's a lack of training that is to blame.

Teachers are often shocked to find themselves in this impossibly difficult position of hearing something they don't want to and something they don't want to believe. Some people simply can't cope with the information. They don't want to believe it's actually happening or they just don't know what to do about it. Sometimes it's not that people don't believe the child, rather that they don't want to because then they have to do something about it. They also don't want to end up being harshly criticised if they get it wrong.

But reporting a child's disclosure is really quite simple. Once you've finished speaking to them write down the day, date, time, place and what you and the child said. Then ring social services immediately, not at the end of the day, immediately.

Luckily Miss Watts and the deputy headmistress did everything by the book and called social services.

The main pooling point for all the information that came through Hackney at this time was Duty and Assessment at

Downham Road, run by social services. Any information that came in was logged into a computer and assessed there. They then referred cases to us by fax.

Sadly, the meagre budget of the social services didn't allow for a half-decent IT system with email back then.* Every so often their machine would jam and by the time they'd realised, we'd end up with a sudden flood of cases pouring through our machine. Sometimes the person at the other end dialled the wrong number and a child's case would whirr out of a random fax machine somewhere else in the UK.

When the fax arrived at Stoke Newington, it was logged and a yellow form was added. Some basic checks were made and, after a telephone discussion with social services, it was decided whether we should act together or separately.

In this case we decided to act together.

Dougie was just eight years old.

He was also Jo's older brother.

I ripped the fax from the machine with a yawn. I'd been up half the night as our newest arrival was teething. I'd then stomped around the house like a bear with a sore head in the morning as our two boys argued and fought around the breakfast table before I started my own argument with my wife about our plans for the weekend. I wanted to head out to a concert with some friends, she wanted me to drive the boys to an equestrian event on the other side of Hertfordshire.

All that was quickly forgotten as I read the fax. I had two concerns: what had happened to Joanne and what made Dougie do it.

We spent a long time chatting to Jo on our sofa. As Dougie was only eight, he was below the age of criminal responsibility

* The fax was finally replaced with email in February 2009.

(it's currently ten). Therefore, legally speaking, no crime had been committed, so there was no reason to put Jo through the formality of a memorandum interview. She was a sweet child; small for her age, with wild curly brown hair and she answered our questions quickly and easily.

Claire noticed that Jo had a rash on her upper arms. There were some nasty scratches there as well. 'Looks like eczema,' Claire said. 'Does it itch?'

Jo nodded. 'Mummy helps me to stop itching it.'

Justine, their mum, was in her early twenties, dressed in black leggings, black boots and a short leather jacket over a black T-shirt. She sobbed after I'd explained what Dougie had done to Joanne.

'Try not to be too upset,' I said. 'This sort of behaviour is surprisingly common and not sexually motivated. Just try to keep matters in perspective. Dougie isn't in trouble, we just need to get to the bottom of why this happened, so we can make sure it doesn't happen again, OK?'

Justine nodded, snuffling consent for a memorandum interview of her son. She looked on nervously as Claire and I took Dougie into the interview room. I had my suspicions about Dougie, hence the formal interview. If I was right, then Justine's day was about to get much worse. Once we were certain he was at ease, we began.

'Who lives in your house?'

'Me, Jo, Mum and Peter.'

'Who's Peter?'

'Mum's friend.'

'Is he your friend too?'

Silence.

'Do you like Peter?'

Dougie shook his head. 'No.'

'Why not?'

'He scares me. I hide in my wardrobe.'

'Why?'

'It's safe.'

'Why do you feel safe?'

'Because he doesn't look for me in there.'

'Who doesn't look for you?'

'Peter.'

'What does Peter do that makes you scared?'

'He tickles me.'

'Where?'

'In my bum, with his finger.'

Children who are sexually abused usually feel unable to tell anyone about their dreadful secret. They suffer in silence and experience very strong feelings: fear, depression, guilt, shame, confusion, helplessness and despair. With all these feelings rushing around inside them, it's hard for a child to keep them under control and they often come out in other ways.

Very often people think that changes in a child's behaviour are simply a difficult phase that they're going through. But the signs are there for anyone who is able or willing to read them. By putting his fingers inside his sister, Dougie had exhibited one of the most obvious signs of abuse: inappropriate sexual behaviour, which sometimes can be – as in Dougie's case – acting out with other children what had happened to them. Sometimes children will draw inappropriate pictures or tell stories that feature sexual activity.

Forty minutes after we'd started, I left Dougie in the interview room with Claire and spoke to the mum. Being the one to reveal the abuse to a young mother is never an easy thing to do. All you can do is be clear and spell it out; don't hold any information back. I explained that her new partner, Peter, had sexually abused her eight-year-old son, who had been left so disturbed that he was now abusing his six-year-old sister.

As I spoke Justine put her hand to her open mouth in horror, shouting out 'No!' before breaking down into uncontrollable sobs.

This was the ultimate betrayal by a man she loved and had enjoyed sex with. She had no clue. As I tried to comfort her she leapt up and ran to the toilet. As I sat there, waiting for her to return, I could hear agonised retching.

It wasn't over yet. Twenty minutes later, after she'd recovered, I outlined what Dougie had gone through in more detail. She became angry. Her whole world had just collapsed.

'What am I going to tell my mum and dad?' she said. 'How can I tell my friends?'

'Tell them as clearly and as concisely as you can,' I said. 'You need them now more than ever.'

Her hatred for Peter was total. I told her that Dougie would need a full medical that afternoon, another ordeal for mother and son.

'I can't believe this. My world has collapsed. This morning I got up and everything was right with the world. Now, three hours later my boyfriend is a paedophile and my son has sexually abused my daughter. I don't think I could have imagined a worse day in my life.'

'I'm so sorry,' I said. 'But your children are young enough to recover from this and I know with you to help them they will.'

Justine nodded, saying nothing.

'There's just one more thing I'd like to know for now. Your daughter has a rash,' I said.

'Yes, it's eczema,' she said.

'She scratches it, does she?'

'Yes, I've been having real trouble trying to get her to stop. She just scratches at night for some reason and I have to sit with her until she's asleep, otherwise she'll scratch herself raw.'

I nodded. Clever Jo had found a strategy to stop her abuser, her brother who slept in the same room, from abusing her. By scratching herself, she made her mother stay with her, at least until she fell asleep.

I have to admit I enjoyed the look of fear and then righteous indignation that crossed Peter's face when he was arrested and brought in for an interview. A tall thin man with a red face, he couldn't stop sweating. It was the sweat of the cowardly, of the guilty.

'He's making it up!' Peter exclaimed over and over. 'Why won't you believe me? He's just a kid. He's trying to get at me 'cos he's jealous of me and his mum.'

He could stick that excuse for as long as he liked. The problem with this is that young children like Dougie have little or no knowledge of sexual abuse – unless they have suffered it in some way. They can't make up stories about something they know nothing about. Adults are (usually) much better at lying than children. Yes, Peter was in a whole heap of trouble, there was no escaping it.

Driving home that night, I was emotionally exhausted. I had watched a family fall apart in the most terrible way right before my eyes. At least these events had brought the reign of terror against Dougie to an end. That was of course hugely satisfying but the distress that I had to wade through to get there had sapped me more than I realised. It was all I could do to stagger into bed – after telling my wife that nothing would give me greater pleasure than to drive the boys across Hertfordshire that weekend.

CHAPTER TWENTY

THE GREAT DIVIDE

The 999 operator asked the five-year-old boy for his address but he said he didn't know, so she put a trace on the phone and stayed on the line with the scared young lad until she had it. It wasn't long before a uniformed officer's boot made short work of the door and the officers stampeded into the flat, finding five-year-old Joshua hugging Julie, his three-year-old sister, in the bedroom. They were both crying, justifiably terrified at the sound of their front door being kicked in. There was no one else in the flat.

When the uniformed officers rang Child Protection the call eventually came through to me. I was in a newsagent's armed with paper and soft drink queuing behind a line of people, every one of whom bought a scratch card once they reached the till. I jammed my paper and drink under one arm so I could extract my phone from my coat.

'It's amazing,' a young female officer told me, 'Joshua was looking after his little sister, protecting her when we came crashing in. Even though he was terrified he put her first.'

I told her I'd be there in fifteen minutes. I could have asked her to take the kids straight over to social services but I didn't like to take children out of their home if possible, as this was where they usually felt safest and where they would be able to respond best to questions from a stranger in a suit. And I hoped that they'd be able to stay at home once we got to the bottom of why they'd been left alone.

I crawled through the Hackney traffic, passing about half a dozen betting shops in about five minutes. It seemed to me as though there were more betting shops in Hackney than in any other borough. I think they sold more scratch cards here than anywhere else in London as well. Such is the desperation and hopelessness of the poor they're prepared to stake what is a small fortune to them on impossible odds to escape the poverty trap.

It must be even worse these days with the nouveau riche rubbing their noses in it, snapping up Hackney's nicer properties for large fortunes. Still, if enough wealthy people moved here then they would bring improvements with them: better local services and amenities, public events such as music festivals in the parks and nicer shops.

Hackney is an amazing place to live and work but it could be a hell of a lot better for its poorest residents. After all, gangs would find it a lot harder to recruit members if they lived in a nice area with plenty of places to amuse themselves. When people live in an area they're proud to call home then they lose that sense of hopelessness and feel they might be able to help the police to make their lives safer and happier.

Nothing could be further from this utopian dream than the Woodberry Down estate, one of the most forbidding estates I've ever seen. Bordered by the huge clay-bottomed East Reservoir to the south that only adds to the sense of desolation, it's impossible to imagine that this area was once considered the posh end of Stoke Newington. But that was back in the 1930s. Work on the current estate began after the Second World War when fifty-seven blocks of flats containing 2,500 homes were built on sixty-four acres of land.

At the time I visited it, most of the estate was awaiting demolition, many flats were already boarded up. There was no sense of community pride here, I can tell you. It looked and felt like a huge, forgotten prison complex where the inmates had been left to run things for themselves.

The flats were crumbling, leaky, cold and it was where you were sent if you were poor, desperate and really, really unlucky. You could sit on your little balcony at night if you wanted but only if you didn't mind the sound of sirens as cops chased teenage troublemakers in and out of the estates. You can even watch mobile footage of these chases taken by residents on YouTube.

The estate held unpleasant memories for me. I'd previously worked on a case here where two 'guardians' had stabbed and then planned to drown the eight-year-old girl they were supposed to be looking after in the reservoir because they thought she was a witch.

I was amazed to discover that the automatic door system was working, so I pressed the flat number and was buzzed in. I strode through the stoved-in door to find a middle-aged male PC playing with the kids. He'd won their trust and when I stuck my head in the room they were both giggling happily at him as he pulled faces and made farting noises.

'Everything OK?' I asked.

The constable jumped and turned bright red, embarrassed at being caught in the act by a senior officer.

'Smashing pair of kids,' he said, clearing his throat and putting on his most professional manner.

I grinned. 'Yes, it sure looks like it. Keep up the good work, don't let me stop you.'

People tend to assume that a young woman police officer will be assigned to look after any children we found but this was rarely the case. The older male officers often have children of their own, so they know how to keep kids amused. The female PCs, who tend to be younger, don't necessarily and may be more focused on their career. In this case, as Craig and Helen rolled up, it was Craig who took over looking after the kids.

Joshua and Julie looked healthy, although their clothes were old and worn. I took a quick nose around the flat. I was pleased to see that it was clean, although the kids' room was in desperate need of redecorating and they had precious few toys.

I entered the kitchen. Holding my breath just in case, I opened the fridge but it was clean and filled with plenty of prepared food neatly stacked in saucepans and bowls, although having said that I had no idea what it was.

I was ignorant of all the foreign foods that are so readily available in Hackney's local stores. You wouldn't find anything so exotic in the leafy part of Hertfordshire where I lived. My ignorance became painfully apparent during a drugs raid when I seized three bags of brown powder and sent them up to the crime lab thinking I'd got the heroin seizure of the year. My heart raced with excitement when they finally called. 'Well done, DS Keeble,' the scientist told me in a deadpan tone, 'you've seized two kilos of pure yam powder, the biggest by the Met this year.' Fortunately for me, the third bag did contain a quarter of a kilo of heroin.

Having checked the flat, all I had to do now was wait. I sent Craig and Helen away and popped a DVD on the obligatory enormous wall-mounted TV. As always in Hackney the definition of poverty included the 50-inch TV, Sky subscription and a mobile phone capable of shooting video.

Joshua stared happily at the TV while Julie played with her ancient-looking dolls. I was amazed. They were so small yet so comfortable in the company of total strangers. I wondered if this was because of the way they'd been brought up. My thoughts were suddenly interrupted by a loud gasp quickly followed by: 'Oh my God!'

Aha. The mother was back and had seen the state of her front door.

I stepped into the hallway and saw a smartly dressed but frightened woman in her twenties standing in the hall. I introduced myself and quickly explained the situation, that the kids were fine.

'I'm so sorry, I had to pop out, just for five minutes; there was no one else.' She rushed past me to check on the children.

I let that first lie of 'just five minutes' pass for the moment. It had been two hours.

'What was so urgent?' I asked.

'I had to go to the chemist,' she said, holding up a white plastic bag, 'you know, ladies' things.'

'May I see?'

Reluctantly, she held open the bag and I peered in.

Well, in a sense she wasn't lying. Hair dye and extensions were definitely 'ladies' things. OK, this wasn't good enough.

'Well, I've been here five minutes,' I said.

She looked extremely relieved.

'But the officers who kicked in your door after your brave little boy dialled 999 got here about two hours ago.'

Her face fell.

'Are you going to tell me where you've really been?'

Looking at the floor she said: 'I just got distracted, shopping, you know?'

Again, not good enough.

I took her details, enough for my report. 'I'm going to talk to Hackney Social Services, who will probably visit you later today and then we will decide what to do. I'm going to arrest you for neglect but I'm happy for you to do this by appointment, OK?'

She looked like she was in shock. Good. 'OK?' I repeated.

She nodded. 'If you want a brief, you're welcome to bring one but I doubt if we'll be long.' I wanted to ease her worry a little, this way I was letting her know that as long as she didn't have any previous that would cause us concern, then we would interview and caution her and social services would keep that all-important eye on her and the kids. This was her only warning. If social services found anything wrong, we'd take her to court and her kids would end up in care.

By the time we'd finished the formalities, she'd offered me a tea, which I declined. I had no time to hang around. My job phone had been vibrating merrily away most of the time we were talking.

'This is no life,' she told me as I prepared to leave. 'I'm twenty-two years old, *twenty-two*. Their dad is out there playing at gangsters or God knows what and I've got to raise his kids in this dump with no money.'

I didn't have any advice for her. All I could do was tell her that I understood it wasn't easy but a five- and three-year-old can't be left alone for two hours at a time.

'If you're all they've got then you're the one who has to make sure they're safe and well. You're lucky. This could have turned out a lot worse for you.'

Despite the depressing circumstances in which the mother found herself I left the estate feeling quite pleased. This was a rare case indeed, one of the few instances where child protection can be quickly wrapped up in a nice little package, a rare event in this world.

Having dealt with various messages back at the office, and having successfully ignored Rob's frown at the huge pile of paperwork that needed sorting out on my desk, I snatched the next fax out of the machine. I read it over and over again. It was one of those borderline cases. Should I stay or should I go?

If I didn't want to go, then I had plenty of excuses on hand: other cases to follow up, paperwork to be signed, emails to be sent, meetings to organise. As usual, some of Rob's wise words materialised as I stared at the referral: 'Always make every decision on the basis of what the hindsight police will say. If the child ends up murdered the following morning then everyone will be looking at you, and you will want to be able to say that you made a good decision the day before.'

A local woman had called in after seeing a woman attack her daughter with a hairbrush while driving her car. She'd written down the car's number and uniformed officers had gone to the registered address, but there was no one there. We had no record of the family. I looked at the mound of ever-present paperwork and then back at the referral.

Sod it, I thought, snatching up my car keys, it can't hurt to make sure.

Lucy and I drove to the address. It was the complete opposite of Woodberry Down: large four-storey Georgian houses overlooked one of Hackney's better parks.

'What do you reckon?' Lucy asked. 'A million?'

'Probably more,' I answered. 'Isn't this the street where Tony Blair used to live?'

'Blair used to live in Hackney?'

'Yup. With Cherie too. I think they were burgled a couple of times and then they moved a mile or so up the road to Angel.'

'He soon forgot his roots, then.'

Angel was one of the most expensive areas in London; that house was where Cherie had opened the door in her dressing gown to receive dozens of bouquets of flowers the day after the 1997 election.

Whenever I thought of Tony Blair I usually thought of his phrase: 'Tough on crime, tough on the causes of crime.' Well, if the causes of crime were paper forms of varying length and colour, we might have been getting somewhere. As it was, I couldn't help thinking that in so many areas, as a society we were further away from dealing with either problem. To be fair, crime-fighting had got better in many areas in the Met without any help from politicians, that's partly why I liked working for Child Protection so much. Things had improved drastically in this field in recent years; we followed every case wherever it led us, whether to the ends of the earth, or to an immaculate million-pound four-storey Georgian house on the edge of Hackney.

I looked across the park. Tall, elegant trees rustled in the wind, a few browned leaves fell to the ground. Although it was early September, it was still warm and a couple of lone book readers lay on freshly cut grass. Hackney is full of contrasts but they don't come much stronger than this. From one side of the park to the other you go from murder and mayhem to *Mansfield Park* and Morse.

Every now and again, a nasty crime happens in that park, a mugging or stabbing, and the crime scene tape goes up, the noticeboards are put up asking for witnesses; an unpleasant reminder to the better-off of their unruly neighbours on the other side of the park.

I lifted the solid brass antique knocker. The front garden was immaculate. Rows of perfectly manicured bushes sat in expensive gravel.

An attractive woman in her mid-thirties answered the door. She had designer sunglasses pushed back on her head and wore a pleasant smile. When I produced my warrant card, she showed no sign of concern and invited us in.

'Sorry about the mess,' she said cheerfully. 'Two kids and I've long given up tidying up after them.'

I wasn't looking at the mess. I was admiring the wide entranceway, the immaculate yellow walls and white coping on the ceiling, the broad hall and the huge kitchen, all glass and light and designer fittings. Was that a walk-in fridge?

'So what can I do for you, officers? Another incident in the park, is it?'

'No,' I said, 'we've received a complaint from a member of the public. You were seen repeatedly hitting a young child with a hairbrush while in your car.'

I kept information to a minimum, a police technique. She might either flood us with details, which we could check against the information we had from the caller, or she could try to say as little as possible, or be overly helpful. All of these could also mean innocence or guilt. Ian Huntley, the murderer of Jessica Chapman and Holly Wells, was over-helpful, giving interviews to Sky News and the BBC and pretending to take part in the search for the girls when there was still hope that they were just missing persons.

The evader usually tries to gauge just how much we know and how much trouble they might be in. Often though this can simply mean that someone has had little contact with police or is recently arrived from another country which has a brutal police force.

The lady, whose name was Martina, took us through the incident.

'Oh that! Mirabelle, my seven-year-old, was fighting with her five-year-old brother over the hairbrush. After numerous warnings, I leaned across the back seat to snatch it from them. Mirabelle wouldn't stop screaming at the top of her lungs at her brother so I whacked her with the brush a few times. Not hard, just to get her to stop screaming.'

Every parent has been there. The screaming, fighting and frustration while you're trying to do something else – especially drive. It can push some parents further than they would normally go. Still, I needed to speak to the kids, alone. No child is likely to disclose anything of interest to us in front of a parent.

'Is it OK if we speak with your children alone?'

'Oh yeah, go right ahead. Good luck at prising them away from the Xbox, though.'

Of course, they had a huge playroom. They were sat next to each other watching a DVD.

'Hi, guys,' I said. 'I'm a policeman. No one's in trouble, I'd just like to talk to you for five minutes, is that OK?'

I talked to kids in their home when I thought the matter was likely to be resolved there and then. If the children started to disclose abuse, however, it was time to stop and wait for a memorandum interview down at Stokie.

Mirabelle started to tell the story about fighting in the car with her brother and how Mummy got cross. As she talked Lucy and I really exaggerated our listening by being overly enthusiastic, making sure Mirabelle felt she was getting the approval she deserved for being so chatty.

Thomas, her little brother, was silent to start with, but he couldn't resist for long and started to relate his own version of events. He was soon in full flow, adding a few graphic descriptions. And, like so many children, because what he said was so well received he felt proud of himself.

Their tale was the same as their mother's; this wasn't abuse, it was parenthood – if gone slightly wrong.

'Why were you fighting?' Lucy asked.

'Because Mummy promised to take me to the fair,' Thomas said, 'and she said she couldn't so I got cross.'

'I told him off,' Mirabelle said, 'Mummy is busy and he shouldn't get angry.'

'But she never takes me anywhere. She's *always* too busy,' Thomas moaned.

Lucy and I rounded off the chat, talking a bit about school and we learned that their mum had missed that year's school play. Then we went back downstairs, noting the original artwork in the hallway, and spoke to the mum. I got her to look at the incident as an observer. I also asked her why the kids were fighting.

I think she knew I knew why but she just shrugged her shoulders.

'It's not easy being a single mum with two young kids,' she sighed, 'but you're right, I was wrong. How do you say it?' she said with a smile, 'I'm "bang to rights", aren't I?'

It's a bit easier here than in Woodberry Down, I thought. And while we'd been in the kitchen I'd seen the numbers for a whole host of babysitters and carers pinned to the giant fridge, alongside a calendar with dates marking parties, manicures and weekends away. I could sure as hell believe it wasn't easy but there was definitely an element of the 'home alone' element here too, with the kids not seeing their mum as much as they would like. Still, in the world of Hackney Child Protection, this was right at the very bottom of our scale. They were bright kids who wanted for nothing but more time with their mother. If she'd been living in a council flat with no money for babysitters then it would be a different story of course. Money can make all the difference.

I told her that we regarded this incident as serious enough to come straight out to investigate, dropping our other cases. Her face fell. This always struck a chord because we don't need to remind most parents of the sorts of cases that we investigate in Hackney, they're in the national press often enough. I saw that my message had hit home, and she now took our visit seriously.

It may not be overtly mentioned in our remit but the police are there to help. We aren't social workers, we're not trained in how to rebuild a family or how to guide them through hard times, but we are there to show the way. When Lucy told the rich single mum about what the kids had told us, she looked guilty as hell. This was a clear and effective warning; her kids had been left wanting emotionally – the difference from most cases was that she could afford to put matters right.

These were two straightforward but crucial cases where the repair of families can begin before they're broken, where we, as police officers, cross the border into the world of social services. A few carefully chosen words of warning can make all the difference. Perhaps these kids would no longer be neglected – it would be hard to tell. For the short term at least, while the Woodberry Down mum would have to follow the rules laid down by social workers, our rich mum could still rely on her army of babysitters.

We left, satisfied that all was well with the family. All I had to do was write up this visit, and my trip to the estate from this morning. I sighed at the thought of all the paperwork and time that entailed for two straightforward cases but at the same time I felt a small burst of happiness.

'Why the smile?' Lucy asked.

'Two cases cleared up in one day to everyone's satisfaction, surely that has to be a record for Hackney Child Protection?'

There was one more thing I had left to do and that was to ring the woman who'd phoned to report the 'hairbrush incident'. I wanted to thank her and to let her know that all was well. I was doing more than I had to; giving her more information than she needed, but I knew I would be instilling confidence in her. As cops, we must never waste an opportunity to make a person feel that they've genuinely made a difference, especially when it comes to child protection. That way she should feel confident enough to call us again in the future. Hopefully she would also tell others that the police cared enough to respond quickly to a call for help from the public, and that for us is a most valuable investment.

Feeling happy with my morning's work, I trotted across Hackney to fulfil a long-standing engagement. One of my roles involved leading training sessions on child protection to doctors, teachers and social workers. This was a role I really enjoyed, I liked spelling out what they had to do when they felt a child was being abused. I could often see their eyes cast back in memory as they wondered about the borderline cases they might have missed and I hoped that in future more children would end up being referred to us as a result.

At this session, which was at a large Hackney school, a teacher put their hand up as soon as I'd finished my presentation. It was a young, serious-looking man, in his late twenties, clearly the sort of teacher the kids couldn't muck about with.

'Detective Sergeant Keeble, I am furious at the way one of these cases was handled by the police.'

I stood dumbfounded. He'd spoken to me like I'd just kicked a ball through his classroom window. All eyes were on me.

'Why is that?' I asked.

'I referred an eight-year-old boy to your team earlier this year and he turned up the next day at school as if nothing had happened while I was left none the wiser. No one had thought to provide me with an update, which I think is incredibly unprofessional. I had no idea whether he was even supposed to be back at school.'

His angry questioning met with murmurs of approval from the other teachers.

'Perhaps you remember him,' he continued, 'a small black boy called Jumu.'

Oh God, as he described the little boy, I realised it was one of mine. He was the one who'd reported young Jumu, who told him he'd been hit by Raymond the lodger.

He had a really good point. Neither the police nor social services updated teachers unless it was somehow relevant to our investigations, which hardly seemed fair since their help was critical to us. We were simply getting on with the case and updating the referrer was way down on our list of priorities.

Lesson learned, albeit in a very embarrassing manner, I apologised and said I would find out and update him about Jumu's case.

'Anyone else need an update?'

A wave of hands rose before me.

Oh boy, I thought, as I promised to see what I could do. I can sense a lot of extra work heading my way.

Before I could do that, however, I had another long-standing agreement to attend: Heather's trial was about to begin.

CHAPTER TWENTY-ONE

REGRESSION

Sitting in a courtroom during abuse cases was a frustrating experience for me. I had no control, no power to act, to jump in and save my witness. All I could do was watch as the case for the prosecution was attacked by the defence, hoping that it was robust enough to withstand the assault.

I looked up at the stand. Heather was bravely facing the defence barrister, an owl-like rotund figure with more than two decades of experience at the bar.

'You alleged in your statement that your father sexually assaulted you.'

'Yes.'

'That he sexually abused you through a period of approximately eight years.'

'Yes.'

'How old were you when your sexual abuse began?'

'I was eight years old.'

'How did it happen that your father began to sexually abuse you; how did it begin?'

'When I was about eight I was sitting on the sofa with him, Mum wasn't home and he had sent my sister to bed.'

'Where was your mother?'

'At work. She worked in a cinema.'

'How did it begin?'

'My father asked me if I knew what different parts of the body were called.'

'And did you?'

'No.'

'And did he tell you?'

'Yes.'

'And what did he say to you?'

'He reached between my legs and touched me. He asked me if I knew what this was called.'

Heather had shown tremendous courage in getting here. Although she had no support from her family as far as the trial went she had her friends from the support group, some of whom had made the trip to be with her in London, as well as my team, victim support and Katherine, the CPS lawyer.

She was so brave. But looking at her then, I realised I wasn't looking at Heather, the 41-year-old strong and righteous mother of two, but at a scared eight-year-old who was about to be abused all over again. I could see it in her expression and I could hear it in the slight tremor in her voice. She normally spoke in a strong and vibrant tone but now sounded so small and alone.

The court lights were bright and clear; she was on a raised stand so everyone could see and all eyes were on her; she was the star of this traumatic show. I don't think I could have gone through that, especially not when the odds were stacked so heavily.

For all rape victims of all ages, the trial becomes a second traumatic experience. Under cross-examination, the victim is obliged to relive the violent experience of physical and psychological trauma; to give an objective, neutral and entirely physical description of an experience packed full of intense emotional and psychological stress. They are expected to recall details of the event but in a way determined by the cross-examiner, not at their own pace.

They're also compelled to answer questions, which all too often in my opinion are posed in a sordid manner. As in Heather's case, the victim often finds themselves accused by the defence of fantasy and make-believe.

Sure enough, Heather's sexual and personal dignity was soon under attack; she had been transformed into the accused and it was as if she were being abused once more.

The defence (and prosecution) do not devise new forensic methods for every trial in a Crown court, they rely on tried and tested methods that have been used for centuries, e.g. 'Never ask a question you don't know the answer to' is one hard and fast rule. They also rely upon standard stories when dealing with rape victims, stories they may actually have little trust in themselves. The defence is there to defend their client, no matter what it takes. Even if, no matter how much they may dislike it, they have to push the boundaries of decency and fairness to save their client, then that is what they will do.

I watched the tragedy unfold in front of me. The jury could not, like I had, sit in front of the alleged victim and the accused and listen as they told me their accounts at their own pace. Heather's powerful and unquestionably honest voice had been silenced, rendered unrecognisable by court procedure. Her account had been transformed, reformulated to fit within the relevant legal categories and to the general conventions of the courtroom.

This question-and-answer form of closed questioning is hard for many witnesses to cope with. It allows only a short time between the question and the yes–no answer before the next question is fired off, giving little opportunity for a witness to elaborate an answer.

This defence barrister had done it all before. As he stood, he looked hard at Heather as if he'd just seen something about her for the first time and checked his notes rather too theatrically, he started to obliterate her testimony with a series of yes–no questions. He was in control. He decided what they were going to talk about and how Heather would answer his questions.

Victims need to be able to tell the story of their abuse without interruption. Heather should have been free to tell her account in a way that was natural for her, free of intimidation by the defence. Instead, she was forced to listen passively as the barrister questioned her motives, her memory, her intelligence, morality, emotional control, reliability and her reason. He trapped her by cleverly steering her into inconsistency and contradiction, unpicking her testimony given under the direction of the prosecution barrister.

All the while her father, the innocent-faced, youthful eighty-year-old in the Marks & Spencer suit sat quietly, watching, knowing the truth but barely speaking one word of it. He had revealed nothing in the interview; he had stuck to the story that Heather was overzealous in her search for affection as a child. He 'admitted' that he probably failed to give her all the attention she needed, that her persistence had in fact made him more distant, and she had concocted this story of abuse to punish him.

The judge watched over his half-rimmed glasses, doing nothing to stop the onslaught from the defence. But why would he? Heather was an adult after all; we were all adults and we knew this was how trials operated. She had been prepared for the courtroom but once she was there, all of that work, all of that preparation went out of the window. It was totally understandable. But I am certain I was the only one who saw that Heather had regressed to her eight-year-old self.

With no supporting testimony from the family for either side it was a straightforward case of he-said-she-said. Her father was acquitted and left the court a free man.

I felt heartbroken for Heather but when I found her afterwards, nursing a coffee with two friends in a side room, she once again amazed me with her strength.

'I'm sorry,' I said.

'It's OK,' Heather replied, 'no need to apologise, you warned me it would be like that. I decided a long time ago that I was going to be a person who was going to talk, instead of being a person who kept secrets.'

She looked at her two friends. 'I no longer feel so different or alone thanks to my group.' She smiled and put on an overly happy TV-announcer-style voice: 'We're a beautiful, courageous bunch of women – and I'm proud to be one!' They laughed.

'Each time we talk about it, the distance increases a tiny bit between me and the pain I feel. After going through that experience' – Heather jerked her thumb in the direction of the courtroom – 'I don't think I could ever be hurt by this again. It hurt like hell being in there, however. For the first time in ages I felt scared, like a child. Good God, I can't believe I even talked like a child, at about the same volume. Still, now I really understand the phrase: "Speak the truth and the truth shall set you free."'

For Heather, being in a group with other survivors proved to be a powerful way to deal with the feelings of guilt and fear.

'When you're with other women and talk about the abuse and are not disgusted, and when you see those same women listen to your story with respect, you begin to see yourself as a proud survivor rather than as a conspiring victim.'

One of her friends jumped in. 'When eight people – who aren't family or counsellors – are telling you it's not your fault, it's very powerful!'

Heather was a strong, capable adult. Listening to her story

had been both a privilege and an honour. She had told her story bravely, adding her voice to the growing army of abused people who have spoken out in recent years in the hope that more victims would now feel able to come forward so that more people would be saved from the horrors they had endured.

The more people speak out, the better-protected society becomes. As Heather said: 'Secrecy is a prison. Going through this has been the hardest thing I've ever done in my life but at the same time it's been the most rewarding thing I've done since that day I was first abused. My father may have walked out of court a free man but I know that his sickness has held him prisoner all his life. Now he's frightened of me, frightened of the truth, of you and all this,' she said, looking around the room. 'He knows now that people are listening and are taking me seriously and you've helped me haul him before a court to stand and listen to what I have to say. Now that's a victory and a half.'

I left the court buoyed up by Heather's incredible attitude. She was so brave, a total inspiration.

I drove back to the station enthused and sat down determined to tackle my paperwork mountain once and for all. As soon as I'd picked up my pen, however, the fax machine started to grind away. I looked around. Everyone else was out or on the phone. I sighed, tore the sheet free, and started to read.

'Oh crap,' I said. 'Just when I thought I'd seen and done it all.'

CHAPTER TWENTY-TWO

CARAVAN OF COURAGE

Downham Road Social Services is right at the heart of Dalston. A flat-roofed, one-storey building with every window covered in steel mesh, it has all the atmosphere of a prisoner-of-war camp.

I struggled to find a parking space, checked I hadn't left anything in view that would tempt any of Hackney's heroin addicts and walked through the icy drizzle into the reception.

Behind the armoured-glass fronted counter, Joy gave me a lovely warm smile of recognition. 'Hi, Harry, how's things?' she asked.

'Oh you know,' I answered as I signed the register, 'Same old, same old. I'm here to pick up Claire.'

'I'll let her know, have a seat.'

In the public waiting area, two children played while their mother studied a form with a frown of concentration. They may have been sat on a threadbare carpet in a building that looked as if it had been made for a paramilitary organisation but they seemed very happy and totally focused on what they were doing. It was very pleasant to watch them, safe and enjoying life, as all children should.

Suddenly, the double doors crashed open, making us all look up. A woman pushing a rickety pushchair violently in front of her ploughed her way up to the reception and smashed it into the desk. Despite the protective glass, Joy shrank back from the window. The woman was tall and thin, had an ice-white complexion, long black hair, white trainers, tracksuit bottoms and yellow T-shirt. She had what some might call a certain 'heroin chic' look – except without any chic.

'I'm here to see Claire!' she yelled at Joy. 'Get her, will you?'

Damn, I thought. I could see our outing was about to be delayed. Claire, who was already on her way out to meet me, appeared a few seconds later, her hands raised in placation.

'Mary, I'm sorry but we can't authorise another emergency payment.'

'Don't fucking tell me that, who's gonna buy her food?' Mary banged the pushchair against the desk again. Nice. I could see a toddler was in there.

Claire spoke softly. 'Mary, I'm really sorry, but another one? No, you have to learn to manage your money.'

Bang went the pushchair, up against the desk. I caught a glimpse of the toddler's face. Her big brown eyes looked scared and stressed, in total contrast to the two others in the waiting area who'd been playing so happily.

'Don't give me that shit; I need the money for her, why won't you give me the fucking money? She needs it, not me. Gimme the fucking money!'

OK, enough's enough. As I got up and started walking over to them, Mary looked at me, smelled copper and wheeled the buggy around towards the exit.

'I just want to feed my kid, that's all, you bitch. Call yourself a social worker, you're a fucking bitch.'

With that she clattered the buggy, which had all the manoeuvrability of a battered shopping trolley, through the double doors. Everyone breathed a sign of relief as they banged behind her.

'Hi, Harry, sorry about that,' Claire said.

I looked through the window and saw Mary angrily waggling the pushchair down the steps and onto the wet pavement. I smiled a greeting at Claire, but my thoughts were with the two-year-old being bashed about in that pushchair.

She would feel the stress of her mother's life. The shouting, the anxiety, the chaos. Mum was on heroin for sure, but 15,000 people in Hackney take hard drugs and as much as we'd love to make them all safe, there was no way we could take all their kids. We were letting them down, simply thanks to the sheer volume of numbers.

I thought about her future. She would watch the inevitable giant TV and see the lives of celebrities unfold before her, in stark contrast to her own. At school she would hear her classmates talk about their stable existences, something that she could only dream of. That innocent look in her beautiful young eyes made me want to step in right at that moment and pull her free from her chaotic upbringing. It was always fatal; making eye contact with children in need always sent waves of pity, even guilt at my inaction, crashing over me. But there was nothing I could do. Her mother's behaviour, although unpleasant, was not nearly enough to separate her from her daughter.

The daughter would have to fight for herself when she was old enough, and in a way I expect she already was, learning to cope without her mother's full attention. I also knew that her chances were not good and I could see her stepping into her mother's shoes in about fifteen years' time, part of the vicious unbroken cycle of drugs, poverty and the overriding sense of hopelessness.

Mary hit the pavement and charged off down the road, back into her chaotic world.

'My car is this way,' I said.

'I saw the look in your eye there, Harry,' Claire said. 'And you can forget it. Mary's been on our books all her life, on heroin since she was fourteen, sexually abused by her mother's boyfriend. I hope by keeping an eye on her the same might not happen to her daughter but I don't know. Heroin is one of our toughest enemies.'

Kids love to copy adults and some become drug addicts just so that they can bond with their parents over the drug they love more than their own children. I'd seen it myself, some youngsters playing with or even trying Mummy or Daddy's stash before they were old enough to even know that it was wrong, that Mummy or Daddy had been breaking the law.

We climbed into my car and began the slow crawl through the lunchtime traffic to a visit. This one was another first for me. I had no idea what we were going to achieve today, as we were about to step into the very private world of the travelling community. A fourteen-year-old girl, Roslyn, had been allowed to sleep in the same bed as her seventeen-year-old boyfriend – a crime in the eyes of the law.

After the fax came in I'd sought Rob's advice. I caught him at lunch in our favourite Turkish cafe; he pushed his spectacles back on his head and folded his newspaper as I pulled up a chair opposite him.

'It'll have to be a surprise visit,' I told him, spooning sugar in my coffee, 'as there's no phone number for the family and I have no idea when she'll be in. She doesn't go to school.'

Like all cops, I had a healthy concern about the travelling community and I told Rob as much, adding that I'd like to see their way of life over and done with. When I was a young constable I'd seen the results of their rip-off handiwork when they charmed gullible old people out of their savings. They'd offer to tarmac their drives, explaining that they'd been on another job and had overestimated the amount of materials they'd need and had loads of tarmac left. All it would cost them would be £20.

They would then cover the driveway with watered-down tar, which looked good, but which would soon be washed away the next time it rained. Once their hapless victim came out to admire their new drive, the conmen hit them with the fact that it was actually £20 per square foot. 'You must have misheard me,' they'd say before escorting their victim to the bank to cough up a good few hundred pounds or worse.

There was an endless list of other cons involving tiling, carpets, double-glazing and so on. Add to that the shoplifting, the lack of education, the inter-breeding and their immoral way of life, well, they hardly seemed to do anything for the country.

Rob sighed in exasperation. 'Have you learned nothing?'

'What do you mean?' I asked, puzzled.

'The travelling community are just that, a community. They have their own values, beliefs and ways. You can't force "normal" values on them; it's just not possible. Besides, in this job, unless you can think like them, you'll fail. To succeed you have to listen to the community you're investigating. You may not like their culture or the crime, but you have to remember, they have children. Therefore you must communicate and educate, not clump through their world in your size tens dictating this, that and the other.'

I wasn't so sure about this. I wanted to tame the travellers. How could we let a fourteen-year-old girl live in a caravan with her boyfriend right under her parents' noses? This had to stop.

'Harry, listen to me,' Rob said. 'You must tread carefully. You must exploit any communication. Talk to them; engage. Unless you put any prejudice about their lifestyle behind you, you will fail. This is about the child and making her life better, nothing else.'

As Claire and I approached the camp, I frowned as I saw a large number of caravans and trailers of varying sizes, shapes and states huddled together under a section of elevated road.

What a truly grim existence, I thought.

My views about the travellers were immediately reinforced as I slowly drove through a gap in the chain-link fence surrounding the site. I watched as a large, ruddy-faced woman hitched up her skirt, squatted and defecated right by the fence.

Rob's advice went straight to the back of my mind. I didn't point this woman out to Claire, my disgust was off the scale. I was glad I'd told Hackney's control room where we were going; although if we did get into trouble then all we could do was run. I noted that Claire was in her flat shoes. Good.

I felt like we'd stepped into another world. As I locked the car door, I looked across the site and stopped dead.

Seeing my stunned expression, Claire turned to look. 'Oh my God,' she gasped.

A young girl of about nine was standing on the other side of the fence, leaning up against it, her fingers hooked through its links. Her face was terribly deformed, the result, I guessed, of a union between sister and brother. Her appearance shocked me so much that I couldn't breathe. Her oversized skull was misshapen, there were bony lumps over her eyebrows, her eyes were buried deep in their sockets and she drooled from a crooked mouth that could never close.

I tried to get hold of myself. A wave of guilt hit me. This was a child. A child with the same hopes and dreams as any other. Whatever the circumstances of her conception were, this was a little girl. As I tried to regain my composure, thoughts flashed through my mind of how she must dream like any other little girl of Prince Charming, ponies and sandy beach holidays. She had just as much right to these innocent aspirations as any middle-class child prancing around her Hertfordshire paddock on her pony. But so many wonderful things were so far from her reach. A child's situation does not dampen their dreams, just their chances of ever seeing them realised.

No doubt I'd reacted in the same way as most people and I was cross with myself. I smiled, too late, and waved a hello. She smiled and waved back. What had she to look forward to in life? A woman in her thirties came around the side of a nearby trailer and grabbed the girl, leading her away while scowling at me. Perhaps she had all she needed here, I thought, a loving family, a community that accepted her for what she was and made her one of their own.

This upset me quite a bit more than usual. Cops are often fixers of difficult situations. A kid gets run over on a crossing and the driver fails to stop, we preserve evidence and go after the driver. Our energy is channelled by the hunt to solve any crime from a murder to a drug deal; we simply go after the bad guys. With this little girl, there was no 'going after'. I felt a tremendous sense of helplessness.

As she walked away she looked over her shoulder at me and smiled again. This had a profound effect upon me. All I could do was stand there uselessly, hoping that some of her dreams would one day come true.

Still angry with myself for my reaction, I walked with Claire up to the nearest trailer. I was about to knock when a voice said: 'What do youse two cunts want, then?'

I knew that travellers – especially their kids – used swear words a lot more liberally than most people but it was still a bit of a shock to hear this word uttered in the high-pitched squeak of a boy whose voice was just breaking.

'We're looking for Roslyn,' I said. 'Which one is hers?'

The boy pointed to a large grey trailer on the other side of the site. 'Thanks,' I said.

'Piss off, copper,' he said with a cheeky grin.

I hadn't told him but he could smell police a mile off.

We were eyed with silent suspicion by the adults while the kids of the camp took great delight in a bit of sportsmanlike name-calling as we made our way over to the trailer.

I knocked and the door opened. It wasn't locked.

'Hello?' I called. 'Detective Sergeant Harry Keeble. I'm here with Claire from social services about Roslyn.'

'Right, youse better come in then.' Stood in the doorway in a vision of brightly coloured designer rip-off clothing (given away by the large 'United Colours of Bennytton' logo) was Roslyn's mother. Her bleached blonde hair was piled high in a cross between a bird's nest and a beehive. A king-size cigarette dangled from the corner of her mouth and she spoke at full volume, as if we were deaf.

'Hello, Molly,' Claire said. 'How's things?'

'It's all arseholes at the minute, my love,' she said in a strong Irish accent, 'but come in quick, for goodness sakes before those fucking kids have youse for breakfast.' She leaned past us and screeched at one of the many kids who'd followed us to the door. 'Terry, fuck off you little rat's cunt, leave the nice people alone!'

She climbed in after us and put on her best speaking voice. 'Sorry about that, now what can I do for you?'

Being six foot five I was stood with my neck bent against the ceiling. 'Mind if I sit down?'

Judging by the amount of stuff, I guessed that the large trailer was full of knocked-off gear. There were fag cartons, saucepans in their packing, piles of DVDs, etc. I tried not to look too closely; that wasn't what we were here for. Even so, I had an inkling that Molly's husband was hiding in the large wardrobe in the middle of the room we were in, thinking that we'd come for him. I was sure I heard a couple of muffled coughs coming from it.

Claire began, outlining their previous meeting, the site, Molly's life and family. Molly chain-smoked the whole time, filling the trailer with a fog of nicotine.

As soon as we got to the point of our visit, Molly surprised me by opening up straight away.

'Yeah, I know Roslyn is sleeping with her boyfriend every

night.' She shrugged her shoulders. 'It ain't right but what can I do? Rozzy's a young woman already. Kids grow up fast here, you know? We're tough and headstrong and don't like to be told nuffink. She's on the pill, that's all I'm worried about. She ain't ready for a young 'un yet. Look, I don't know how much you know about our community but our girls usually marry young, about sixteen to eighteen, and start courting at fourteen. Rozzie's a bit ahead of the game but they're going to marry, you know.'

Claire nodded. 'Can we speak to Roslyn?' she asked.

'I'll get her,' Molly said. Without moving she took a deep breath and yelled at the top of her voice: 'ROZZIE!'

'WHAT?' came the reply from somewhere deep within the trailer.

'GET YOUR ARSE OUT 'ERE, NOW!'

Roslyn emerged from the back and sat down with us in the cloud of smoke. She was tall for her age and slim. She wore black leggings, a large baggy T-shirt and her long dark hair hung open. As she sat down, she reached for a cigarette from her mum's packet but Molly slapped her hand away.

'Tommy and me are in love,' she told us. 'I want to share his bed with him but I don't want to get pregnant just yet. We're careful.'

Roslyn quickly shattered my preconceptions; she was intelligent and alert and was happy to talk to us. There was something refreshing about her attitude and her willingness to debate the issue with us sensibly – and this was despite a severe lack of a traditional education.

All my thoughts of threats of police protection orders were soon put to one side as Roslyn mentioned there was no such thing as 'underage sex' in Spain and that there this would not be an issue. I was impressed. I certainly hadn't expected to be lectured on European law. Roslyn was clearly mature enough to make the right decision; we just had to be sure she was going to make it.

'I understand what you're trying to tell us but UK law is very clear and whatever the case in other countries, despite the fact that you love each other and are trying to go about this sensibly, I have to enforce the law.'

'I understand,' Roslyn said.

I was amazed as we quickly reached an agreement. Tommy would no longer stay the night and she would go back to school.

'You can trust Rozzie,' Molly said. 'She ain't one for the fob-off. If she says it, she means it.'

'You got it, Ma,' Roslyn said.

'Of course, no one else here of Rozzie's age is at school,' Molly said as she showed us out.

'Why not?' I asked.

''Cos they's fulla Gorgia.* But we'll see. Maybe she'll see it through. She got nothing else to do till she gets married anyways. Cheerio then.'

The trailer door slammed in our faces.

'Well, that went a bit different than expected,' I said.

'They're a nice family,' Claire said with a smile. 'Rough as hell but nice.'

I was certain I could hear a gruff male voice coming from inside the trailer, arguing with Molly. Had I been right? Had her husband been hiding from us in the wardrobe?

Of course Rob had been right; I knew he'd give me that 'I told you so' look over his glasses when I next spoke to him. I should have known better; this was a community, just like any other, it had its quirks (although I still believed that those quirks included a lot of criminal behaviour) and traditions which I, as a white male cop who lived in Hertfordshire, found hard to understand.

---

* Gorgia is the catchall term for non-travellers.

While I thought there was still much that was wrong with their way of life, it was something they had been born into and that was Rob's point, these kids would lead the travelling community in the future. It was our duty to create stable relationships with people living on the edge of society if we were ever going to understand them and coexist peacefully and lawfully.

By engaging with people like Mary the heroin addict, social services were improving the chances of her two-year-old daughter having a brighter future but the challenge was an extremely difficult one. Dealing with Roslyn in a calm and considered manner was another small step forwards. Claire would re-visit the site to make sure Roslyn had stayed true to her word and would use the visits to build a useful relationship with a normally impossible to reach group of people. She would perhaps eventually connect with other children that needed our help. That, of course, was what it was all about.

CHAPTER TWENTY-THREE

NOT THAT INNOCENT

I sat bolt upright in bed, sweating. I looked at the bedside clock. 3 a.m. My heart was pounding. Mary's pushchair had been banging over and over against the doors to the police station in my nightmare.

Should I have intervened? Should I have taken her? At 3 a.m. it's easy to let worry overtake you. What would happen to the little girl if her mum overdosed in the night? She was only two. When would she be found? How long before the neighbour called the police? I'd once kicked the door in on a Hackney council flat when I was a young PC after a neighbour reported that he hadn't seen the old man who lived there for three days. I held my breath as I entered the flat, dreading what I was about to see; you always hear so many horror stories from the older cops of maggots and exploding corpses (due to a build-up of gas). He was naked on the kitchen floor, covered in his own excrement, and he nearly gave me a heart attack when he suddenly moved. Would that little girl end up waiting three days for us to come looking? I looked back at the clock. Enough was enough. I had to be up in two hours; unless I stopped my runaway train of macabre thought, I was going to be awake until dawn.

At 10 a.m. that morning, trying to swallow a massive yawn, I walked into the little room at the side of the station office to find my suspect, Andrei, a Polish man in his late sixties, trembling with fear. He was dressed in an open-necked shirt and jeans.

'Now what's this all about?' he asked, pale-faced and clearly panicked. His solicitor stood by him, briefcase in hand.

'Your granddaughter, Nadia, has alleged you indecently assaulted her,' I said.

He buckled at the knees; his solicitor grabbed his elbow.

'You OK?' the solicitor asked.

Andrei, nodded.

After I'd formally arrested him he whispered, 'It's not true', and I escorted him through to the custody suite where Craig joined us.

It was what we call a 'minor' indecent assault. 'Minor' is a police term; no indecent assault is ever 'minor', it just helps us to categorise crimes when we process them. It's not something we say to a suspect or victim, that the assault was 'minor'.

I leaned over and pressed play on the tape recorder. The machine buzzed loud and clear, signalling its activation. Andrei flinched. I began the introductions, just like I'd done a hundred times before.

Andrei was attentive; he leaned forward, his hands clasped in front of him on the table. His solicitor, reserved and professional, rattled off his details.

'Do you understand why you've been arrested?'

Andrei nodded.

'You need to speak for the machine.'

'Y-yes. Yes I do.' His voice shook.

'You've been arrested on suspicion of indecently assaulting Nadia.'

Andrei winced at the sound of her name. I started to talk about his upbringing, going through all the characters that made up his family until we came full circle, back to his granddaughter.

Craig had already interviewed Nadia, who had just turned fifteen. She'd made it very clear that she didn't want to take the matter any further. As usual we kept investigating in case there were other children at risk or other victims waiting to be discovered. We also needed to know if Andrei was a risk to others or not. If we could prove he was, then we could put him on the sex offenders' register. I wasn't sure; Andrei was squeaky clean with no previous, a model citizen. Or was he?

On the other hand, social services had a record on Nadia. Her childhood had been troubled; her mother had been cautioned for neglect several years earlier. Nadia had fled the family home on a couple of occasions, both times staying away overnight before she was found.

The alleged incident had taken place in Andrei's car as he drove Nadia back from the cinema. I asked Andrei to describe the evening.

He took a deep breath and started to tell us. As he spoke, he occasionally closed his eyes, as if in deep thought, conscientiously making sure he got the details exactly right. He corrected himself a couple of times and was serious, purposeful. I noted that his eye contact was good; it came and went as he searched his memory, which was perfectly normal.

'Do you want to know the route we took?' he asked.

'No, that won't be necessary, thank you.'

He was being helpful, extremely helpful in fact.

In essence, he'd picked his granddaughter up, taken her to see *High School Musical*, bought her a Coke and popcorn and sat through a film he didn't enjoy. After the film, he'd taken her home, by the same route.

This was where I slowly took him through the allegation. As

soon as I started I saw his face redden; tears started to well and he struggled to control his voice. He was still trying to work with me however. This made a huge impression on me and I tried to resist the urge to react to it, to tell him that it was OK, that he was doing really well – and that I believed him.

Normally when interviewing paedophiles and men who had slept with teenagers I got one of two basic reactions:

1. Avoidance. The unemotional, emphatic denier or non-com.
2. Enjoyment. Those who get pleasure from discussing the allegation.

Andrei was either a bloody good actor or genuinely distressed. I ploughed on. Paedophiles are clever, they can manipulate. 'Was this happening to me?' I wondered.

'She alleges that you stopped the car and grabbed her breasts,' I said, finally getting to the key moment.

'It never happened,' he said, tears running down his cheeks. 'I can't understand why Nadia would say such a thing. I love her very much, I would never, ever do something like that.'

I waited for a moment after he finished, waiting for him to take the obvious line but he didn't. This would be to say that Nadia was 'troubled' and had made the allegations up. He knew she had had a difficult childhood; that her mum had been in trouble and that Nadia had run away from home, but he wouldn't use this against her to get himself off the hook. He was prepared to let me do my own homework to find this out.

I also took this to be a sign of loyalty towards his granddaughter. He wasn't going to 'shop' her, no matter what the situation. As far as Andrei was concerned, she was above criticism.

As the interview continued, I found myself really struggling to stay objective and I was relieved when I wrapped things up and gave Andrei a date to come back.

As Craig and I strolled to the canteen for a caffeine hit, I ran back over the interview in my mind. I'd previously heard of one case where a father had begun the sexual abuse of his twelve-year-old daughter in a similar manner to Nadia's allegation, turning a corner a bit too fast so he could excuse the brushing of his hand over her breasts. But I simply didn't feel like this was something Andrei was capable of.

I felt extremely comfortable with Craig; although we often had different views we shared the same passion for child protection. And although I was his boss, I sought his counsel on many occasions. Rank makes you accountable, but it doesn't make you right.

'Well,' I said to Craig when I sat down with our coffees, 'what do you think?'

His reply came without hesitation. 'Innocent, no doubt about it.'

Andrei's interview had left a deep impression on both of us and it seemed clear-cut. The suspect, who had a clean record, had given a clear in-depth account of the evening, in contrast to our victim with the troubled past. Of course, Nadia was just the sort of child that a paedophile would go for – an unreliable witness known for making false allegations.

Whatever our views, we had to run the case by the Crown Prosecution Service but as I passed on the case, which I felt weighed heavily in Andrei's favour, I felt uncomfortable, as if I was betraying my 'victim'. These sorts of jobs can gnaw away at you and make you wonder over and over if there was anything obvious that had been missed, whether you could have spent more time looking for evidence, but of course the fax machine was still grinding away and more urgent cases that wouldn't wait spooled onto my desk.

As it turned out, this case would come back to haunt us all.

CHAPTER TWENTY-FOUR

THE HAUNTING

'Please help me, my daughter is in danger. Her dad's just driven off with her and he's abusing her now. She's only thirteen, please help!'

The 999 operator at the Central Communications Complex in Hendon calmly began to set the wheels in motion. The desperate voice gave her number. The operator radiated reassurance; help would be there soon.

Emergency operators can never predict what they're about to hear next, from a cat stuck up a tree to a child rapist caught in the act, every imaginable human tragedy and more besides. Then, just when they'd thought they'd heard it all, another new drama arrived. It's a tough job, every word, every second counts as response times can make the difference between life and death, but it's not easy getting the right information from a frightened and distressed caller who hardly knows what they're saying, thanks to the shock. People who abuse this system simply don't receive the sanctions they deserve.

The caller's details were taken, then the name of the father, the car's make, colour and registration number. The call was fired out, responding units 'shouted up' as they began the hunt. A child in immediate danger really gets cops' blood pumping.

When I pulled the urgent referral off the fax a short while later, I sighed.

'Oh, for God's sake, not again,' I groaned. 'That's the third time this month!'

'Mad Margaret, is it?' Clara said.

'Yeah,' I replied, before adding with sarcasm: 'How did you guess?'

'You know the rules, Harry. Your fingers touched the fax first so it's all yours. At least you know the routine.'

I was truly sick of this. Back in the 1970s we would have just ignored Margaret's allegation and notified the mental health team. But now she took up valuable resources as we played hunt the paedophile for a paedophile that did not exist. She rang a short while later, demanding action to 'safeguard her child'. I went through the motions, but not for long; I knew I was wasting my time.

I spoke to her daughter Sandra at home where she lived with her father, a good-sized terraced house not far from Broadway Market, which, after a decade or three of being a total dump, had suddenly been trendified overnight by young up-and-comers spreading out from the hip areas of Shoreditch.

I rang the doorbell and rubbed my hands together. The season's first frost had coated everything in ice.

Sandra reacted to my badge with a shrug and invited me in. She'd been through it all before and knew the routine. Various injunctions had come and gone to try to stop the torrent of unfounded allegations from her mother, but to little avail. Sandra was a precocious teenager, smart and into the world of romantic vampires, a good way of escaping the trials of her everyday life. She was dressed in black, had made herself up to look suitably pale with dark ringed, shadowy eyes.

'Dad won the custody battle fair and square,' she said. 'Mum's mental issues won't go away though, you know? Mum's really been trying to make Dad suffer, especially since he started going out with Amy.'

'Is your dad in?'

'He'll back in a minute, he's just dropping off Amy at work.'

'Is Amy your stepmum?'

'That's a good question,' Sandra replied in a tone of mock seriousness. 'Amy's very "hot", closer to my age than my dad's, immature but gorgeous, much better-looking than me. Honestly, I don't know if she's supposed to be my stepmum or my older sister.'

'How's your mum?' I asked.

'Mental.'

Seeing my shocked expression, Sandra laughed. 'I'm joking. She's not that great to be honest. Look, I'm so sorry about this, you must hate me. You've got other, more important cases to see to, haven't you? You should go, there's nothing for you to worry about here.'

A wave of guilt washed over me. I was a cold-hearted bastard. Sandra needed our attention just as much as the next child. Her emotions were being yanked about all over the place at this traumatic time, just as she was entering the rollercoaster ride of adolescence. Somewhere under her vampire disguise was a confused and lonely little girl, trying to understand why her family had fallen apart. This was another instance where our job crossed the line of social services.

'I've definitely got time for a cup of tea,' I said, looking towards the kitchen. As Sandra put the kettle on, I settled down to talk, properly, just for a little while; enough time for Sandra to offload a little.

'It's better that Mum and Dad aren't together; the rows were terrible, particularly when Mum had a manic episode, which happened whenever she laid eyes on Dad. It was scary, but I miss her. I wish she was well, so very much. She's all alone now and won't find anyone else, she's too difficult. The doctors can't fix her. The drugs don't work.'

'What happened this time?'

'I'd been staying with her for the day but it was really hard to get through to her, to talk. Sometimes she looks straight through me, you know? Whenever it's time for Dad to pick me up she just flips. She started by sulking when I said goodbye. I tried to peck her on the cheek but she stood there, all cold with her arms crossed. It was horrible. Then Dad is all stressed in the car, he can't wait to get away and he doesn't want to talk about it. You should see her when she does catch sight of him; he's pretty much the ultimate trigger to send her into a manic episode. I don't know why. I love him too. He's not perfect but he's a good dad, you know?'

For thirteen, Sandra was an amazingly mature young woman. The easy solution would be for me to step in and end the visits but there was no way Sandra wanted that. No cop should stand in her way, especially if all it means is a mountain of paperwork, a thousand or so boxes to be ticked and crossed as we put the reports through as a 'no crime'. This was all I had to do to support Sandra.

Of course, a serious problem could conceivably arise one day if her mum made an allegation that turned out to be true. The hindsight police would pull us to pieces. We would always respond, if only for that reason. Many would see this as a drain on our resources, but if it helped Sandra, then maybe that was a price worth paying.

Next time the fax rolled off the machine with Sandra's name on it, I was determined to make sure I was the one who tore it free. I was rapidly learning that so much good can be done in this job by building relationships, but by the very nature of the work, which made us jump from case to case, it was rare for us to get the chance.

Just as I was finishing up with Sandra, her dad walked in. He was a youthful-looking forty, trendily dressed and friendly. After shaking my hand, he said: 'I hope that's not your car I've just seen being towed outside. Parking's a nightmare round here.'

'Oh no!' I ran outside to check and sure enough, it wasn't my lucky day. Parking can be a real hassle in an unmarked police vehicle. I couldn't care less about parking tickets but getting clamped and towed really screws up your day. I'd been parked in a 'residents only' bay.

I made my way over to the pound. You have to be a brave person to work here. In front of me in the queue of outraged car owners was a young black man, effing and blinding at the bloke behind the counter. He was so agitated I could barely understand him but I could tell he was throwing quite a few accusations at the towing company about the damage to his souped-up Golf with special chrome hubcaps and tailfins.

There were two ways of dealing with this. One was to show my warrant card and say 'I'm a policeman, stop shouting and swearing or you're under arrest', but I didn't fancy risking a roll around on the dirty floor.

Instead, I crossed my fingers that option two would work. I put my hand firmly on his shoulder (risky, I know) and said: 'Listen, mate, I'm a police officer and I have come here to pick up my police car, how do you think I feel?' The man grinned at me and stopped his tantrum. Now at least he had a good story to tell about the copper who got his car clamped. He still muttered as he handed over his hard-earned cash to get his car back but at least the queue could at last move forward again.

Soon I was back in my car and on the phone. It was Clara. 'I've got some bad news, Harry,' she said grimly. 'I thought I'd better let you know.'

Oh God, what now?

'You remember Andrei?'

'Yeah, of course.'

'He's dead. His wife is blaming the granddaughter.'

'Not suicide, surely?'

'No, it was a heart attack but the wife said he might as well have killed himself.'

Good God. It had been a few weeks since we'd interviewed Andrei and the CPS had cleared him. He was clearly innocent in the eyes of the law. It turned out that while we'd forgotten the case and put it behind us, things had turned out rather differently for Andrei.

His wife said that several members of his own family had disowned him and only his daughters' insistence that he was innocent, and that Nadia had made it up, saved his other kids from having nothing to do with him. Andrei had been due to retire but somehow they found out and he was asked to leave early with no party, no goodbye, just clear your desk and leave. He had collapsed at home. Shortly after he arrived at the hospital he had a massive and fatal heart attack.

It wasn't as if word had got out that he was being investigated for abusing his granddaughter and the local community had decided to take matters into their own hands. Bricks hadn't gone through his front window, his car hadn't been vandalised, people hadn't yelled 'Paedo!' whenever they saw him in the street.

Why hadn't he thought to come to us about this? Did he think we would make things even worse if we got involved? I couldn't understand it. We could have helped him explain things to his family. Perhaps he hoped that being cleared would be enough. Obviously it hadn't. Some members of his family had made up their minds and assumed that being cleared was simply a sign of a lack of evidence, not innocence.

His wife was determined to have the funeral cortège pass by

the estate where his granddaughter lived. She wanted Nadia to see the consequences of her allegations. If it had I think we may have ended up with a riot and I didn't think Nadia, who was already guilt-ridden, was going to benefit from such a gesture, but luckily it never happened.

But I could well understand Andrei's wife's anger. Should there be more done to protect people accused of child abuse? I wasn't sure. We'd sometimes sent men home who we were sure were guilty of child abuse on a 'never to return' and they'd practically begged us to lock them up to keep them safe from the community that was up in arms. Usually we didn't pay too much attention to their complaints, at least not until a crime was committed – after all, in the eyes of the law they were as deserving as the next person of our attention.

Andrei should never have suffered as he did. What happened to him was not only a sign of people's strength of feeling and ignorance with regard to child abuse, no matter how 'minor' or spurious the allegation, it also showed us that we need to do what we can to protect the accused until they're proven guilty. Andrei had needed the help of the police and social services but he either hadn't thought to ask for it or simply didn't want to. Perhaps he didn't believe we would help him, or thought that we thought he deserved what he got. It's a sad fact that we will never know.

CHAPTER TWENTY-FIVE

YOU CAN'T ALWAYS GET WHAT YOU WANT

It's hard, I thought as I looked at Alan, to stay in control sometimes.

He was stood in the entranceway to his sister's flat, exactly where I'd been hoping to catch him. Alan was short and stocky, and looked like he'd be able to handle himself in a fight. His fat, bulging forearms were covered in badly drawn tattoos. All that was missing was the matching pit-bull accessory. He was the definition of a thug, the perfect realisation of an ugly stereotype.

Alan was clearly used to getting into rucks, the sort of ape-like fights that football hooligans seem to enjoy, the kind that involves a lot of arm waving and shouting at the enemy like baboons before throwing a few punches and kicks and then down the pub for lager and slaps on the back all round. Yes, Alan was a man who could throw a punch and follow it through. I knew this for a fact; he'd done exactly that to his son Joel, aged four.

I couldn't disguise my contempt. He was pathetic, a coward, a child abuser. I almost wanted him to resist arrest so I'd have to subdue him.

*

I'd interviewed four-year-old Joel that morning. Four years old is about as young as we can go in terms of getting a useable statement from a memorandum interview.

Mandy, Joel's mum, had been too scared to give evidence about her own beatings by the fists of Alan her 'boyfriend' (their relationship was more like client and prostitute) but at least she gave us a statement about Alan hitting Joel. 'It's one thing to hit me,' Mandy said through a cloud of cigarette smoke, tears streaming down her cheeks, 'but hitting my little boy like that is something else.'

Despite this, she'd left it long enough for Joel's injuries to heal before telling us. Still, Joel painted a very clear picture of his sad little life for us during the interview. He spoke clearly and honestly, as only a child can. Kids are free of all the verbal tricks and turns of phrase that adults use. They just tell it how it is, no matter how bad.

'When Daddy comes home I run to my room.'

'What do you do in your room?'

'I hide under my bed, listening.'

'And what does Mummy do?'

'Gets hurt by Daddy. I told her to hide too but she lets him in.'

'What can you hear?'

'The punch.' Joel clapped his hands together. 'Like that.'

'You hear Daddy hitting Mummy?'

'Yes. And shouting.'

While Joel stayed hidden under his bed, crying and alone, Alan, who usually visited Mandy when he was drunk (which was often), had sex with her and then usually beat her to a pulp, perhaps throwing her a tenner as child support for Joel.

Afterwards, when Alan had left, it was Joel who would comfort his mum.

'What did he hit you with?'

Joel made fists and held up his hands.

'He hit you with his fists?'

'Yeah. Really hard. I fell over.'

All this drink-fuelled violence was affecting Joel. He understood in his own way what 'drunk' was. It was a time not to be around, a time to hide.

Whenever his dad found him during these drunken episodes and he was in a good mood, he'd force Joel to bare-knuckle box with him, calling him his 'little fighter', wanting him to take after his dad. In the 'boxing matches' that followed, Alan would punch Joel harder and harder to build up his resistance to pain.

Joel was extremely worried about his mum. We all have worries in our lives, but imagine being four and worried that you or your mum is going to get punched again and you've no way of preventing it. Now that's a serious worry, a huge amount of stress. No childhood should include that kind of fear.

He really loved his mother and wanted to stay with her. She was obviously a victim as well as Joel but this was going to be tricky. We needed to make Joel's environment safe and that would usually mean splitting the family, but in this instance if we were going to keep Joel with his mum then we were going to have to find a way of keeping the dad away from the family home. Once Alan had a few beers inside him and was feeling horny again, I doubted whether any injunctions would put him off.

I tracked Alan down to his sister's flat in a low-rise council block, where he was sleeping on the sofa. He was out. At work, she said.

His sister kicked off the moment I put the allegations to her. She was the spitting image of her brother, the same ugly face creased with lines of bitterness. I suspected they'd had a crap upbringing but it really was impossible to feel any sympathy for them.

'What the fuck you sayin'?' she spat. 'Alan ain't done nuffink.

Youse just picking on 'im. She put youse up to it, dint she? That evil witch of a girlfren'. She ain't even fit to lick the ground Alan walks on.'

I wasn't able to rationalise with her, it really was like trying to get a raging pit bull to sit up and beg. I did make a mental note, however, of her vicious attitude and of the fact that she had kids of her own, young kids of Joel's age that Alan had access to. As soon as I got out of there I'd alert social services to her attitude and to my doubts as to whether she would be able to protect her children from Alan's violent urges.

It was always shocking to hear a mother offering such blind support to someone in circumstances such as these, even if that someone was her brother. Allegations like this need to be taken seriously and discussed rationally. Cops are used to family loyalties when shoplifting or burglary is involved but not when someone is accused of beating up a four-year-old child.

Just then Alan rocked up. He was similarly dismissive of all of the allegations.

'I don't know what 'er problem is. I provide for 'em, don't I?' he said, sticking out his pompous round chest. 'No son of mine will go short.

'I weren't even there, were I, sis?' he added, turning his head towards the kitchen where his sister was boiling something in a pan. 'I was 'ere wiv ya, weren't I?'

'Damn right.'

'I haven't even said when this was.'

'Tell me when and I bet I was here. Look, mate, no one is gonna stop me from seeing my boy. No one, all right? I'd never 'arm an 'air on 'is 'ead and I don't smack women, OK?'

He had a low brow. I seriously began to wonder whether he was missing a part of his frontal cortex, the part that allows us to reason and argue coherently with others.

Maybe I couldn't hit him but I could nick him, so I did, and despite a great deal of indignation, he came 'quietly'. Alan was soon bailed, however, and there was nowhere else for the investigation to go. It was yet another hopeless case of 'he-says-she-says'. Mandy, who was clearly terrified of what Alan might do to her, didn't want to take it any further, and of course Joel sided with what his mum wanted out of fear. But in Child Protection we don't stop there. In this case it was intervention time. She had to choose: Joel or Alan?

Dev was put onto the case and he soon called me. 'Sorry, Harry. This is a bad one, I'm afraid. Mandy's covered in bruises. She won't stop him, she's too scared and all the injunctions on planet earth won't bring Alan to a halt if she's not prepared to work with us. We have to protect Joel now. Trust me, it won't be long before something far worse happens.'

That was it then. There was no way we could risk Alan belting little Joel in the head when he was drunk, so as soon as I could I drove down to Mandy's flat with Dev and we took the little boy into our protection.

Mandy screamed in torment once we told her what we were there for.

'NO!' she screamed, doubling over in mental agony.

'I'm sorry, Mandy, but you've given us no choice,' I said. 'We have to protect Joel from Alan.'

'At the moment this is the best option,' Dev said. 'It is not ideal but at least Joel will be safe.'

Joel started to scream as we took him away. 'Mummy!' he cried, panicked further by his mum's screams.

'JOEL! No! Mummy loves you, Joel, never forget that!'

Joel wept quietly all the way to the emergency foster carer.

'She's one of the best, is that foster carer,' Dev said reassuringly. 'She'll spend a great deal of time loving Joel, don't you worry.'

I nodded, saying nothing, staying tight-lipped.

Not everybody wants what's best for them. But now Mandy had suffered a hard lesson. If she wanted her little boy back as much as he wanted to be with her, then she was going to have to help us deal with Alan.

The wait was long and fruitless. Today, little Joel is somewhere deep within the care system and every day he moves further away from his mother.

I hated it when this happened. It felt so wasteful, so hopeless.

And then Craig called. I told him what had happened.

'Looks like you're having one of those days, Harry. Sorry, old boy, but I've got another one for you.'

'Can't it wait? I've just put a mother and child through the worst day of their lives.'

'Sorry, mate, no can do. We're short-staffed as ever and Rob said you have to take it; he said it sounded like this one could use your delicate negotiating skills.'

I smiled ruefully. Terrific. It sounded like Rob was testing me with a tricky one, a case that we would go over together later to see how well I'd coped.

'What is it?'

'It's a bit delicate,' Craig said, 'so tread carefully, won't you?'

CHAPTER TWENTY-SIX

THE NIGHTMARES OF MY FATHER

The man's eyes were wild with rage. 'What have you done with my daughter?' he yelled in a powerful West African accent. Beads of sweat lined his forehead as he struggled to his feet and tried to take a step towards me; his anger had made him forget his crutches. He staggered as he leaned across to get them, wincing in pain. Groaning as he straightened up, he then looked me hard in the eye.

This wasn't going nearly as well as I'd hoped but as I stared into his face, which was heavily wrought by anger and physical pain, I didn't feel as if I were actually about to be attacked. The man, who was called Moses and whom I judged to be in his early forties, simply wanted to express his anger and frustration. I was a trespasser both in his sparsely furnished flat and in his private life; I, a pawn of the state with too much power, had intruded into his home only to criticise his fatherhood, something he saw as grossly unfair and inappropriate.

'Please, calm down,' I urged, placing my hand on Moses' left arm and looking him in the eyes. This was not the heavy and restraining 'you're nicked, sunshine' hand but the 'it's going to be

OK, trust me' hand. His eyes, which still bored into me, softened ever so slightly.

I withdrew my hand and, to my relief, he sat down. But let's see how the next part goes first before patting myself on the back, I thought to myself. I'd earned his tolerance, not his respect. I'd managed to keep my voice level, relying on reassurance and gentle communication as opposed to shouting and screaming. Ninety-nine per cent of the time, this job is about restraint, about controlling anger. Once you ended up in a shouting match, you had nowhere else to go, except back down or fight it out.

'Are you OK?'

He nodded silently, looking resentfully at the floor as he did so.

'Do you want a glass of water?'

'No.'

No eye contact now. He still didn't trust me.

'What happened to you?' I asked, gesturing at the crutches.

'You really want to know?'

'Only if you want to tell me. You don't have to.'

'Well, all our problems stem from this,' he said, gesturing with one hand at his legs. 'Back in Sierra Leone I was a water and sanitation manager. Do you know what that is?'

'No, I don't.'

'I'm not surprised. Here all you do if you're thirsty is turn on the tap. If you're sick you go to the hospital. In Sierra Leone, you drink water straight from the ground and sometimes it isn't clean. People only go to the hospital to die. I taught people how to rehydrate themselves when they have sickness, like cholera and diarrhoea, by drinking boiled water mixed with salt and sugar. I also chlorinated the village wells; that made the water safe to drink.

'I would travel between the villages using a little motorbike.

One day I was attacked by rebels who shot me in the back, stole my bike, and left me for dead. When someone found me they took me to a hospital, to die, so I thought.'

He looked up at me: 'But I didn't die.' He was pleased at this victory, overturning the expected outcome.

His expression quickly darkened, however. 'Sometimes in the weeks I spent there, I wished I had died. You know what the worst thing about that hospital was?'

'No.'

'The power cuts.'

'Power cuts?'

'Yes. The first night there was a power cut I didn't think much about it to start with. They had a back-up generator, which they ran using petrol. I could see there was panic after an hour or so. They didn't have enough fuel for the generator and the power hadn't come back on by the time it ran out.

'Four babies who were on oxygen support died because the hospital didn't have enough fuel for the generator. Four young lives for the sake of a few litres of petrol. I lay on my back, helpless as they died, one by one. Every time we had a power cut, I lay there, listening as someone else died.'

'That sounds absolutely awful. I'm so sorry,' I said helplessly.

'It is just me and Jemi now. Her mother, Kadie – well, I'm sure you know that giving birth in my country is a lot more risky than here. After the birth, Kadie started bleeding from a tear in the cervix. There was so much blood on the floor that I slipped on it. The doctors ran in and pushed me away. They stitched her up. I gave my blood so they could pump it into her, the oxygen tank kept conking out, that damn generator was useless. I watched my blood hanging on a filthy, rusty old stand, as it was pumped into my wife's body. Jemi was on another bed, alone, crying. I could hear her but I could not take my eyes off my wife. One of the nurses told me to hold the baby close and I did and I said to

Kadie that we had a daughter and she was fine. Then Kadie died.'

He paused. I didn't want to hear this story, nor did I need to, but Moses was in full flow and at least he was calm.

'Do you know how many mothers die in Sierra Leone trying to give birth, Detective?'

I shook my head.

'One in eight.' He leaned forward. 'Here it is one in *eight thousand*. But do not think for one moment, Detective, that we grieve less because we see so much more death in our country. The whole village mourned for Kadie. The whole village helped me bury her.'

He fell silent.

OK, I thought, I'm there now. Time to start talking to this guy. Every now and then, some of the troubled people I met just needed someone they could talk to – just someone who could listen, to whom they could unburden. Visits from the police often work as a great motivator for people to open up, often excusing their current situation and/or behaviour. I'd heard many a sob story created out of thin air to try to elicit sympathy and this had made me a healthy sceptic. I knew that Moses' story wasn't fake, however. He wasn't after my sympathy. He would much rather have physically kicked me out of his home.

We sat in silence for a few more seconds. The sun came out and the pale yellow winter light lit up the sparsely furnished lounge. Chairs, sofa, coffee table, no TV, just a portable radio and hi-fi system circa 1985.

'You know why I'm here,' I said, a statement rather than question.

'No, you have no business here, how should I know? All you've told me is that my daughter is not coming home. What has she done?'

'She hasn't done anything.'

'Yes, she has, she is disrespectful of her father; she is a wilful child.'

'Did you punish her last night?'

'Yes, of course, she refused to do as she was told.'

'How did you punish her?'

'I beat her with my cane. You want to know why?'

I nodded.

'She wanted to wear a short skirt and refused when I told her she would not go out like that. Of course I beat her, do you think I want to let her become a prostitute?'

'There is no evidence of that. She's only fourteen.'

'No evidence!' he boomed. 'I don't give a damn about your evidence. My daughter will not be a prostitute, you understand me? Is that what you want? Do you want her to become a prostitute? Do you want her for yourself?'

'Hey, stop it, you're going too far now.' I kept my voice level but it wasn't easy.

'No I'm not, I do not want my daughter to become a prostitute. How do you think girls become them, huh? Do you know? Can you guarantee me? In this area? Have you seen what it's like out there at night?'

I had, practically every day since I joined the police. We were but a stone's throw from Lordship Lane, a well-known red-light district, where the prostitutes stalked the streets. They walked up and down, up and down into the small hours, past the cafes and barber shops before taking their clients round to a variety of well-established back alleys and warehouse car parks.

'Whatever your fears, you can't beat her so badly that she ends up with marks on her legs. It's a criminal offence.'

'I hit her with my cane,' he said crossly, pointing to the other side of the room where the ebony walking stick rested against the edge of the door frame. 'I didn't hurt her much and she will not be a prostitute. I don't care what you think. Do you have a daughter?'

I ignored the question. We went round and round in circles. I needed to find a different tack. Was he simply a father alone and out of his depth, was he a bully or was he doing what he thought was normal? I'd seen first-hand how corporal punishment was used in schools in Ghana when I'd travelled there looking for witnesses in a case of child rape.

This was tricky. I'd normally arrest the father in these circumstances, but fourteen-year-old Jemi had begged me not to, telling me her father had nightmares about all the horrible things that might happen to her. If she'd been thirteen I would have had no choice as the offence would have been that much more severe in the eyes of the law. I had relented, even though I would've felt a lot more comfortable if Moses was in the controlled environment of a police interview room. Still, something was holding me back from arresting Moses, some unexplainable gut instinct.

Jemi had told me she could stay with her aunt while I talked to her father. I'd checked the aunt out and agreed that this was indeed a safe place for her.

'Go easy on Moses,' her aunt had told me earnestly, 'he's had a hard time; he just doesn't want to lose his daughter. She was eight years old when they came to England. She is a beautiful English child now. Moses finds this very difficult. He is still in Sierra Leone.'

I decided to try a different tack. 'You do realise that you've frightened your daughter, don't you, Moses? She's scared of you.'

'You are a liar.'

'No really, I mean it, she is really scared. Is that what you want?'

'Of course not. I love her, I am just protecting her.'

'But you aren't, you are frightening the hell out of her. She is scared.'

I spotted tears glistening on the rims of his eyelids. I'd struck a chord. He didn't want to lose his daughter but at the same time he was pushing her away by being far too over-protective. Moses was a proud man who had seen far too much tragedy; his wife lost in childbirth, himself crippled, watching his child become a British teenager, wanting her independence and to be like her friends.

'Moses, Jemi will stay away tonight, with her aunt.'

His tone softened. 'She belongs with her father,' he said quietly.

'Just one night to start, then you can speak to her on the phone, and see how it goes. She can't live here if she's scared, can she?'

'No,' he said, hanging his head low. 'I am sorry. I did not want to frighten my daughter. I am the one who is frightened, frightened of what might happen to her. I do not want her to hate me for trying to protect her. I will not hit her again.'

As he spoke, Moses started to stand. 'I'm OK!' he said, crossly waving me off as I stepped forward to help him up.

Using one of his crutches, he limped across the room and picked up the cane. He leaned his crutch on the wall, turned to face me, holding the cane in both hands, and snapped it in half.

CHAPTER TWENTY-SEVEN

A MATTER OF
LIFE AND DEATH

It was mid-morning on the day of the office Christmas party and I was on my way in to join in the fun when Brenda called.

'I'm in Evergreen Square,' she said, 'and I'm trying to get an answer from Sharon. I think something's wrong. Her neighbour said she's in.'

'What do you need me for?'

'Guess.'

Christ. Had it been nine months since we'd taken Sharon's last baby?

'She hasn't given birth, has she?'

'Not yet, but she's due in a few weeks. I'm worried she might have given birth in the flat.'

'OK, I'm on my way.'

How you described this part of town depended how long you'd been here. To some it will always be the Holly Street estate, a doomed government tower-block flagship that replaced several streets of neat Victorian terraces in the 1960s and was itself demolished after twenty years spent fostering crime. This had in turn been rebuilt as Evergreen Square, which had been visited by Tony Blair when he was prime minister.

Speaking in 2004, he said: 'I got used to the society of fear in the eighties canvassing on the Holly Street estate in Hackney – now thankfully greatly improved – when people were too scared to open the door and the letterboxes had burn marks around them where lighted rags had been shoved through them.'

Well, looking round it a few years later, I'd say the improvements were hard to see – apart from all the CCTV cameras, which as I mentioned earlier, had pushed the dealers and troublemakers, including a gang called the Holly Street gang, to conduct their business in the stairwells.

Stevens Nyembo-Ya-Muteba was a forty-year-old British national who found refuge in Evergreen Square after leaving the war-torn Democratic Republic of the Congo. He lived here in a first-floor flat with his wife and two daughters. He had been offered a place at Cambridge but turned it down in favour of Greenwich University, so he wouldn't have to move his family and look for another job. By day he studied for his BSc in maths and finance. By night he worked as a driver for Tesco to support his family.

Nineteen-year-old Joseph Ekaette, aka 'Tiny', had arrived in Hackney with his mother from Nigeria. They were here illegally, having overstayed their visa. Ekaette was standing in the stairwell outside Stevens's flat with members of the Holly Street gang when the father of two opened his door and asked them to leave. They were making so much noise that his family was unable to sleep. Ekaette refused and in the tussle that followed he stabbed Stevens in the chest. Stevens died before the ambulance could get him to the Homerton.

Later that night, Ekaette drugged and raped a fourteen-year-old girl, filming the attack on his mobile phone. The life sentence he eventually received was of small comfort to Stevens's wife and daughters who had lost the man they loved, the man who was going to provide for them and had been well on the way to proving himself as one of Hackney's greatest success stories. Yes, the name and buildings might have changed, but underneath the same old estate lived on.

I saw that the pavements were slippery with ice as I climbed out of the car and walked cautiously towards a shivering Brenda. She wiped a large drop from her bright red nose. 'Hello, Harry, merry Christmas.'

'Likewise,' I said with a smile and banged on the door.

'Sharon! It's the police, you have to open up!'

'Are you heading home for the holidays then?' I asked as we waited for an answer.

'Yep. Yourself?'

'Just a quiet one in Hertfordshire with the family, all being well.'

I banged on the door again.

'Sod it,' I said, 'it's too cold to hang about all day, time to go in, police style.'

I'm getting too old for this, I thought as I took a running jump at the Yale lock. The door flew open, and hit the hall wall with a satisfying crash.

It was very quiet inside.

'Sharon?' Brenda called.

We looked at one another.

'Perhaps she's out,' I said. 'The neighbour might be wrong. Stay here, I'll check it out.' I started to walk down the hallway.

I found Sharon in the bedroom. I knew she was dead the moment I saw her. I touched her skin; it was ice cold, her fingers had already stiffened; some veins had darkened as her blood set in the cold.

Her murderer lay next to her. Chalk two more up, a mother and unborn baby to hard drugs.

'Oh Jesus Christ.' I turned. Brenda had come in and was standing behind me.

Thirty minutes later, as the ambulance prepared to leave, I was ready to go and asked Brenda if she'd like a lift.

'Yeah, thanks,' Brenda said. She still looked to be in shock.

'I don't suppose you fancy joining our Christmas party, do you?'

'Thanks, Harry, but I don't think I'd be much fun right now.'

'You'll fit in just fine, all we're going to end up doing is talking shop over fizzy pop and sausage rolls.'

'I've got to get back to the office, paperwork, you know.'

We climbed into the car and sat in silence as I drove.

'If you want to talk about it—'

'I'm OK, Harry. It's just that I'd known Sharon for so long, from when she was a beautiful and confident young girl. Why did this have to happen?'

'If only I could answer that,' I said. 'Look, you've saved six of Sharon's babies and they've got the best start in life they could possibly have, all things considered.'

We sat in silence again. Suddenly I stopped the car. 'I don't believe it!'

'What is it?' Brenda asked, looking worried, 'what now?'

Brenda looked at me like I was mad as I smiled and then started laughing.

'Dev never told me, cheeky sod!'

I climbed out of my car. Just on the edge of the estate, on the corner of a street was a flat-roofed one-floor building. It had once been a very small community centre, which had been closed for many years. Now it was surrounded by a wire mesh fence. A sign said: 'Smile, your [sic] on CCTV!' I grinned like a Cheshire cat.

Above the fence was a colourful sign, painted in yellow and red and dotted with flowers.

It said: *Auntie Rose's Nursery*.

And less than a mile away on Highbury Corner, Anne Marie, Will and Jo sat through their first Christmas without Emma. Anne Marie was free, albeit under a supervision order. Her many saving graces had been her frank confession, her determination to find a solution to her depression, her love for Jo and the strength of support that came from her husband. Will had left his job and was determined to pursue a less demanding, more satisfying career working from home.

Jack and his mum were celebrating Christmas in another town; his father was eventually put away for a very long time for attempted murder and child abuse.

In Downham Road Social Services, Mike's desk had been cleared and cleaned and was waiting for a replacement. Mike believed that he wouldn't be able to cope with all the Jacks he would inevitably face in the future. I understood but wished he could have stuck it out. We're so short of social workers it's criminal.

I'd followed up as many of the teachers' referrals as I could manage. Anna, now fifteen, had decided to keep her baby and despite the offer of a place at a young mum's refuge she was living at home with her mum Karen and Sue. Although school had, for the moment at least, fallen by the wayside, her mum had promised to help care for the baby and would make sure Anna finished her education once it was born. David was still on the run; we would catch up with him eventually but that was still a couple of years away.

Anh had been reunited with Ly and Qui after a spell in full-time psychiatric care and apologised, via Claire, for the machete attack – very gracious considering I punched her in the face.

Aisha and Nadifa had stayed in Hackney and Aisha was back

at school. With support from their own community the threat of cutting had eventually faded.

Tanesha and Sefu were still at home and under the careful watch of social services, and Matabe had turned a new leaf.

Joanne, Dougie and their mother Justine were getting on with their lives. Peter was in jail, and would be for some years before he was released and put on the sexual offenders' register. Joanne and Dougie had put the past behind them; although it would be some time before Justine could start to forget that terrible day she spent in our interview room.

Checking on the teacher referrals was a bit of a revelation to me. It seemed that between us all, the system was working – for the most part. It was easy to miss this fact because we were so busy and were used to moving quickly from one traumatic scene to the next, often never knowing the end of the story. The problem was of course that there were so many cases out there that we simply didn't know about.

Some of the cases that teachers asked me to find out about went back years. They'd never forgotten. Why would they? Some of these kids were practically family and suddenly they had either been yanked out of their lives or returned to school with no further explanation.

There was so much we didn't get to hear from the youngest kids. They often didn't understand what was happening to them. It was only when they were older that they were able to explain thoughts and feelings as well as fully understand the actions of adults who abused them. I would perhaps never get to know some of these stories but I vowed to keep the teachers updated when I could.

Back at the office party, we all agreed it had been quite a year, one that for me had started with a rooftop chase and ended with Hackney's own tragic version of the nativity, a cop, a social worker and a paramedic stood over the dead body of a mother carrying an unborn, fatherless and wholly innocent child.

I thought it was odd how we all loved this area so much considering how much misery we saw here. No other job allows for a closer look under the lid of the more difficult aspects of modern life and into the lives of families from all over the world, from so many different cultures.

'That's what I love about Hackney,' Dev said, 'it's an adventure every time I go out. There's a lot of misery but there's a spirit too, a heart, you know? A feeling that we're all in it together; I suppose it's a strange kind of community spirit.'

We were getting there but there was still so much to do, so many children that needed saving.

Soon, we would be heading home to be with our families but none of us would be away for long. Christmas being Christmas, that supposed time of happy families and forgiveness, it was a stressful time in Child Protection. There were a lot of dreams that weren't going to come true on Christmas Day.

Sure enough, Rob tapped me on the shoulder. He was wearing a gold paper crown. Very appropriate, I thought.

'Sorry to interrupt, Harry, but I need you for one more memorandum today. Claire's on her way here with Craig; they're bringing in a little girl with a black eye.'

'No problem.'

'Thanks, Harry,' Rob said. 'Finish your mince pies,' he said as he walked quickly away, 'I'll make sure the room's ready and will come and get you when they arrive.'

I called after him. 'Hey!'

Rob turned a quizzical look. 'What?'

'Merry Christmas.'

Rob smiled and pushed his glasses back on his head. 'And a Happy New Year.'

Yes, another day in the life of Hackney Child Protection was well and truly under way.

A WARNING

It takes a special kind of courage to knock on certain doors, knowing that anger, resentment and goodness knows what else could be waiting on the other side. As a cop I can always call for urgent back-up or arrive with a vanload of highly trained, heavily armoured and baton-wielding officers.

At the moment, social workers travel alone to high-risk areas, sometimes visiting children with violent parents without police support. In my opinion, the police and social services should all work in the same child protection office. This would allow for easier and faster information sharing, faster referrals and would also make meetings extremely easy to set up, saving thousands of hours in travelling time each year.

Sharing the same offices would also help us assess potentially dangerous cases very quickly; allowing us to travel with a social worker to an address that they might have previously gone to on their own using public transport. We would also be able to provide access to important information outside of office hours.

Unfortunately, no matter how practical this may seem, it looks like it may never happen as right now we're facing a real crisis: a shortage of social workers in child protection. Lord

Laming identified this UK-wide shortage during his inquiry into the child protection failures that led to the death of Baby Peter, Peter Connelly, in Haringey in August 2007.

In some London boroughs, 40 per cent of social work positions are vacant. A 2009 survey carried out by the *London Evening Standard* revealed that Hackney was at the top of this chart with 41.5 per cent of positions unfilled, while Haringey was not far behind at 33.8 per cent. The national average is 14.6 per cent.[1]

Social workers like Mike are leaving all the time, demoralised and exhausted. No one is rushing forward to replace them. It seems as though red tape, low morale, low pay, lack of support, high workloads and the fear of being made into a scapegoat has understandably put people off.

Councils became so desperate that they started recruiting social workers from abroad. Unfortunately, a new temporary immigration cap imposed by the new government has scuppered this possible solution. One local authority with 16,000 employees has been told by the UK Border Agency that it may only have a total of five work permits for 2010 – and this includes any existing overseas staff. They employ forty overseas workers and had been expecting a further eleven social workers from Canada. Another local authority had been expecting twenty-five social workers from the United States.[2]

Other councils have come to rely on privately employed agency social workers. For example, in 2009 Windsor and Maidenhead said that twelve out of fifty social worker posts were vacant, which led them to hire seventeen agency social workers. Each agency social worker cost them about £20,000 per year more than directly employed staff.[3]

Councils are now approaching retired social workers, asking them to return to work. The Local Government Association had hoped to tempt 5,000 former social workers back into the job. But this is now looking just as unlikely.[4]

And this is the really scary part. The government is looking for any way it can to save money so they can pay off the national deficit and so are planning to impose some pretty hefty cuts to council budgets. Guess which one of the services is going to be worst affected? Unbelievable as it seems, the answer is child protection. Councils have been told to freeze council tax for the next two years and to expect severe cuts to their government funds. The consequences are barely comprehensible to anyone working in child protection.

Take Buckinghamshire County Council, for example, who are planning a £317,000 cut in child protection that they say will 'reduce our capacity to manage high level preventative work'. This includes a £226,000 cut in front-line child protection staff that will hit 'our capacity to manage the assessment process of children in need'. More cuts are inevitable, the council says, as it is committed to saving £52 million over the next four years 'through efficiencies'.[5]

For Bexley Council a £1.4 million deficit in the government's Area Based Grant is to be recouped by slashes to Children and Young People's Services and Environmental Services (Finance Services and the Chief Executive Department will be left untouched, however).

This was after Bexley Social Services saw a 37 per cent rise in child referrals, a 55 per cent increase in children subject to a child protection plan and an 8 per cent increase in children being taken into care, following the death of Baby Peter.[6]

A massive cut in Wirral fell heaviest on Children's Services, which lost £2.6 million. They've made it perfectly clear that child protection will suffer, with fewer children's social workers recruited.[7]

The London Borough of Richmond in south-west London is cutting £2.4 million from education, children's and cultural services, while in North London, Barnet has come up with the concept of an 'easyCouncil', a plan to model local authority services on the no-frills approach of budget airlines.[8]

Such a move was described as 'Armageddon' by Barnet Council's head of children's services, Robert McCulloch-Graham, when he was interviewed by the *Guardian* newspaper. His department has been struggling with a 50 per cent increase in the number of referrals to its children's social care department over the past two years.

Suffolk County Council is taking an even more radical approach to public sector reform by proposing a 'virtual' authority that outsources all but a handful of its services – including child protection. How can we possibly even dream of entrusting something as sensitive as child protection to commercially run companies?[9]

In Edinburgh, the number of children feared to be at risk of abuse has soared by more than 40 per cent. A new report on protecting vulnerable youngsters revealed that the demand for services has 'increased significantly, and it is anticipated that this trend will continue'.[10] Cuts mean that the council will focus on those most at risk, i.e. in immediate danger, leading to well-founded fears that some youngsters vulnerable to physical injury, sexual abuse or neglect, but not immediately considered at high risk, will slip through the cracks. These are the children who will be in 'immediate danger' in the not too distant future.

Anthony May, director of children and young people's services at Nottinghamshire County Council, recently wrote: 'We have seen a 56 per cent increase in referrals over the last year, an 83 per cent increase over the past two years in the number of children subject to child protection plans and a 24 per cent increase in the number of children coming into council care over the same period.'

As a result, Nottinghamshire is trying to spend an extra £1.7 million a year for the next three years on the safeguarding of children, at a time when the council needs to take £150 million out of its budget over the same period, a virtually impossible task.[11]

As for Haringey, the borough where Victoria Climbié and Peter Connelly died, the council needs to make savings of £60 million over three years. Its children and young people service is a big contributor to the council's projected £6 million overspend as it too struggles to cope with increasing numbers of referrals and children taken into care.[12]

Other councils reportedly contemplating cuts to children's services include: Birmingham (£13 million, 1,500 jobs to go); Somerset County Council (£17 million); and Hampshire County Council (£24 million, 180 jobs) where managers are planning to chop £24.8 million from the £170 million children's services budget for 2011–12.[13]

The inner city London Borough of Lambeth is also bracing itself for cuts. However, Jon Rogers, Unison Lambeth branch secretary, said he had been given an undertaking that, for the moment, current social workers' jobs were safe thanks to the high vacancy rates! That's all right then![14]

Many councils are looking to focus almost entirely on the services that look after children most at risk. This means that 'non-core' children's services will be cut – such as early intervention projects aimed at tackling problems in high-risk families before they spiral out of control and require the input of expensive safeguarding services. Needless to say, crude cuts to early intervention will result in more referrals to child protection services further down the line.

Not surprisingly, a survey carried out for the Local Government Association found that only 1 per cent of the public believe social care for older people or child protection services should be cut to save public money. People were much more keen to see the numbers and salaries of NHS managers reduced – 69 per cent of people said they should face cuts.[15]

If reading all this makes you want to run around the room shouting 'We're doomed!' then join the club. However, Hackney's children's social services recently managed to find a solution to their lack of staff by turning the system on its head, so that fewer social workers are able to take on more cases.

Instead of the usual hierarchy, with front-line social workers at the bottom, Hackney created a system of small units of five people, each headed by a consultant social worker. These consultants are key. They are highly experienced, able, well-trained and paid more than £40,000 a year. One social worker focuses on the child while others look at the adults' needs and crucially an administrator (not a social worker) handles the mass of paperwork each case generates. The units include therapists, clinical practitioners and coordinators. All work closely together on cases, with the consultant taking responsibility, usually handling between thirty and forty cases in total.

When dealing with a large family of six children one person works with the younger ones and another with the older ones. If one is on leave, there's always another team member available to take a phone call. This means that the decision-making is shared, as is the stress of difficult decisions. Any decision then rests on the instincts of the whole group, rather than on an individual. As a result the number of children in care in Hackney has fallen by about a third,[16] completely reversing the national trend where the numbers of children in care have shot up in the wake of the Baby Peter case.

Let me just repeat that. Hackney is lacking more social workers than any London borough but has managed to reduce the number of children in care by a third. It is keeping more children safe in their families instead of sending them to foster carers and care homes. Of course, this system is more expensive than the one all other boroughs are currently operating, but having 30 per cent fewer children in care will save the UK an absolute fortune in years to come. Hackney no longer hires expensive agency staff and Hackney social workers no longer want to leave.

Now, like everywhere else in the UK, Hackney's child services departments are on the chopping block as the government tries to make savings by cutting local authority budgets. The examples I've cited here are just the tip of the iceberg – space precludes me from covering every single borough in the UK, but they are all facing cuts and children everywhere are being put in even more danger from those that would wish to harm them. We simply can't let this happen.

Call me a cynic but it looks to me like the UK's most vulnerable children are being punished for the mismanagement of the economy. Cuts to child services are a false economy. If we don't look after the vulnerable in our communities now then it will cost us a fortune, economically and socially, in just a few years' time. Overstretched social services will miss cases like Victoria's and Baby Peter's.

Write to your MP. Start Facebook campaigns. Write blogs. Do all you can to help save our most vulnerable children and help recruit more social workers.

While I understand that money is not limitless, when it comes down to it, in the words of Jumu's father, Obi:

'How can lust for money possibly outweigh a single baby's life?'

END NOTE

If you have been the victim of sexual abuse, whether yesterday or twenty years ago, it's vital to report it. Even if you don't want to follow it up with a police investigation, you hold valuable criminal intelligence that could be used to help protect other children. Also, by coming forward, you will have taken the first step on the road to achieving some kind of closure.

You can do this by contacting your local police (alternatively, this can be done anonymously by calling Crimestoppers), local social services and various voluntary organisations. You are also more than welcome to approach me directly via my website: harrykeeble.com

Crimestoppers: crimestoppers-uk.org, telephone 0800 555 111

Help and information for adults can be found via the National Society for the Prevention of Cruelty to Children (NSPCC): www.nspcc.org.uk, telephone 0808 800 5000.

For children see ChildLine: childline.org.uk, telephone 0800 11 11

Do also please feel free to email me for advice: harrykeeble@btinternet.com

If you'd like to work in child protection then visit my website: harrykeeble.com

Please support my Facebook campaign: Save our Social Workers

NOTES

CHAPTER ONE

1. School staff get 1,700 complaints, BBC News online, 10 August 2010, http://www.bbc.co.uk/news/education-10918940

CHAPTER TWO

1. Hackney's Key Facts and Figures 2007, pdf downloaded from http://www.hackney.gov.uk/xp-boroughprofile.htm
2. Babycentre: The Cost of Childcare, http://www.babycentre.co.uk/baby/workandchildcare/costofcare/
3. The policewoman branded an illegal childminder – for looking after her colleague's toddler, by Andy Whelan, *Daily Mail*, 27 September 2009. http://www.dailymail.co.uk/news/article-1216370/Leanne-Shepherd-policewoman-branded-illegal-child minder-looking-colleagues-toddler.html

CHAPTER THREE

1. 'Shaken baby' convictions quashed, BBC News online, 21 July 2005, http://news.bbc.co.uk/1/hi/uk/4702279.stm

CHAPTER FIVE

1. Weighed down by caseloads, Amy Taylor, CommunityCare.co.uk, 5 June 2009, http://www.communitycare.co.uk/Articles/2009/

06/05/111742/Children39s-social-workers-struggle-with-high-caseloads.htm

Arthurworrey wins 10-year battle for registration, Kirsty McGregor, CommunityCare.co.uk, 11 March 2010 10:17 http://www.communitycare.co.uk/Articles/2010/03/11/113989/arthurworrey-wins-10-year-battle-for-registration.htm

'Victoria is always there. She never goes away ...' as told to Diane Taylor, *Guardian*, 19 February 2007 http://www.guardian.co.uk/society/2007/feb/19/childrens services.socialcare

CHAPTER SIX

1. World Health Organisation: Zimbabwe Summary Country Profile For HIV/AIDS Treatment, 2005 www.who.int/hiv/HIVCP_ZWE.pdf

2 and 3. Scourge of Child Rape in Rural Zimbabwe, by IWPR – Africa, ZIM Issue 49, 13 March 2006, http://iwpr.net/report-news/scourge-child-rape-rural-zimbabwe

CHAPTER SEVEN

1. An excellent feral/confined children resource can be found here: http://www.feralchildren.com

CHAPTER EIGHT

1. Diagnostic and statistical manual of mental disorders: DSM-IV-TR, American Psychiatric Press Inc., 4th Revised edition (31 July 1994). Page 308. Schizophrenia: Prevalence

CHAPTER NINE

1. Illegal workers found in East End sweatshop, by Alison Richards, *London Evening Standard*, 18 September 2009.

2. A Scoping Project on Child Trafficking in the UK, June 2007, produced by CEOP on behalf of the Home Office and the Border and Immigration Agency, June 2007. Section 1.7.4: Vietnamese Children, page 31.

3. Police target cannabis factories, by Neville Dean, PA, *Independent*, 25 September 2006 http://www.independent. co.uk/news/uk/crime/police-target-cannabis-factories-417505.html
Untold profits fuel the violent gang world of London's cannabis farms, by Tony Thompson, *London Evening Standard*, 2 September 2010.
http://www.thisislondon.co.uk/lifestyle/article-23873247-untold-profits-fuel-the-violent-gang-world-of-londons-cannabis-farms.do

4. Children trafficked from Asia to UK to work in cannabis factories, by Nina Lakhan, *Independent*, 23 September 2007, http://www. independent.co.uk/news/uk/crime/children-trafficked-from-asia-to-uk-to-work-in-cannabis-factories-403251.html

CHAPTER TWELVE

1. The facts and figures for FGM and the lives of Somali people in London can be found from the following three sources:
Somali Housing Experiences in England, Ian Cole, David Robinson, the Centre for Regional and Social Research, Sheffield Hallam University, 2003.
Forward FGM Information Pack, The Foundation for Women's Health, Research and Development (FORWARD), 2002.
http://www.forwarduk.org.uk/key-issues/fgm
First steps in a new country: baseline indicators for the Somali community in LB Hackney, Holman, C., Holman, N., Sahil Housing Association Ltd, April 2003,
http://www.researchasylum.org.uk/?lid=75

2. See Forward FGM Information Pack, FGM: The UK Situation, page 18.

CHAPTER FOURTEEN

1. A great deal of information in this chapter can also be found in more detail in *The Language of Sexual Crime*, edited by Janet Cotterill, Palgrave Macmillan (31 July 2007), in particular in the section entitled 'Just Good Friends: Managing the Clash of Discourse in Police Interviews with Paedophiles', by Kelly Benneworth. This is an excellent resource for anyone who interviews children, survivors and perpetrators of abuse.

2. E. L. Rezmovic, D. Sloane, D. Alexander, B. Seltser, T. Jessor (1996), 'Cycle of Sexual Abuse: Research Inconclusive About Whether Child Victims Become Adult Abusers' (PDF). US Government Accountability Office General Government Division United States. http://www.gao.gov/archive/1996/gg96178.pdf.

Ward, T., Hudson, S. M., & Marshall, W. L. (1995), 'Cognitive distortions and affective deficits in sex offenders: A cognitive deconstructionist interpretation', *Sexual Abuse: A Journal of Research and Treatment*, 7, 67–83.

3. Linda S. Grossman, Ph.D., Brian Martis, M.D., and Christopher G. Fichtner, M.D. (1 March 1999). 'Are Sex Offenders Treatable? A Research Overview'. *Psychiatric Services* 50 (3): 349–361

CHAPTER SIXTEEN

1. A great deal of information in this chapter can also be found in more detail in an excellent examination of courtroom questioning in 'The Questioning of Child Witnesses by the Police and in Court: a Linguistic Comparison', Michelle Aldridge in *The Language of Sexual Crime*, edited by Janet Cotterill, Palgrave Macmillan (31 July 2007).

EPILOGUE

1. Tim Ross, Education Correspondent, *London Evening Standard*, 4 February 2009, http://www.thisislondon.co.uk/standard/article-23633478-capitals-shortage-of-social-workers-leads-to-child-abuse-fears.do

2. UK Border Agency turns down requests for non-EU social workers, Les Reid, *Guardian*, 26 September 2010, http://www.guardian.co.uk/uk/2010/sep/26/uk-border-agency-social-workers

3. The cult of council tax cuts, by Heather Wakefield, Public Finance, 9 February 2010, http://opinion.publicfinance.co.uk/2010/02/the-cult-of-council-tax-cuts-by-heather-wakefield/

4. Jobs plea to ex-social workers, BBC News online, 3 March 2009, http://news.bbc.co.uk/1/hi/uk/7919725.stm

5. In depth: council cuts meeting, Oliver Evans, Bucks Free Press, 5 August 2010, http://www.bucksfreepress.co.uk/news/8316121.In_depth__council_cuts_meeting/

6. Youth services and jobs to go in £2 million Bexley Council budget cuts, Kate Mead, *Bexley Times*, 17 September 2010, http://www.bexleytimes.co.uk/news/youth_services_and_jobs_to_go_in_2million_bexley_council_budget_cuts_1_652378

7. Labour raise budget cuts fears, Liam Murphy, *Wirral News*, 14 June 2010, http://blogs.wirralnews.co.uk/hamiltonsquared/2010/06/labour-raise-budget-cuts-fears.html

8. Library and day centre services threatened by Richmond Council, *Richmond and Twickenham Times*, Chris Wickham, 23 September 2010, www.richmondandtwickenhamtimes.co.uk/.../8410001.Services_threatened_by_budget_cuts/
Barnet 'easyCouncil' project lacks proper business plan, audit finds, Robert Booth, *Guardian*, 23 September 2010,

http://www.guardian.co.uk/politics/2010/sep/23/barnet-easy-council-costcutting-plan-criticised

9. Suffolk council plans to outsource virtually all services, Anna Bawden, Guardian, 22 September 2010, http://www.guardian.co.uk/society/2010/sep/22/suffolk-county-council-outsource-services

10. Budget cuts leave children facing higher risk of abuse, Alan McEwan, Edinburgh Evening News, 28 August 2010, http://edinburghnews.scotsman.com/news/Budget-cuts-leave-children-facing.6500511.jp

11. Cuts to children's services like 'Armageddon', Patrick Butler, Guardian, 8 September 2010, http://www.guardian.co.uk/society/2010/sep/08/childrens-services-spending-cuts

12. Cuts to children's services like 'Armageddon', Patrick Butler, Guardian, 8 September 2010, http://www.guardian.co.uk/society/2010/sep/08/childrens-services-spending-cuts

13. ibid.

14. Lambeth special education needs team to go in cuts package, Molly Garboden, Community Care, 26 July 2010, www.communitycare.co.uk/.../lambeth-special-education-needs-team-to-go-in-cuts-package.htm

15. Spare elderly and child protection from cuts – survey, Vern Pitt, Community Care, 5 July 2010, http://www.communitycare.co.uk/Articles/2010/07/05/114841/spare-elderly-and-child-protection-from-cuts-survey.htm

16. Government orders review of child protection in England, BBC News, 10 June 2010, http://www.bbc.co.uk/news/10280710